TURKISH
COAST

Kaş to Dalyan
Second edition

Michael Bussmann and Gabriele Tröger
with walks by
Dean Livesley

SUNFLOWER BOOKS

Second edition © 2009
Sunflower Books™
PO Box 36160
London SW7 3WS, UK
www.sunflowerbooks.co.uk

ISBN 978-1-85691-367-6

Important note to the reader

Apart from the walks, this book is a translation from a series of *general* guides originally published in Germany (see Publisher's note on page 8). We have tried to ensure that the descriptions and maps are error-free at press date. The book will be updated, where necessary, whenever future printings permit. It will be very helpful for us to receive your comments (sent in care of Sunflower Books, please) for the updating of future printings.

We also rely on those who use this book — especially walkers — to take along a good supply of common sense when they explore. Conditions change very rapidly in this part of Turkey, and *storm damage or bulldozing may make a route unsafe at any time*. If the route is not as we outline it here, and your way ahead is not secure, return to the point of departure. *Never attempt to complete a trip by car or on foot under hazardous conditions!*

If you would like to offset the carbon dioxide emissions for your trip to Turkey, go to www.climatecare.org.

Cover photograph: Ölüdeniz

Text (except the walks) translated and adapted from *Türkei — Lykische Küste, Türkei — Westküste* and *Türkei — Südägäis;* text, town and site plans © 2005, 2006, 2008 Michael Müller Verlag, Erlangen, Germany; translation: Thomas Wilkes and Pat Underwood
Photograph credits
  © Michael Bussmann: cover and pages 11, 17, 27, 30 (bottom), 33, 45 (bottom), 61, 70, 101, 106, 109, 115, 129 (bottom), 156, 170 (top), 174
  © Brian Anderson: 20
  © Dean Livesley: 9, 32, 94, 104, 120
  © i-stockphoto: pages 5, 6, 18, 22, 29, 30 (top), 32, 37, 38, 41, 45 (top), 47, 49, 50, 57, 62, 69, 120, 127, 129 (top), 132, 136, 143, 145 (both), 147 (both), 163, 170 (bottom)
Walking maps: © Sunflower Books
Sunflower Books is a Registered Trademark.
A CIP catalogue record for this book is available from the British Library.
Printed and bound in China: WKT Company Ltd

Contents

4 Turkish Coast: Kaş to Dalyan

Preface

If Lycia had its own flag, the colours would be aquamarine or emerald for the shimmering sea and, above, a fine gold line for the beautiful beaches, then various shades of green for the fresh-smelling forests and bright white for the summits of the Taurus Mountains, capped with snow for so much of the year. The star in the centre of the Turkish flag would be replaced by the constantly shining sun, and the crescent moon beside it by a column, symbolising the many ancient sites.

The Lycian Peninsula takes in a very large area — running between Antalya and Lake Köyceğiz south to the sea. It is impossible to do justice to the entire spread *and* feature walks in one book, so this volume concentrates on the region between Kaş (including Kekova to the east) and Lake Köyceğiz. A companion book, covering the stretch from Antalya to Demre, takes in the rest of Lycia. When you've got all that under your belt, you might like to move further west to visit the Bodrum, Reşadiye, and Bozburun peninsulas, covered in a third volume.

Historical descriptions of the wild, fissured Lycian coastal region abound with superlatives. Mustafa Kemal Atatürk, 'Father of the Turks', called this area the most

Tour boats clustered at the foot of Butterfly Valley near Ölüdeniz

beautiful in Turkey. And the landscapes that sent so many writers into raptures have not changed for centuries.

Despite all the hymns of praise, the peninsula's thinly populated coastal strip long remained untouched by tourism. It was so isolated that for a short time it even became a place of exile (see, for instance, the reference to Turkey's great man of letters, Cevat Şakir Kabaağaçlı, under 'Blue cruises' on page 19). Today, thanks to the many flights into the airports at Antalya and Dalaman, millions of visitors happily spend their holidays in the places where unwanted dissidents were once forcibly detained.

But the consequences of developing the coastal strip into one of the top locations for mass tourism cannot be

Carian rock-tombs on the cliffs facing Dalyan

concealed, even during the most beautiful times of the year. Many of the once-tranquil fishing villages have changed substantially in the last decade or so. Bay after bay is being opened up but, fortunately, the bulldozers still face several hundred kilometres of coast to plunder, so it will probably be at least another decade before the last idyllic places fall prey to big business.

Kaş to Dalyan highlights ...

... for lovers of beautiful beaches

If you love sun, sand and sea, the long stretch of coast between Kaş and Dalyan will enchant you, with scores of wonderful beaches and quiet bays. There are compelling attractions almost all the way along; the following stand out.

Bay of Kaputaş — not far west of Kaş, this small but exquisite turquoise bay has a golden beach with a collar of steep cliffs.

Patara — one of Turkey's longest sandy beaches (14km), still unspoilt, and with a fascinating dune landscape.

Ölüdeniz — a dream lagoon with a flair of the South Pacific. Ölüdeniz vies with Patara as the 'best beach in Turkey'. But you have to visit Ölüdeniz in spring or autumn to see the lagoon as it's pictured in all the brochures — in summer it's far too crowded.

Bay of Katrancı — a semicircular picture-postcard bay backed by a small wood, ideal for camping.

... for archaeology and culture freaks

A wealth of ruined cities testifies to the importance of this coastal region in ancient times. In addition there are the rock tombs — a cultural inheritance from the puzzling Lycian civilization, which are only found here. Amongst the plethora of sites, the following are musts.

Xanthos — declared a UNESCO World Cultural Heritage Site in 1988, Xanthos was one of the most powerful Lycian cities. It is famous for its rock tombs, but the most imposing finds are no longer at the site — they are in the British Museum.

Letoon — near Xanthos and another UNESCO World Cultural Heritage Site, this was the main religious centre of the Lycian League.

... for nature and landscape enthusiasts

Off the beaten track there are still many unspoilt places left to discover. The harsh Lycian Taurus Mountains are characterised by summits rising up to 3000m, barren plateaus, extensive pine forests, and impressive ravines gouged out of the rock by roaring rivers over the millenia. Below this backdrop lie hidden bays and sandy beaches from where you look out to a sparkling sea ranging from palest turquoise to deep blue. Below is just a selection of the most beautiful places to explore.

Kekova — or, more particularly, the sea between Simena and the island of Kekova. In this lake-like area, with its many small islets, you can explore the famous 'sunken cities' on a boat trip.

Saklıkent: There are two Saklıkents in Lycia; this book covers the magnificent Saklıkent Gorge between Fethiye and Kalkan. You enter the gorge on a narrow footbridge over a rushing river— where trout jump straight onto the plates of the nearby restaurants.

Dalyan Delta — between Lake Köyceğiz and the sea, the delta is a nesting site of the loggerhead turtle and a sanctuary for many birds — an ornithologist's paradise.

Publisher's note

A couple of decades ago we published 'Landscapes' walking and touring guides to the Antalya and Bodrum/Marmaris areas. These best-sellers eventually went out of print: there was so much building work going on that they needed annual revision — far too costly an exercise for UK-based authors. In the intervening years, tourism to the area between Kaş and Dalyan flourished.

Thanks to finding two German authors who have been visiting and writing about Turkey for many years and an Englishman who has his own guiding business in the area, there are now three titles available: *Antalya to Demre, Kaş to Dalyan* and *Bodrum to Marmaris.* Dean has provided all the walks in this book, and everything else is down to Michael and Gabi, the main authors. Naturally this can lead to slightly different writing styles, but we hope it won't be a case of 'too many cooks'. A few notes follow.

Keep in mind that if a hotel or restaurant entry says 'recommended by readers', this refers to recommendations by *German* users of the original guides (in print for decades and revised every two-three years). This does *not*

Dean's walks take in many lesser-known ancient sites — not on tourist routes or the Lycian Way; these sarcophagi are at Hoyran (Walk 8).

mean, however, that the establishment is predominantly frequented by German clients; what Michael and Gabi always seek out is the place with a personal touch, whatever the price category or clientele. Just log on to some of the hundreds of web addresses they provide!

Dean was a find; he has lived in Turkey for almost 20 years and helped research and implement the famous 'Lycian Way'. He has been involved in conservation for many years and now runs his own company organising activity, nature and cultural/historical tours from his base at Kayaköyü, near Fethiye. If you want to explore in depth — on foot or by boat, as a day trip or camping out under the stars — contact Dean at Seven Capes Sea Kayak Centre, www. sevencapes.com; (0252 6180390 or (0537 4033779.

One common thread binds all three authors: a shared love of Turkey's ancient history, landscapes and traditional hospitality. This shines through all the pages of the book — from the humorous boxed asides about mythological characters and carpet-sellers to their delight in retracing ancient walking routes.

Key to the maps and plans

touring map

▬▬▬	motorway
▬▬	trunk road
▭▭▭	secondary road
▭▭▭	minor road
──	track
▲	mountain peak
✲	viewpoint
Δ	campsite
∴	ancient site
9	location of walks

town plans

P	parking
🏖	beach
M	museum
☾	mosque
i	tourist office
☎	post office
BUS	bus stop
🚕	taxi rank
🚗	car hire
✚	hospital, clinic

walking maps

▬▬	dual carriageway/trunk road
▭▭▭	secondary road/motorable track
-----	jeep track/path or old trail
6▸	main walk and direction
6▸	alternative route and direction
🚐	bus, *dolmuş* stop/petrol station
◇ ✦	*sarniç*/tank, tap, water source
⚑∏	mosque/ancient site
✗☞	windmill/viewpoint
▪∎	building/castle, fort or tower

Country and people of the crescent moon — Turkey in facts and figures

Official name: Türkiye Cumhuriyeti (Republic of Turkey)

Geography: With a surface area of 779,452 square kilometres, Turkey is more than three times the area of the United Kingdom. Just three percent of the area is on the continent of Europe, with the remainder (generally called Anatolia) being in Asia. Turkey's highest mountain is Mount Ararat (5165m) in the easternmost part of the country. Turkey is one of the most seismically active continental regions of the world, with a long history of earthquakes due to tectonic activities in the fault line and the drifting together of the Eurasian and Arabian tectonic plates.

Political system: Turkey has been a parliamentary democracy since the constitution of 1982. The last elections were held in 2007, at which time the reigning conservative AKP party gained 341 of Parliament's 550 seats (followed by the social democratic CHP with 112 seats). The AKP party is headed by Recep Tayyip Erdoğan, Prime Minister since 2003. After the 2007 elections, Parliament selected Abdullah Gül, a close associate of Erdoğan, for a five-year term of office, but the next president will be elected by the people. Parliament is also the law-making body; after a four-year legislative period, there will be new elections in 2011. Laicism (separation of church and state) is guaranteed in the constitution.

Economics: Thanks to the AKP, which brought in long-awaited and much-needed structural reforms (privatisation of unprofitable state enterprises, transparent tendering procedures, central bank autonomy, better terms for international investors, etc.) Turkey has recently experienced some boom years, with economic growth of 5-10%. But the overstretched budget is worrying. The national debt amounts to about 50% of GDP — and as long as only one out of ten people in employment pays tax, it's difficult to see how the deficit will be overcome.

The annual inflation rate has decreased strongly over the last few years; in 2001 it was 54%, in 2005 — for the first time in 30 years — it was below 10%. The latest figures show unemployment standing at around 9.9%, with annual income per head at between £4000-7500. (depending on the source consulted). Income in the Istanbul area runs at about double the national average, in the poor eastern provinces it's only about half the average. Countrywide, agriculture contributes only 11% towards GDP (although it employs 40% of the total workforce), industry brings in 25%, the building trade 4.5%, and the service sector 59.5%.

Military: The armed forces number 515,000 men and therefore are among the largest in the world (the second-largest in NATO). Military expenditure as a portion of gross national product is approximately a third higher than the world average. One reason for this is the long conflict with the Kurds in the east of the country. Soldiers are highly respected by the Turkish people.

Population structure: In 2008 Turkey had approximately 73 million inhabitants (1960: 28 million); the average age is 28 (UK: 38.6). The population density is very varied. The administrative district of Istanbul with 1330 inhabitants per sq km is clearly the most dense. The lowest population density is in the underdeveloped provinces in eastern Anatolia with only 16 inhabitants per sq km.

Sub-populations: 85.7% Turks, 10.6% Kurd, 1.6% Arab, and 2.1% mixed (Armenians, Greeks, Laz, Circassian, Georgians and Muslim Bulgarians).

Health/social: one doctor per 723 inhabitants. The average life expectancy for women is 73 years and for men about 68 years. Old-age pensions do not exist, nor are there any unemployment benefits.

Education: Over the last few decades much has been done for education; over 50,000 schools have been built since 1950. The estimated illiteracy rate for women is approximately 18%, for men about 6%. However there is a strong contrast between east and west: in the western part, illiteracy is mostly confined to the older generation, whereas in the east (where child labour is still common) the figures include children as well. Since 1997 eight years' schooling has been compulsory.

Religion: 99% of the Turkish population are Muslims. The remainder are Jewish and either Syrian or Greek Orthodox Christians.

☀ *Introduction*

This book covers the coast and hinterland from Kekova (east of Kaş) to Dalyan and the area around Lake Köyceğiz. Most people staying here will be probably be arriving at/departing from the airport at Dalaman. If you plan a longer stay and hope to explore more of Lycia, there is the option of moving east with *Turkey: Antalya to Demre* and returning from Antalya; inexpensive one-way flights are easily bookable, and tour operators offer two-centre holidays.

When to go

Up until late autumn, the south coast of Lycia is shielded from the cool air mass coming off the Anatolian highlands by the 3000m-high peaks of the Taurus Mountains. Thus long hot summers alternate with short mild winters. There is very little rainfall during the hot season, while the winter months are wet. The **bathing** season lasts from Easter until around mid-October, and outside this period many hotels are closed. April, May and October, when the daily maximum temperatures rarely exceed 30°C, are the best months to visit (unless you will be spending *all* your time on the beach).

Getting to the area
By air

At time of writing, there were **(charter) flights** to **Antalya** from Birmingham, Bristol, East Midlands, Exeter, Glasgow, Humberside, London Gatwick, London Luton, London Stansted, Manchester and Newcastle. **Dalaman** has even more flights

— from all of the above airports plus Belfast International, Cardiff, Doncaster Sheffield, Edinburgh, Leeds Bradford, Liverpool, Norwich and Teeside.

Kaş is about halfway between these two airports; Dalyan and Fethiye are best reached from Dalaman.

Scheduled flights (with Turkish Airlines or BA) necessitate a changeover in Instanbul. From the United States it's rather a long haul, with flights by Turkish Airlines in cooperation with American Airlines and BA, stopping over in the UK.

Flight-only options are ideal for anyone who wants to make their own accommodation arrangements — or fly into Dalaman and return from Antalya (or even Bodrum). It's very easy to make your own arrangements on the internet, and perhaps book a **fly-drive** as well.

Prices are highest between April and October, when there are also more flights: expect to pay around £270 *including taxes*. But 'off-season' there are some very economical deals — around £130

return or less *including taxes.*
Obviously, booking well ahead
(or at the last minute!) you may
well be able to better these
prices.

The **travel documents** you'll
need are listed on page 52 in the
'A-Z' section. For information
about Dalaman Airport, see page
171; for connections from Kaş to
Antalya's airport see page 63.

Package tours to the area
between Kaş and Dalyan are
offered by a huge number of
companies and are perhaps the
easiest option if you just want to
stay in one place and haven't the
time to make your own arrangements. All the major UK tour
operators offer packages based
on Dalaman, but there are other
specialists for Turkey: for a list,
visit www.gototurkey.co.uk and
click on 'Specialist Tour
Operators' (in the USA/Canada
see www.tourismturkey.org and
click on 'Tour Operators'). The
most popular resorts, from east
to west, are Kaş, Kalkan, Patara,
Hisarönü, Ölüdeniz, Fethiye,
Göcek and Dalyan.

Naturally all tour operators will
be only too happy to book you
excursions to tourist sights
outside the region, *gulet* trips
along the coast, or even hiking
tours. Often these excursions are
offered at time of booking, or ask
your tour rep about them.

The **baggage** allowance is
usually limited to 20kg on
flights, but if you are flying with
a Business Class or other seat
upgrade, or are staying longer
than 28 days, you may be able to
get this lifted to 30kg. Otherwise
you are likely to have to pay
about £3-7 per kilo for excess
baggage (although if you're just

a few kilos over they are likely to
turn a blind eye). For **sports
equipment** the rules vary
between airlines: golf clubs and
diving equipment are usually
carried free, but sometimes they
are classed as extra baggage for a
flat rate of between £20-40.
Bicycles, paragliders and
surfboards can be charged at
anything between £20-£100.
Naturally you will want to check
all this in advance — in any case
you are legally bound to give the
airlines advance notice of
oversize baggage.

By *car*

Driving to the area is *possible* for
those who have plenty of time
(allow 4-5 days), especially if you
want to tour and camp (campsite
details are listed under 'Accommodation'). You will need an
international driving licence, the
vehicle's registration documents
and valid Third Party insurance.
On arrival, details of the vehicle
will be logged in your passport,
and you won't be able to leave
the country without it. After
crossing the Channel, you would
make for one of the Italian ports:
Ancona or *Brindisi* for ferries to
Çeşme in western Turkey (Mar-
mara Lines; www.marmaralines.
com) or *Ancona* or *Venice* for
ferries to Igoumenitsa in Greece
(Anek Lines, www.anek.gr). The
option via Greece is cheaper, but
it's still another 1000km to the
Turkish south coast.

By *train*

This option is only for those
really keen on rail travel; it is far
more expensive than air. There
are daily departures from
London via Brussels or Paris to

Istanbul (several routes, each taking three nights and with multiple changes of train). For details of these trips, see www.seat61.com. At the same web site there are links for onward travel in Turkey itself but, since no trains serve the coast, at some point you have to change to a bus.

Getting around the area
By car or motorcycle

Having your own wheels makes travelling along the Lycian coast uncomplicated, but some caution is required. Once warrior-like Turks hunted on their steppe horses; today their great-great-great-grandchildren handle themselves with equal prowess in traffic — the combat cry has simply been replaced by the horn. For many drivers there is only one lane — the middle of the road. Overtaking on blind corners, driving the wrong way on a one-way traffic lane or street, not stopping for red lights: these things happen all too frequently. You will witness all this for yourself in time, but it pays to be aware of it from the start.

You can **rent a car** in the tourist centres on nearly every corner whereas, in comparison, the number of places offering **mopeds, motorcycles** and **bicycles** is pretty modest. If you are interested in renting any sort of vehicle, you must of course have your driving licence and passport or ID card. Some rental companies require that the driver is at least 21 or even 23 years old and has had their driving licence for at least one year. The large international rental companies usually forbid you from leaving asphalt roads so that, strictly speaking, you would not be allowed to drive to any bays or ancient sites only accessible via tracks. If you plan to do a lot of driving, look for a car that uses less expensive diesel.

Prices are usually substantially lower from local hire companies than from the large international chains. Depending on the season, you'll pay between £15-30 per day with the smaller companies. They offer this price advantage by having an older and usually less well-maintained fleet of vehicles. The prices of the better-known hire firms differ little — again, depending on the season, they charge about £35-55 per day for the cheaper models. Whichever you choose, the mileage is usually free. The best value is to book by the week before leaving home, and can be cheaper still if booked straight away as a **fly/drive**. Prices for motorcycles begin at approximately £20/day, scooters start at £15/day and mopeds at £10/day.

Do read the **small print**: make a note of the **insurance cover** specified in the contract, and particularly personal liability in the event of a claim. Note for instance that even with fully comprehensive insurance, under-body damage and flat tyres are not covered. Various rental companies accept credit card payment; gold cards usually offer an additional insurance protection/cover, which makes it unnecessary to take out passenger insurance or the like. If in doubt, ask your insurer.

Should you be unfortunate enough to be involved in an **accident**, you must *not* move the vehicle, but summon the police, no matter how remote your situation or seemingly minor the damage. A police report is mandatory for any insurance claim. *Do not sign any report which you cannot read* — or else make a note on the report that you could not read it. There are a few scare stories around about accidents involving personal injury to the effect that it's better to put your foot down and drive to the nearest police station as quickly as possible, lest you meet with summary justice at the scene. However well meant, this is totally irresponsible advice. You would be charged both for hit and run and for not giving aid, with far worse consequences than any possible reprisals at the scene of the accident.

Keep the following **traffic regulations** in mind: the **maximum speed** in built-up areas is 50km/h (with a trailer 40km/h); otherwise 90km/h (with a trailer 70km/h); motorcycles 80km/h. On motorways the limit for both cars and motorcycles is 120km/h. The **blood alcohol limit** for drivers of *cars without trailers* is 0.5mg/l (generally equivalent to two glasses of wine), for everyone else (including motorcyclists) there is *zero tolerance*, no alcohol permitted at all. **Mobile telephones** may only be used with a hands-free device while driving. **Petrol stations** are frequent along the main roads and open seven days a week. Lead-free (*kurşunsuz*) petrol is readily available. Petrol prices in Turkey

Special advice for motorists

• Avoid driving at night if at all possible. Badly lit lorries and cars will be on the roads — to say nothing of people on completely unlit bicycles and farmers in dark clothing on their way back from work. The risks of an accident are also higher at night because you can't see the potholes and building works ahead, and they may only be marked off with some stones. Add to that carefree pedestrians of all ages — the road is regarded as a pavement, especially in the country areas.

• If you are in the first row at a red light when it changes to green, look right and left before going ahead — not all your fellow road-users are interested in the colour play of traffic lights…

• In Turkey it is common practice to sound your horn before a blind bend. If the oncoming traffic does not hear anything, they assume the road is free. It is also common practice to sound your horn when overtaking!

• Exercise special caution on loose chippings, particularly on newly built stretches of road. Thousands of windscreens are broken every year. Keep well back from lorries!

• In order to curtail speeding, frequent radar controls are in place (minimum fine £35), and speed bumps have been added in recent years at the entrances to built-up and populated areas. For those who don't yet know their way around, these speed bumps can be treacherous, because there are usually no signs to make you aware of them, nor are they marked in colour (apart from large oil marks!).

Traffic signs — what's what?

Bozuk satıh — bad stretch of
  road
Dikkat — be careful; caution
Dur — stop
Düşük banket — unfinished road
Kay gan yol — slippery surface
Park (yeri) — car park
Park yapılmaz — no parking
Şehir merkezi — city centre
Tamirat — roadworks
Taşıt geçemez — road closed
  (driving through prohibited)
Yavaş — drive slowly
Yasak — forbidden/no entry

are higher than those in Britain at
time of writing, with a litre of
normal unleaded costing approximately £1.62 (diesel £1.42).
Don't worry if you have a
puncture; the Turks are very
helpful. Ask for the nearest *Oto
Sanayi* — a group of workshops,
usually on minor roads at the
entrance to or exit from the
larger communities.

By bus

The bus is the king of cross-
country travel. The number of
companies with networks
serving the whole country is
incredible, and the price
differences are small.

The busiest companies use
modern Mercedes or Mitsubishi
buses, which are manufactured
in Turkey under licence. Air
conditioning (take a jumper with
you on the bus!) and video are
standard; the majority of the
buses also have toilets, tinted
windows, special seat cushions,
etc. Well-known companies are
Metro, Ulusoy, Kamil Koç,
Pamukkale and Varan. The
better bus companies give you a

token for your stowed luggage,
so it's easily retrieved at the end
of the trip. During the journey
passengers are usually catered
for by a young steward. Biscuits
and drinks are distributed free of
charge, as well as a Turkish eau
de cologne *(kolonya)* for sticky
and sweaty palms.

All the buses are non-smoking
(but they stop for breaks
approximately every two hours).
The departure times listed in this
book serve only as a rough
indication and refer to data from
the larger bus companies.
Journeys with the smaller
(predominantly local) bus
companies invariably take
longer, since they make so many
stops along the route. Further
information about bus travel can
be found with introductory
details about the towns and
villages covered.

Bus fares vary little; on average
one pays 3-4 pence/km, with the
up-market companies charging
somewhat more. So a trip from
Kaş to Antalya would cost about
£4.50. Booking a ticket also
includes a **seat reservation**, and
you can choose your seat from a
plan. Naturally the front seats
are usually the best and most
coveted, but wait: you may be
exposed to the driver's cigarette
smoke — unlike the passengers,
the drivers *are* allowed to smoke
on the bus!

Arrive well in advance of
departure time! Buses leave
punctually — and often up to
five minutes early!

Turkish **bus stations** *(otogar,
terminal* or *garaj)* are very like
British and continental *railway*
stations, with toilets, waiting
rooms, kiosks, restaurants and

shops. If there is no official 'left luggage', you can usually leave your things at the counter of your bus company. Bus stations are usually located several kilometres outside the city centres, so to get to them you often first have to take a service bus or *dolmuş*. But the well-known companies and local bus companies normally offer a feeder service with mini-buses from the centre of town. Smaller towns frequently only have a collection of simple bus company offices near the market, and the buses either leave from just outside the office or stop briefly on the town bypass.

At larger bus stations, **touts** working for different bus companies will try to persuade you to one ticket counter or other. Just ignore them, so that you can compare departure times and prices in peace.

By *Fez Bus*

The 'Fez Bus' (www.fezbus.co. uk) is a hop on-hop off service aimed at backpackers and independent travellers. From the beginning of June until the end of October a Fez Bus leaves Istanbul every two days and makes a circuit round half of Turkey before going back to the Bosphorus. With just one pass (which is valid for the whole season), you can get on and off as often as you want on whichever route you've booked, and you do not have to start at Istanbul. The basic route (Istanbul — Gallipoli — Selçuk — Köyceğiz — Ölüdeniz — Kaş — Antalya — Cappadocia — Ankara — Istanbul) is called the 'Turkish Delight Pass' and costs about

Waiting for the bus

£175, including an English-speaking tour guide. There are a great many add-ons, too — from detour routes on the mainland to *gulet* cruises and trips to Greece and its islands.

By *dolmuş* (shared taxi)

Shared taxis are one of the most popular ways to get around in Turkey. *Dolmuş* means 'full up'; in practice, this means that they do not operate to a strict time-table, but instead set off when the driver is happy that he has enough people on board. A *dolmuş* (usually a mini-bus seating from 14-20 people) can be recognised by a sign on the roof or hanging in the window indicating the destination. In cities there are special *dolmuş* stations for connections to outlying parts of the region, otherwise they leave from the town markets. In large connurbations some routes will have intermediate stops. Moreover, you can stop a *dolmuş* anywhere along its route by waving it down. The *dolmuş* is a boon for walkers!

Dolmuş **prices** (specified by the city councils) are somewhat higher than bus prices in city traffic, but a bit less once outside the built-up areas. The fare is usually collected once you are underway. A new law demands that prices for different distances must be shown, but this is not always adhered to — in which case take note of what your fellow (Turkish) travellers are paying, or you may end up paying an additional 'tourist fare'. The longer routes are broken down into sections, and you only pay for the stretch you travel.

The idyll of a 'blue cruise'

'Blue cruises'

The 'blue cruise' business is booming on the Lycian coast. A blue cruise is an all-inclusive holiday on a *gulet*, a beautiful, broad-beamed wooden yacht. While they do have masts and sails, they are usually motor-powered, and the only sail which is always raised is the protective awning. *Gulets* are usually very comfortably equipped, since blue cruises don't cater for yachtsmen but for tourists who enjoy seeing the coast from the water, bathing in isolated coves … and sharing the 'on-board' experience with others. The only disadvantage is that, once the initial excitement has worn off, sharing a confined space with strangers can be trying. Backpackers will be used to this kind of accommodation and have the right attitude, but for more mature travellers it's a good idea to book as a group and charter your own *gulet.*

Blue cruises are named after trips made by a famous circle of philosopher friends who gathered round the bohemian journalist Cevat Şakir Kabaağaçlı. This 'Turkish Jean-Paul Sartre' published his work under the alias 'Fisherman of Halicarnassus', after he had been exiled to Bodrum because of his anti-militaristic stance. He fell in love with the area and stayed on. In the early 1960s a group of his disciples joined him in Bodrum, where they all sailed along the Aegean coast on sponge-diving boats, trying to live as close to nature as possible and surviving primarily on fish and *rakı*. They called their soul-cleansing travels 'mavi yolculuk', or 'blue journeys'.

By taxi

In the tourist centres you can find a taxi on every corner. The fares for longer journeys (for instance to some tourist attraction, site, etc.) are usually posted in the taxi in various currencies. For trips within the cities it's best to take a taxi with a meter or negotiate the price in advance. *Caution:* sometimes taxi drivers 'inadvertently' press their meter button, so as to make the fare higher. During the day *gündüz* must appear on the display (*gün* = day, *gündüz* = daytime; *gece* = night).

By train

Railways are not, so far, a significant element in Turkey's transportation network, and there are no trains operating along the Lycian coast.

By ferry

Ferries no longer ply the west or south coasts of Turkey. The only regular connections are from Marmaris and Fethiye to Rhodes. All the other Greek islands off the Lycian coast are served by excursion boats.

By chartered boat

The Lycian coast and the southern Aegean are among the most popular sailing waters of the Mediterranean, as you can tell from just one look at all the top yachting magazines on sale in the area. Boats can be chartered locally, with or without a skipper. The main yachting centres for tourists in the area covered by this book are Göcek and Fethiye, but nearly all the other larger resorts have a marina. Or you can anchor in many secluded ports and bays.

You can easily reach Kastellórizo (Walk 1) on an organised boat trip.

By **organised tour**

Take a helicopter to Pamukkale, a bus to Ephesus or a boat to the 'Sunken City' at Kekova: by air, land or sea, all the tourist centres offer innumerable half-day, full-day and two- or three-day excursions to local and surrounding sights. If you haven't time to plan an independent excursion or you prefer not to travel on your own, these organised trips are an enjoyable way to learn more about Turkey. From the price point of view, they are most economical for those travelling on their own, since a couple could probably hire a car for the same money. Even better value are the boat trips to secluded bays which you cannot reach by car.

The big catch with many bus tours and boat trips, of course, is that most of the routes are nearly identical, so many bays and tourist attractions are inundated with huge crowds for a just few hours of the day. What's on offer, and where, is listed for each area in the section 'Practicalities A-Z'

under 'Boat trips' and 'Organised tours'.

Prices for these excursions do not vary greatly between tour operators. If you *do* find a tour that is substantially cheaper than that offered by the majority of operators … then you can expect far more shopping breaks for carpets than are normally in the programme! The tour guides of course earn commission on everything you buy.

By **bicycle**

It's rare to find bicycles for hire — and when you do, they are usually poor quality. Cycling here is still in its infancy so, if you want to tour this area by bicycle, take your own bike — and a helmet as well (you must wear one by law). Combined moped/bicycle workshops offer help with punctures and repairs — provided no exotic spare parts are needed.

By **hitchhiking**

It's not common to hitchhike in Turkey, since public transport is so inexpensive, but in principle it's possible everywhere and once in a while is the best option at the end of a walk. But unaccompanied female travellers should *not* hitchhike on their own.

Walking

In recent years the development of the Lycian Way, Turkey's first long-distance trail, has been widely publicised. If you hadn't read that this is one of the world's top walks, your first glimpse of the towering chain of mountains which runs the length of the peninsula might utterly discourage you from exploring the area on foot.

But you are in for a pleasant surprise. In spring and autumn there is no more beautiful way to discover Lycia than on foot. If you plan to tackle the 'Way', or just parts of it, there is information galore on the official website (see panel). In contrast, this book describes **16 *day* walks**, with many variations, using local transport — or a car if suitable. There are walks for all ages and abilities; all are graded. Many of the routes take in parts of the Lycian Way, but you will always return to the comfort of your base in the evening.

Seasons: **April/May** and **October** are the best months for walking in this part of Turkey. In **spring** the air temperature is moderate (although the sun is still very hot), and there is a delightful freshness in the mountains. But remember that there is always the danger of typical mountain weather. As the temperature climbs after the winter months, the warm maritime air rises to meet the coolness around the snow-covered mountain peaks and condenses to cloud. This does not happen so much when the drier winds from the north are blowing but, when the warm southerlies with their moist air are gently sweeping in on a bright, clear morning, then the first tell-tale signs appear as wispy cloud around the high peaks. Around midday the cloud thickens and spreads, sometimes covering the sun — only to disperse and vanish as the day cools.

Autumn in this part of the country is often long and warm and provides ideal conditions for walking, but you cannot always rely on this. **Winter** is even more variable and, although temperatures never fall very low at sea level, the number of rainy days increases, and the rain is invariably heavy. The sun remains strong and warm

---

Likya Yolu — The Lycian Way

The 509km long-distance footpath runs along the coast from Fethiye (Ölüdeniz) and through the steep Taurus Mountains almost as far as Antalya. The 'Sunday Times' described it as one of the most beautiful walks in the world. It takes about five weeks to complete the whole route — and a few months of training beforehand! Anyone who wants to complete the whole walk, or even parts of it, will find a wealth of details on the official website: www.lycianway.com. The official guide to the route is available from this site or from your usual supplier — it's a good read in any case.

throughout the autumn and winter, and the spells of fine weather can create very clear visibility which make for ideal walking conditions.

High **summer** provides the most difficult conditions for walkers; temperatures get very high and anything more than a short stroll to the nearest beach is not advisable because of the constant danger of heat exhaustion and dehydration.

Guidelines: The **time checks** given at certain points always refer to the *total* walking time from the starting point, based on an average walking rate of

In the Taurus Mountains

4km/h and allowing an extra 20 minutes for each 100m/330ft of ascent. These time checks are not intended to pre-determine your own pace but are meant to be useful reference points. Do bear in mind that they do not include any protracted breaks. Before tackling one of the longer hikes, compare your pace with Dean's on one of the shorter walks. Depending on your level of fitness, you may also consider some of his 'easy' walks to be 'easy-moderate' — or even 'moderate'.

Please accept some words of caution: keep to the routes described (all of which Dean checked in the months prior to publication) and do not try to make your own way in this vast, rugged and difficult terrain. Points that may look close can sometimes take many hours to reach. Except for the Lycian Way, there is virtually no signposting or waymarking, nor are there any accurate large-scale topographical maps. For any walks except those graded 'easy', it will help to have some walking experience, a good sense of direction, a little good will, perseverance and stamina.

If you are an **beginner walker** or you just want an undemanding ramble, look for walks graded 'easy', and be sure to check all the short and alternative versions. Otherwise, turn back at some point of interest part-way along — perhaps a good viewpoint or ancient site.

Experienced walkers should be able to tackle most of the walks in the book, taking into account the season and weather conditions of course. Quite a few full walks are very long, so be sure of your fitness before you attempt them.

It is never advisable to walk alone, and this is especially true for women. If you must go alone, carry a mobile and a loud whistle to use as a distress signal in case of an accident. Whether you are alone or in a group, *do* inform a responsible person where you are going and what time you plan to be back.

Maps: The **maps** in this book have been drawn up from a wide variety of base maps — all very different, none of them accurate. Detailed large-scale maps for Turkey are not yet available, and it remains an area of some sensitivity. (Do *not* try to obtain large-scale maps in Turkey; at the very least you will be regarded with suspicion.) Before publication, we found a fairly modern 1:250,000 military map (not on general sale). Despite its small scale, we have overlaid the UTM grid from this map on our walking maps for GPS enthusiasts to puzzle over (details on the individual maps). Unfortunately, Dean did not have time to track his walks, and we have only calibrated one or two maps ourselves to check known coordinates. These seemed fairly accurate, but others will no doubt be *wildly* out. If any volunteers send in edited tracks for Dean's routes, we will post them on our web site and use them to update future editions.

Equipment: Give careful thought to **basic gear** before you go. Many footpaths are steep and stony; comfortable **walking boots** with ankle protection and good grip are strongly recommended. Long (and fairly thick) **trousers**, tucked into **long socks**, will help you avoid being scratched by prickly bushes and will keep ticks at bay too. **Sun protection** is crucial: sunhat, suncream, sunglasses, and a long-sleeved shirt. Always carry **plenty of fluid and food**: depending on the length of the walk, you will need 1-3 litres of liquid per person (many mountain springs are dry from mid-September until the winter rains). Your day **rucksack** should of course contain a **first-aid kit**, small **torch** and **mobile phone** (emergency numbers are shown on page 50). You may also want to take an **anti-venom kit** (available from specialist camping stockists); see 'snakes' below. If you are walking between October and May, you should also take a **windcheat** and **waterproofs**; in winter a **fleece** or two, **woollen hat** and **gloves**. Any other special gear will be listed under 'Equipment' at the top of each walk.

Nuisances: **Dogs** are generally no bother, as the Turks tend not to keep them as pets, and any stray dogs are usually harmless. (If dogs worry you, take a 'Dog Dazer', an ultrasonic device which persuades aggressive dogs to back off; they are available from the Sunflower website, www. sunflowerbooks.co.uk.) But you will have to be on your guard against **snakes**. Most are harmless and will move out of your way rapidly but, if they don't, the best advice is to quietly move out of their way. There are **vipers** around and, since it would be dangerous to step on a viper, it is *imperative*

that you do not walk in the countryside in open sandals. Always have your feet and ankles well covered and, as a sensible precaution, wear your long trousers tucked into your long socks. Take special care near water, when you are about to sit down, or when you rest your hand, so unthinkingly, on a drystone wall. If you do have the misfortune to be bitten by a snake, seek medical help urgently — and if you cannot identify the species, kill it and take it with you!

In comparison with snakebite, the sting of the **scorpion** is painful, but not dangerous to most people. Again, as a precaution, don't leave any of your clothes on the ground. **Wild boar** forage for food in the mountains, but they are nocturnal creatures, and unlikely to be seen.

You can avoid **ticks** by keeping your body covered. If a tick does get to your skin, it is necessary to make it withdraw before taking it off; an easy way to do this is to touch them with a solvent such as methylated spirits or alcohol. **Bees** and **wasps** are around in summer, so make sure you carry the necessary medications if you are allergic to insect bites. In any case, always give beehives a wide berth!

Accommodation

Accommodation in the area varies from up-market resorts where you will be handed cocktails in the jacuzzi down to places where you wouldn't go into the toilets without shoes. Most hotels and guest houses are located along the coast. There is a very welcome increase in the number of '**boutique hotels**' — small stylish places to stay (some marketed as guest houses), which are often housed in old, restored natural stone buildings. *This book places particular emphasis on this type of accommodation.* The standard of most hotels is in direct relation to the price; Turkey is still an inexpensive destination. During the Turkish holiday period, July and August, reserving in advance is recommended, particularly in larger tourist centres. But outside these months you should have no problem finding a place to stay on-the-spot — on the contrary, your problem will be choosing from the large selection on offer. In principle, bartering is possible in small cheap hotels and guest houses, but fortunately this is not usually seen.

All recommendations in this book mention facilities like air-conditioning or telephones only in establishments where you would not expect to find them.

All-inclusive resorts

The bulk of all-inclusive resorts in the area is clustered around Fethiye. These places, often behind high-security fences and with up to 2500 beds, are not geared up to receive individual travellers at short notice, so booking is either impossible or very difficult. If you do manage it, the walk-in rate is often well above double the normal rate that you would have paid booking through a brochure. Note, too, that the term 'all-inclusive' is not clearly defined, and some hotels give themselves this accolade without actually

earning it. So make sure in advance whether for example the drinks or the sports facilities on offer are included in the price. At many hotels where 'all-inclusive' doesn't mean what it says, some crafty tour operators will advise you never to eat or drink anywhere other than at your base, to prevent being ill or even attacked. This is utter rubbish! The advice is only intended to bind you to the hotel bar, where the beer costs four or five times more than it would outside the resort.

Prices for the all-inclusives depend on equipment, service, size of the buffet, sports facilities, number of hosts and hostesses, etc. and range from £50-£165 per night for a double room.

Hotels

All hotels are registered with the Ministry for Culture and Tourism and are assigned categories. If you choose your accommodation depending on the number of stars, be aware that the classification is based on *equipment* (mini-bar, television, lift, restaurant, air-conditioning, etc.); criteria like location, architecture, friendliness of the staff, and the like are not considered. Moreover the rating is often out of date, because many Turkish hotels were built 'on the cheap', so the equipment often wears out quickly. This applies particularly to three-star hotels. Luxury boutique hotels are not categorised by stars. In hotels at the bottom end of the market and in many guest houses you will just have to accept the fact that there isn't always hot water and the amenities are often unreliable.

Prices: The larger, sophisticated hotels charge from £65 for a double room in peak season. Prices are up to 50% lower between September and May. Small hotels offer double rooms with shower or bath from about £17. A room in really cheap accommodation, without bath or WC, starts from £5.50 per person.

Pansiyonlar (guest houses)

When comparing simpler hotels and small *pansiyonlar*, the latter are usually the better choice, since their operators usually care more about the well-being of their guests. Even when compared with some of the top hotels, the *pansiyon* may be preferable, because the friendliness of the owners makes up for the (rarely missed) luxuries. A number of cosy *pansiyonlar* can be found along the coast in places like Simena/Üçağız, Kaş, Kalkan, Patara and Dalyan. Many campsites (see below) also let rooms — the equipment is spartan, but the rooms (often in bungalows) are usually very well done.

Prices for *pansiyonlar:* a double room with shower/WC ranges from £17-42. Singles are usually given a double room at a reduced price.

Aparthotels

The number of aparthotels has been rising constantly in recent years. Basic equipment includes a kitchenette or small kitchen, a living room with a sofabed and TV and — depending on size — one or more bedrooms. Naturally the **prices** of aparthotels vary substantially depending on size, equipment and location. You should be able to get a good apartment for 4 people from about £42/day.

Youth hostels

In the whole of Turkey there are very few youth hostels, not least because many private *pansiyonlar* (see above) offer inexpensive rooms. There is *no* youth hostel in the area covered by this book.

Tree houses

These are wonky huts on stilts or built in trees. Simple bungalows are also widely marketed as tree houses. Tree houses offer no comforts or amenities — just madly romantic nights starting from £3.50 per person. They are meeting places for international backpackers. If you want to stay in a tree house, head for the Saklıkent Gorge or Butterfly Valley.

Campsites

The **official, licensed campsites** are, like the hotels, under the control of the Ministry for Culture and Tourism. The normal amenities include showers (not always warm), camper kitchens and power sockets, restaurants and (usually) supermarkets. Prices here are commonly around double the price of **unlicensed campsites**, where the amenities leave something to be desired. Many campsites also let bungalows and parking bays for tents and camper vans. The 'bungalows' are usually simple wooden huts without much in the way of creature comforts, but they usually have tiled floors, bath and WC, terrace, etc.

'**Wild camping**' isn't a problem on the Lycian Way or in the mountains (where there is no other option), but not otherwise recommended: between curious villagers and police checks it can be a very unnerving experience.
Prices: For two people and a tent, reckon on paying £5-17 — the price is the same whether you have a tent or camper van.
Opening times: Many campsites are only open from May to October. They are only crowded in high summer. By the end of September you may be the only guest on the site … and find that the bar, restaurant and super-market have closed.

Food and drink

'The iman fainted', when asked to taste 'women's thighs' and the 'lady's navel'. 'The ruler was pleased' when served the 'vizier's finger'… Whole dramas can be performed based on the names of Turkish dishes! They also hint at which tradition the recipe falls back on and how much fantasy the chef puts into his creations.
'Life comes from the stomach' is a Turkish proverb. And in fact Turkish cuisine can claim to be of as high a standard as French. The basis for the dishes is usually fresh vegetables, including some that are either unknown or seldom used in Britain and Europe (like chick peas, broad beans, okra, rocket and purslane). It's different with spices: they virtually never use Eastern exotica, but rather trusted classics like pepper, paprika or parsley. Garlic is also used, but not as much as you might imagine.

Outdoor restaurant in one of Kalkan's alleys

Where to eat

In the larger tourist centres you can of course find anything from Chinese restaurants to Italian pizzerias, Bavarian beer gardens, and cuisine from around the world. For Turkish specialities the choice is primarily between *lokantas* and *restorans*.
Lokanta: You eat in a *lokanta* to get a meal under your belt rather than to enjoy the 'dining out' experience. *Lokantas* are found on every street corner; they are simple, good and cheap (prices start at £3.20). The décor — tiled walls and cold neon lighting — is spartan to say the least. The pre-cooked meals are kept warm in glass cases, and you select from meat and vegetable dishes, soups

Tipping

In simple lokantas no tip is expected, but in restaurants it is. If the service is *not* included in the total (note that quite often it *is* included), about 10% of the total bill is expected (15% in more expensive restaurants). In restaurants where they have no menus and prices on boards, it is advisable to enquire about the prices before ordering — some waiters are sly foxes…

and stews. The busier the *lokanta*, the fresher the meals usually are. There are many variations on the *lokanta*, too: depending on what the speciality of the house is, it may be called a *kebapçı*, *köfteci* or *pideci*. At an *işkembeci* they serve soup with entrails and other innards. Most *lokantas* do not have an alcohol licence.

Restoran: Restaurants normally have an alcohol licence, more tasteful décor, better service and of course higher prices. But the menu does not always differ from that of the simpler *lokantas*; this applies in particular to mid-range restaurants. A full meal with a beverage starts at about £6.50. For the better restaurants there is no set limit: if you want to enjoy a candlelit dinner at an elegant restaurant by the water's edge, expect to pay £17 or more per person (without wine). Fish restaurants rank price-wise with the more expensive restaurants, and for a three-course set menu expect to pay £17-26 per person.

Breakfast

In the larger hotels in tourist areas, an 'international' breakfast is nearly always served as a buffet; how sumptuous or otherwise depends on the grade of hotel. Even in the less expensive establishments, you can expect coffee, jam, cheese spread and eggs.

But try a traditional Turkish breakfast *(kahvaltı)*! You will be served fresh white bread, jam, eggs (usually hard boiled), olives, cucumbers/gherkins, tomatoes, butter and sheeps' cheese. Turks enjoy sheeps' cheese on bread with honey. With all this, tea is the drink of choice. Filter coffee is not usually available; those who want it will have to settle for *neskafe* or something similar. Turks also eat *pekmez* (thickened grape juice) as a spread with *tahini* (sesame paste) on bread for breakfast — and it's delicious!

Starters

You can choose from things like piquant creamy yogurt *(haydari)*, spicy vegetable purée *(ezme)*, cold vegetables in plenty of olive oil *(zeytinyağlı)*, stuffed vine leaves *(yaprak dolması)*, melon with sheeps' cheese *(peynirli karpuz)* and similar delicacies. The Turks call such starters *meze*, and display them in glass cabinets for you to take your pick. It's also fairly common to do without the main course altogether and select only starters; in many restaurants it's no problem. Fresh white bread *(ekmek)* is always served on the side.

Turks rarely choose **soup** as a starter. They have soup as a replacement for breakfast, occasionally in between meals … or to nurse a hangover. Many

Spices on display always stop photographers in their tracks.

Turks swear by the Alka Seltzer effect of entrail soup (*işkembe çorbası*) … but this may not be to your taste! If you would like some hot soup as starter, try the hearty lentil soup (*merçimek çorbası*) — another speciality.

Caution: Avoid having starters in small beach-side restaurants which are not connected to mains electricity. Dishes with fish and mayonnaise that have been out in the heat for some time can lead to a bad stomach upset or food poisoning.

Meat

The most popular meat dishes are *kebaps* and *köfte*. **Kebap** is the generic term for meat dishes of any kind (usually lamb, some-times poultry), which can be baked, grilled, or roasted. There is probably no need to dwell on

döner kebaps. *Şiş kebap* is a tender meat dish roasted on charcoal, served with rice or bulgar (cracked wheat). *Patlıcan kebaps* are skewered minced meat with aubergine. If the meat is arranged with yogurt and tomato sauce on roasted round flat bread it's known as a *bursa kebap* (or *ıskender kebap*). Also try the *adana kebap*, a strongly peppered mince meat kebab. Or *güveç*, a tender pot roast with vegetables cooked in a clay pot.

Köfte are essentially meat patties or meatballs made from minced mutton, lamb or beef; they can be roasted or grilled. The tasty 'women's thighs' (*kadınbudu*), with added rice and a coating of breadcrumbs, get their name from the elongated shape of the meatball.

Turks love offal — like roasted liver (*ciğer*) or kidneys (*böbrek*). *Kokoreç* is a snack on offer at many street corners — grilled intestines with onions and tomato in bread. There are many, many other curiosities to try, like grilled sheep testicles (*koç yumurtası*), stewed sheep heads (*kelle*) or feet (*paça*).

Vegetables

Vegetables (*sebze*) are used as the base of Turkish dishes rather than as a supplement to a meal. The choice of pot-roasted, baked,

Fishermen drying their nets

and stewed vegetables is enormous. A particularly popular dish is *dolma*: this consists of stuffed vegetables, like zucchini (*kabak dolması*) or aubergines (*karnıyarık*) filled with minced meat or bite-sized pieces of lamb. It is usually eaten with yogurt.

Various stews are also tasty; try *kıymalı ıspanak* (spinach with minced meat). Chick peas (*etli nohut*) or okra with lamb (*etli bamya*) are also delicious. *Caution:* Take it easy, at least to start. The food is often swimming in olive oil — on stomachs unaccustomed to this diet, this can have the same effect as a dose of castor oil.

Fish

Salt-water fish frequently on offer are sea perch (*levrek*), turbot (*kalkan*), Mediterranean mackerel (*kolyos*), plaice (*pisi balığı*), mackerel (*uskumru*) and freshly-caught sardines (*sardalya*). Tuna (*palamut*) features on many menus, too, prepared in several different ways. Trout is a particular fresh-water favourite, and there are many trout restaurants in the hinterland (some feature in our walks).

Sweets and fruit

One of the most popular **sweets** (*tatlı*) is *baklava*, a pastry made from several layers of dough, interspersed with almonds and pistachios. The small rectangles have a syrup of sugar, lemon juice and honey poured over them. *Helva* is just as sweet and sticky, a calorific 'bomb' made of white flour, sesame oil, honey and sugar. Easier perhaps on the British stomach (and conscience) are almond pudding *(keşkül)* or rice pudding *(sütlaç).*

Those who enjoy experimenting should try *aşure* at least once — a jelly-like dessert: when prepared properly in a top-quality restaurant, this contains more than 40 ingredients, including rose water, nuts, cinnamon and even beans! It was inspired by the legend of Noah's ark — you mix all the left-overs together and boil them up.

The recipe for *tavuk göğüsü* is equally unusual — a mixture of chicken breast chopped into small pieces, rice flour, milk and sugar. All these and many others are on offer at the *muhallebici,* snack bars specialising in sweets. If you are happiest ending your meal with **fruit** *(meyve),* there is a wide choice. Depending on the season, melons, figs, grapes, peaches, cherries, strawberries, pomegranates or citrus fruits are available. Washing all fruit thoroughly is good, but peeling it is better!

Snacks

Snacking is an art form in Turkey, and *börek* can almost replace a complete meal; this speciality is a filo dough triangle filled with minced meat, spinach or sheeps' cheese. Similarly delicious fillings are hidden in *pide,* a crispy flat bread. Also worth sampling is *lahmacun,* the Turkish pizza topped with minced meat and herbs.

Mantı is known as the Turkish ravioli — so small that 30 fit on a single spoon; you eat it with garlic-flavoured yogurt, melted paprika butter and mint.

Simit salesmen are always around; their sesame rings are at their crispiest early in the morning. One often sees women in traditional dress as well, preparing *gözleme,* a kind of pancake filled with different kinds of sweet or hearty ingredients. And try *kumpir,* if you get the chance, giant stuffed potatoes.

Soft drinks

Pepsi, Coke and all well-known brands are on sale everywhere. Water *(su)* is often placed on the table with the meal. If it comes from the tap, you should *avoid* drinking it. Freshly squeezed fruit juices *(meyve suyu)* are recommended. Delicious fruit juices are also sold everywhere in cans. *Ayran* is a refreshing drink made from yogurt, salt and cold water — a little like buttermilk.

Turkey for vegetarians

A tired smile is all that most Turks can offer a vegetarian — because those who voluntarily choose to do without delicacies like *şiş kebap, köfte* or entrail soup must be either ill or mad. Don't worry: even without meat one can enjoy delicacies in Turkey. The bulk of the starters are purely vegetarian, and there are plenty of tasty vegetable stews, creamy soups, salads and filled pastry dishes awaiting discovery. In order to avoid any nasty surprises, make sure by asking 'Etsiz mi?' ('Is it without meat?', pronounced 'Aytsis mee?') and follow this up by saying 'Et yemiyorum' ('I do not eat meat', pronounced 'Ayt yaymeeyorum').

Tea, served in a bulbous glass, is the national drink.

Hot drinks

The Turkish national drink is *çay*. This good black tea from plantations on the Black Sea coast is drunk at every opportunity. Whether at breakfast, business meetings, in carpet shops or at the hairdressers, the small bulbous glasses are found everywhere. Tourists seem to have taken a shine to *elma çayı*, apple tea. Turkish mocha (*Türk kahvesi*), which can de ordered either sweet (*şekerli*), slightly sweet (*orta şekerli*) or without sugar (*sade*), is usually taken after a rich meal. Those who don't mind grit between their teeth order *neskafe*. In chic cafés you can of course also get cappuccinos, espressos or macchiatos.

Alcohol

Rakı is the favoured tipple — about 45 percent aniseed liquor — and tasting rather like the Greek *ouzo*. The Turks prefer to drink it diluted with ice and water from high, narrow 0.2 litre glasses. It then takes on a milky colouring and so is also called 'lion's-milk'. *Rakı* counts as a digestive and medicinal aid against all possible ailments, and 70 million litres are consumed each year in the interests of keeping the population healthy. 'Tekirdağ' is the brand most highly recommended. You can tell good quality *rakı* from inferior brands because it makes a film on the glass.

Beer (*bira*) is also a popular drink with meals, the Efes brand being the most common. You can also find Danish Tuborg (brewed in Turkey); it's somewhat drier than Efes.

Less known are Turkish wines (*şarap*). The better varieties are normally excellent — especially the Dolucas and Kavaklideres. Turkish wines are stomach-friendly due to their modest acid content.

Patara's propylon *(see 'Ancient sites' opposite).*

Practicalities A-Z

Ancient sites — the most important terms

Acropolis: castle hill, also the upper part of town

Agora: market and meeting place in ancient Greece; the major part of a colonnade, surrounded by shops

Architrave: a main beam (usually stone) resting across the top of columns

Basilica: central Roman hall, in which the side aisles are lower than the main aisle (only later was the term used for churches)

Bouleuterion: council hall of the senate in Greek and Roman times

Cavea: auditorium of an ancient theatre, in Roman times usually semi-circular, in Greek times usually facing outwards

Cella: main hall of a temple, usually with one or several religious statues

Gymnasium: centre for athletic training, originally part of a school

Heroon: religious building in honour of a hero or dignitary

Capital: uppermost end of a column

Necropolis: graveyard

Nymphaeum: fountain

Odeon: theatre-like building for small cultural events

Orchestra: performance area of the theatre

Pantheon: a temple for all gods

Peristyle: a space surrounded by columns

Propylon: gate building

Stoa: roofed colonnade or portico

Beaches

The search for sun, sand and sea attracts millions to the Lycian coast every year. Some of the most beautiful and best-known

Patara is rated one of the top beaches in all Turkey — 14km long, with wonderful dune habitats.

long sandy beaches lie along the coast, but there is a multitude of idyllic 'hidden' bays as well. **Naturism** is forbidden in Turkey (although it is quite usual to see Turkish men bathing in their underpants). There have been quite a few police raids on beaches frequented by naturists.

Average water temperatures			
January	15°C	July	24°C
February	14°C	August	25°C
March	15°C	September	24°C
April	16°C	October	22°C
May	18°C	November	19°C
June	21°C	December	17°C

Books for background reading

Louis de Bernières, *Birds without Wings* (Vintage, 2005); see page 149

John Julius Norwich, *A Short History of Byzantium* (Penguin, 1998)

Richard Stoneman, *A Traveller's History of Turkey* (Cassell, 1993), and *Alexander the Great* (Routledge, 2004)

Freya Stark, *Lycian Shore* (John Murray, 1956) and *Alexander's Path* (John Murray, 1958)

Kate Clow and Terry Richardson, *The Lycian Way* (Upcountry, 2005)

Chemists

Turkish pharmacies (*eczane*; open Mon.-Sat. 09.00-19.00) have more or less everything you would find at home. Many medicines are called by a different name, however, and are often available without prescription (for instance, antibiotics) — and they are cheaper too.

The nearest **24-hour chemist** (*nöbetçi*) will be shown in the window of the *eczane*.

Children

Turkey is paradise for those travelling with children. If your offspring plays sailboats with plates in the restaurant or cries out from world-weariness on a long bus trip, nobody will get worked up over it, the pieces of broken glass will be removed with a smile, your child will even be comforted and probably given sweets.

You will be welcomed with children wherever you stay, whether in a simple *pansiyon* or a luxury hotel. The latter often provide babysitters who arrange an interesting children's programme, the former will welcome you with unbelievable warmth — with the host even taking the little ones fishing on his boat.

For alternatives to building sand castles there are camel rides on the beach, aquaparks with giant water slides, dolphin shows, etc. The best nappy brand in Turkey, by the way, is Ultra Prima, available in pharmacies.

Climate and weather

See 'When to go' on page 12 and the detailed information for walkers on page 21. Below some statistics.

Monthly averages		
air temperature*	hours of sun	rainy days
Jan. 10°C (7/16)	5	11
Feb. 11°C (7/17)	6	10
Mar. 13°C (8/18)	7	7
Apr. 16°C (11/21)	8.5	4
May 20°C (15/25)	10	3
Jun. 25°C (19/30)	12	0
Jul. 28°C (23/34)	13	0
Aug. 28°C (23/34)	12	0
Sep. 25°C (19/31)	10	1
Oct. 20°C (15/26)	8.5	5
Nov. 15°C (11/21)	6	7
Dec. 12°C (8/18)	4.5	11

*followed by minimum/maximum

Consulates/embassies

Embassies for the English-speaking countries are located either in Istanbul (℅ prefix 0212) or Ankara (℅ prefix 0312).

UK ℅ 0312 455 3344
Ireland ℅ 0212 259 6979
USA ℅ 0312 455 5555 (Ankara) and ℅ 0212 335 9000 (Istanbul)
Australia ℅ 0312 447 2391
New Zealand ℅ 0212 244 0272

There are also British consuls in Antalya and Fethiye:

British Vice-Consulate, Antalya
☎: 0242 244 5313
✆: 0242 243 2095
e-mail: britconant@turk.net

British Honorary Consulate, Fethiye
☎: (90) (252) 614 6302
✆: (90) (252)614 8394
bhcfethiye@superonline.com

Crime

Thefts and robberies are quite rare in Turkey. The country's worst crime is corruption, but that's another story and not a problem for tourists. But be aware that, like everywhere else, there are cheats and con artists around — especially in the big cities and tourist centres. If you have a problem, contact the nearest police or tourist information office. They will help you because tourism is critical for the economy.

Of course it is a good idea to take the usual precautions of leaving valuables (including unneeded credit cards) in a hotel safe (*never on view in a car or on the beach*), carrying no more cash than you need, and keeping to well-lit streets at night. And make sure no one is 'spying' on you when you key in your PIN number.

Illegal drugs are on sale in Turkey: marijuana, hashish, opium and heroin. The punishments for bringing drugs into or out of the country, or drug use are severe — and Turkish prisons are known the world over for their dreadful conditions. *Never take a package out of the country without knowing what is in it.* (By the way, many drug dealers co-operate closely with the police…)

Currency

The Turkish lira was devalued in 2005, when the new Turkish lira (*yeni Türk lirasi*, abbreviated YTL) was introduced.

Notes to the value of 1, 5, 10, 20, 50 and 100 YTL are in circulation. One new Turkish lira comprises 100 *kurus*, and **coins** have been issued for 1, 5, 10, 25 and 50 *kurus* as well as 1 lira.

The prices quoted in this book were as accurate as possible at the time of writing (late autumn 2008), but will no doubt differ greatly from the prices you find on the spot! This is partly due to the fact that prices in Turkey do not rise or fall in line with inflation, but remain stable for longish periods and then jump steeply. But of course the chief factor is the instability of all exchange rates at present, coupled with the drastic fall in the value of the pound.

At the time of writing £1 = 2.40 YTL.

Turkey's **foreign exchange control regulations** require you to declare cash amounts to the value of US $5000 (about £3300) or more on departure.

You can **exchange currency** at banks (normally open Mon.-Fri. from 09.00-12.00 and 13.30-18.00) or the many exchange bureaux in the area (Turks keep their savings in hard foreign currencies, thus the multiplicity of exchange bureaux). The difference in rates between the two is generally small. Always remember to keep a record, as proof that you exchanged your money legally.

Cash machines (ATMs) are thick on the ground, too, and the exchange rate on withdrawals using a debit card is often better than in an exchange bureau.

Credit cards are accepted in all of the better restaurants, hotels and shops.

Not every branch of a bank is authorised to redeem **travellers' cheques**. American Express Travellers' Cheques can be cashed (as long as it's by the person who signed them) at branches of Akbank and Türkiye İş Bankası.

Tipping: in restaurants the rule is generally 10% of the bill; hairdressers, masseurs, chambermaids (per day) around 2YTL. You needn't tip taxi drivers, but rather round up the fare. In bars and cloakrooms just leave some small change.

Students reductions and other **concessionary prices** are shown with the relevant entry fees.

Dress

Away from the holiday centres in Turkey, great importance is attached to cleanliness and proper dress. For what to pack check the table of monthly averages on page 34. For a beach holiday on the coast, light clothes — preferably cotton — are enough, but remember that in the spring a cool breeze blows off the water in the evening. For visits to mosques see under 'Mosque etiquette' on page 43.

Electricity

The power supply is 230 volts as in continental Europe, and two round-pin plugs are the norm, so take your continental or international adapter.

Festivals and holidays

The tourist centres on the coast have surprisingly little infor-

Shave ... or lose out

Whether bushy and magnificent or fine and delicate, they are always well trimmed: only a moustache makes a Turk a man — at least in Anatolia and in conservative circles. Even today village men who have worn moustaches for years keep an eye on the younger generation, to make sure that no young rascal grows a moustache before the 'proper' age.

But in many places on the south coast the young don't want to know about such antiquated traditions, so they are smoothly shaved or sport designer stubble. To them, the classical moustachioed male, with his standard grey department store jacket, has all the status of the village nincompoop from the Anatolian countryside. Even the young women see them as sleazy perverts with x-ray eyes. In some trendy clubs, the bouncers make sure that anyone with a moustache is barred.

Those who wear full beards also remain outsiders, at least when it comes to public offices and universities. In secular Turkey (see page 42) the full beard is seen as a symbol of the wearer's Islamic faith — the equivalent of women covering their heads.

mation about national holidays — probably because it's always 'holiday time' (but only for the tourist, not for them!).

1st January: New Year's Day

January or February: Kurban Bayramı (movable dates, four days); see page 43.

23 April: Independence Day, commemorating the first time

the parliament sat in Ankara (on 23 April 1920). Is also celebrated today as 'Children's Day'.

1 May: Spring Festival (an unofficial holiday replacing the former Labour Day).

19 May: Youth and Sports Day; it marks the start of the Turkish War of Independence in 1919.

30 August: Victory Day, commemorating victory over the Greeks in 1922.

29 October: Republic Day; Turkey was proclaimed a republic on 29 April 1923. This festival is celebrated with parades.

October or November: Kadir Gecesi (movable dates); see page 43 and Şeker Bayramı (moveable dates); see page 43.

10 November: while not an official holiday, the day of Atatürk's death (1938) is 'semi-official', since a large part of the population stays away from work.

See also 'religious holidays' on page 43.

Flora and fauna

The Lycian coast is characterised by typical Mediterranean vegetation, with forests of pine and cypress as well as bushy macchia comprised of oleander, holly, kermes oaks, box trees, myrtles, lavender, carob trees, etc. On the higher elevations, the prevailing tree is the Turkish pine (*Pinus brutia*), but you will also find isolated firs, black pine (*Pinus nigra*) and the Lebanese cedar. Timber from the high Taurus Mountains was exported as far as Egypt in ancient times, for use in boat-building. The Taurus range stretches the length of the Lycian

Setting off to work in the Taurus Mountains

Peninsula, shielding the southern coast from the cool air mass coming off the central Anatolian highlands; below the mountains, olive groves and cotton fields flourish — as do greenhouses for growing vegetables. Everything from tomatoes to melons is cultivated, including bananas, grapes, figs, citrus fruits and the like.

Uncontrolled hunting of wild game has led to the decimation of animal numbers roaming free. Stags and roe deer once played in the forests of the Taurus, today one only sees them rarely. With a bit of luck you can still come across foxes, wild boar, badgers, polecats, tree martens, stone martens and the almost-extinct porcupines or rodents like the cute ground squirrel. Wolves and bears are found only in the most secluded parts of the Taurus, jackals and leopards only extremely rarely in distant eastern Turkey. Lions became extinct in Turkey during the 19th century.

Fauna with 'lower profiles' can be seen darting or waddling

along on the ground — lizards, geckos and turtles. When you're out hiking, you will also see snakes once in a while; 37 different types of snake have been recorded in Turkey, including vipers and adders. Most are not dangerous but, if you are going out walking, read more about snakes on page 24. Chameleons are not uncommon, but hard to spot because of their camouflage.

Of the birds, the storks (under protection in Turkey) are fascinating. There are also many birds of prey such as eagles, falcons and buzzards. Ornithologists will be in their element on the beach at Patara and by the Dalyan Delta, where they can see grey and purple herons, kingfishers, white storks, songbirds, night swallows, and many more.

Finally, just another piece of advice regarding 'animal pests': mosquitoes, fleas and cockroaches don't only see the forests as their habitat!

Gays and lesbians

Homosexuality is frowned on in Turkey, where being outed leads to merciless discrimination. A decree by the Ministry of the Interior even forbids organised groups of homosexuals to gather on Turkish streets. Because of this decree, some 800 participants on a gay cruise were turned away, when their ship was prohibited from docking in the Aegean coastal town of Kuşadası. Turkish gays and lesbians can only avoid discrimination in the anonymity of Istanbul with its millions of inhabitants. Only in Istanbul can gays and lesbians find the same variety of clubs and pubs as they would find around the rest of Europe. To find gay- and lesbian-friendly bars and hotels, see www.turkey-gay-travel.com.

Import and export regulations

You are allowed the following **duty-frees** for personal consumption when entering Turkey:
200 cigarettes (400 if bought in a Turkish duty-free shop before going through customs)
50 cigars or 200g of tobacco
0.7 litre spirits
gifts to the value of £255.
If you come into the country with anything extremely valuable (a high-carat diamond for example), it must be registered in your passport by the Turkish customs on entry.

To **export antique objects** from Turkey, one needs the written permission of a museum director. This also applies to old seals, medals, carpets, etc. Offenders are threatened with harsh punishments. The export of **minerals** also needs written permission (from MTA in Ankara, ☎ 0312 2873430). To take or ship out **carpets**, you must produce a receipt.

When you leave the country, items bought for private use (clothing, for instance) up to a value of £145 can be brought back into the UK tax free (at time of writing). Check with the airlines before leaving about the latest regulations on bringing back duty frees.

Information about Turkey

All the international branches of the Turkish Ministry of Tourism (www.gototurkey.co.uk or, in the USA, www.tourismturkey.org) have mouth-watering brochures that they will send on request (direct from their web sites). Otherwise you can contact:

UK
Turkish Culture and Tourism
   Office
First Floor, 170-173 Piccadilly
London W1V 9DD
(020 7355 4207 or 020 7629 7771
(᠂ 020 7491 0773

USA (New York)
Turkish Centre
821 United Nations Plaza
New York, NY 10017
(212 687 2194/5/6
(᠂ 212 599 7568
ny@tourismturkey.org

Inoculations

No inoculations are *required,* but it is advisable to be vaccinated against tetanus, diphtheria, polio and hepatitis A before your trip. Double-check with your airline, tour operator or the Department of Health (www.dh.gov.uk), to see if there are any changes.
By the way, if you are plagued by a cold during your stay: blowing your nose in public is considered very unrefined in Turkey!

> **Tip on info**
> *Compared with many other destinations, there's relatively little information on Turkey's 'official' web pages, so it's worth surfing the names of places in this book — from hotels to sites. For practicalities, a brilliant site is www.turkeytravelplanner.com*

Internet access

There are plenty of internet cafés in Turkey for those who want to surf the web or send e-mails during their stay. The more stylish the café, the more expensive it is to be on-line: half an hour costs £0.45-0.80. The addresses of internet cafés have *not* been listed in this book, because they change so frequently. Many hotels and even *pansiyonlar* also offer internet access.

Invitations

The Turks are extremely hospitable. Those who enjoy mixing with the locals, whether on bus journeys or on visits to simple restaurants, are frequently spontaneously approached or even invited to tea. Invitations to their homes, on the other hand, for example for the evening meal, are much more rarely extended, because of the sanctity of the family. If you are ever invited into anyone's home, you can take it as a sign of special esteem. Because of this, it is important to remember some of the host's customs and conventions (although small breaches of etiquette will obviously be forgiven).
Guests usually bring a **gift** —

nothing lavish, just something simple that would please the host or family.

Shoes are removed at the entrance. If there are no indoor shoes ready, socks will do.

For a hearty welcome, one traditionally exchanges a double **kiss** (right cheek, then left cheek) — this is more common between people of the same gender than the opposite gender. If you are uncertain, just politely offer your hand and let your Turkish host take the initiative before committing a *faux pas.*

Speaking loudly in the presence of older people is considered poor manners. Seniors are treated very courteously. In traditional families it is even usual to stand when the head of the family appears.

To refuse something offered is impolite. The hosts have undoubtedly made a great effort to please you, possibly spending well beyond their means.

Islam

Islam (in English 'submission' or 'surrender') is the youngest of the major world religions. Like Judaism and Christianity, it is a strictly monotheistic religion; its followers believing in one omnipotent God. According to Islamic belief, Allah is the creator and guardian of all things and all life. He cares for, guides and judges human beings; on the day of the Last Judgement, 'the saved' enter paradise, while 'the condemned' descend to hell.

The religion's founder was Mohammed (around 570-632), who grew up as an orphan in Mecca. His religious and political work began around 610, after the Archangel Gabriel appeared to him in a vision, but his first sermons were received with scepticism in his home city. It was only when Mohammed moved to Medina in 622 (the start of the Islamic calendar) that he became established as a world and religious authority, generally accepted as a legislator and prophet. Some of Mohammed's messages were revolutionary for the times — for instance the condemnation of slavery in the name of God.

The role played by the Islamic faith in Turkey varies from region to region. For many inhabitants of the Westernised coastal towns, it means almost nothing. But just a few kilometres inland, things look very different. For the military, the swirling currents of Islam are a thorn in the side. To prevent the preaching of hate, the government names the *imams* (who are government employees) and prescribes both what they are allowed to preach and what they can teach in theological lessons based on the Koran.

The Koran and *Sunna* are the fundamental teachings of the Islamic faith. The **Koran** (Holy Book of Islam), which consists of 114 *suren* (chapters), is believed to be the true word of God, as told to Mohammed by the Archangel Gabriel. This explains the infallibility attributed to the Koran. The Sunna ('Tradition') is a collection of 9th-century stories *(hadith)* about the life of Mohammed and his followers, giving an insight into how some of the Koran's more obscure chapters can be put into practice. In contrast to the Koran, the

Sunna is *not* considered infallible.

Islam teaches that since human beings are morally weak and fallible, God sends **prophets** to them, who teach them how they should live. In Islam, Jesus also ranks among these prophets, beside Abraham and Moses. The Christian view, in which Jesus is seen as the son of God, is not shared by Islam. Muslims believe that the long line of prophets came to an end with Mohammed, and that the Koran is the final true word of God.

Disputes after Mohammed's death about who should succeed him led to **a splitting of Muslims into two main groups: Sunnis and Shiites**. Over 70 per cent of Turks are Sunni. The Sunni saw

Fethiye's old mosque

The Five Pillars of Islam

The Koran dictates five obligations for all Muslims:

— profession of faith (kelimei şahadet): 'I testify that there is no God except Allah, and Mohammed is His prophet...')

— prayers (namaz) five times a day, washing before you pray

— extending charity to those in need (zekat)

— fasting during daylight hours during the month of Ramadan (oruç)

— a pilgrimage to Mecca (hac)

With some of the duties there is a bit of flexibility. Thus the Muslim need only make his pilgrimage to Mecca if he is healthy and can afford it; washing before prayer can be just done as a ritual, if no water is available; pregnant woman, the sick, and young children can postpone fasting.

the caliph as Mohammed's legal successor and the head of the Muslim world. For the Shiites (the name comes from the Arabic word *schia, or* 'party'), however, only a blood relative of the prophet could stake their claim to leadership. Since Mohammed left no surviving sons, the Shiites saw Ali (Mohammed's cousin and son-in-law) and his descendants as the legitimate successors *(imams)*.

Around 25 per cent of Turks (including many Kurds) are **Alevis**, who are Shias. But the only thing Alevis have in common with Iranian Shias is the belief in blood-line succession.

Laicism: separation of religion and state

'Islam will one day govern Turkey, the question is only whether the transition will be easy or hard, sweet or bloody.' Statements like this, from the former party chief Necmettin Erbakan, were one of the reasons for the banning of the Islamic Welfare Party (1998) and the Virtue Party that succeeded it (2001). From the broken pieces of the latter, the Party for Justice and Development (AKP) was formed, winner of the parliamentary elections in 2002. The banning of religious parties was justified on the grounds that Turkey had been a secular state, with a strict separation of state and religion, since Atatürk founded the republic ('any politician who needs the help of religion to run the government is an idiot').

For the revolutionary modernisers, supported by the military and Western-orientated politicians, Islam was the largest obstacle in the way of modernising the country. Atatürk rejected the Islamic calendar and withdrew Islam from its position as state religion. The Turkish experiment was the first and most successful example in the world of the secularisation of an Islamic state.

But even after all these years laicism is still exposed to many dangers, as was pointed out by the former Turkish President Süleyman Demirel (1993-2000): 'Our state is laical, but its population is not'. The secular way presents a constant potential for conflict, insofar as the basic Islamic social philosophy is the principle that all spheres of life form an inseparable unit, whether spiritual, social, political or economic. While radical forces militate for a religious state, moderates look for ways to preserve traditional Islamic values in today's secularised world and not play off one side against the other. A popular advocate of this approach is Yaşar Nuri Öztürk, Dean of the Islamic Faculty at Istanbul University. His publications rank among Turkish best-sellers.

For example Alevis reject the strict Islamic *Sharia* law: unchanged for over 1000 years, this interpretation of the Koran and Sunna sets out the rights and obligations of individuals in the community and covers every conceivable aspect of life.

Mosques (*cami*) are not only intended for prayer; they are also used for community meetings, theological lessons, political meetings and temporary accommodation for pilgrims and the homeless.

Usually one enters a mosque via a forecourt (*avlu*), where the ritual washing is done at the cleansing well (*şadırvan*) before prayer. The prayer hall, spread with carpets, consists of a prayer niche (*mihrab*) which always points toward Mecca, a pulpit for the Friday sermon (*minbar*) and a chair or kind of throne (*kürsü*), from which the prayer leader (*imam*) reads out passages from the Koran.

Men and women pray separately, always however in the direction of Mecca. By kneeling and bending the head to the ground, one shows Allah humility and respect.

The muezzin calls followers to prayer five times a day from the mosque's minaret. Minarets were only introduced in the 8th century — before that the muezzins climbed onto the roof. But today the call to prayer, so alluring and 'Eastern-sounding' to the European ear, usually only comes from loudspeakers.

The exact timing of **religious holidays** (see also 'Festivals and holidays' on page 36) is determined each year according to the Islamic moon calendar. In Islamic convention a holiday begins at sunset the evening before. When it comes to important holidays, all shops, offices, etc. will close at noon the day before. The following holidays are of particular importance.

Kadir Gecesi (Night of Power) falls on the 27th night of the fasting month of Ramadan. This holy night celebrates the Revelation of the Koran to Mohammed through the Archangel Gabriel. People believe that wishes and prayers expressed on this night will be granted.

Şeker Bayramı, the Sugar Festival, is the feast marking the end of Ramadan, the month of fasting. One visits relatives, and children go from house to house asking for sweets — hence the name. All businesses and public offices are closed for this three-day holiday.

Ramazan

This is the name the Turks give the Islamic month of fasting, which is called Ramadan in most other Islamic countries. Followers may not eat, drink, smoke or have sexual intercourse between sunrise and sunset for 30 days. After darkness falls however … everything is possible. In conservative rural areas, you may find many restaurants closed during Ramazan, but of course in the holiday centres one hardly notices any difference.

Kurban Bayramı, the Sacrifice Festival, is the most important Islamic holy time and a four-day public holiday. This festival is rooted in the story of Abraham, who was willing to sacrifice his son Isaac, in order to prove his loyalty to God. At the last moment God provides a ram instead. The Turks follow in this tradition, with a lavish meal of newly slaughtered sheep for family and friends. All left-overs are donated to charity.

This is the time of year when pilgrims travel to Mecca, so that both domestic and international travel in Turkey is at a peak — be aware of this and try to avoid travelling on the first or last day.

Remember, too, that banks will be closed and some ATMs will run out of money.

Maps

The most reliable map of the area for general purposes is only for sale in Turkey itself: look for *A map of Ancient Lycia*, prepared and distributed by Sabri Aydal (scale 1:250,000), on sale in many shops. Large-scale topographical maps are impossible to find at present. Apart from the maps in this book (see notes on page 23), your best option is to use the maps published with the guide to the Lycian Way (see website, page 20), but they have little detail and no grids.

Medical care

There is no reciprocal health agreement between Turkey and the UK (or any other English-speaking country); it is strongly recommended that you take out **private health insurance** and read the conditions carefully if you intend to take part in any potentially dangerous sports like paragliding or rafting.

For minor ailments, it often suffices to visit one of the many chemists' shops and describe your symptoms to the pharmacist. Although they are very unlikely to speak English (use gestures), they have been dispensing remedies for the usual tourist problems for years. If by chance you are suffering from 'tourist tummy', straight away you might try drinking some black tea with a bit of salt in it.

Music and belly dance

To European ears, all Turkish music may sound the same, but it is in fact divided into different styles.

Folk music: With traditional Turkish folk music (*halk müziği*, also called *Türkü*) a *saz* (Turkish lute, usually with three strings) takes pride of place. Soloists or small combos sing about the simple things of countryside life — birth, love, death. After decades of absence, Kurdish folk music is also making a comeback. One hears this music mostly in cosy oriental taverns — ask for a '*Türkü-bar*'.

Classical (art) music: In contrast to folk music, *fasıl* or 'art music' is performed in restaurants. It had its origins in Ottoman palace music, but there are traces of more modern influences. The singers are usually accompanied by the *kanun* (zither), *darbuka* (hand drum), *tef* (tambourine) and *ud* (lute). One of the most successful interpreters on the Turkish art music scene is busty Bülent Ersoy: gaudily made up and clothed in mink and glitter, this corpulent 50-year-old Barbie Doll was a man until 1979.

Turkish **pop music** addresses the same topic as most English hits: love. 'Türkpop' mixes traditional Turkish melodies with modern influences, so the interpreter has a wide-ranging palette — from top songwriters like Sezen Aksu ('the Madonna of the Bosphorus') to trendy teen stars and even schmaltz.

Arabesque music, as the name suggests, has its roots in Arabian music: the topic is unrequited love. This rather monotonous oriental 'wailing' is often heard on the TRTint TV station … or on the *dolmuş*. Top among performers is Müslüm Gürses,

Belly dance today is just a colourful pageant put on for the tourist market.

who looks like a love-sick dachshund. There have been some notorious Arabesque concerts frequented by 50-year-olds (usually stoned) who fall about howling in ecstacy and cutting themselves with razor blades.

Many Europeans see **belly dancing** as the epitome of Turkish-oriental sensuality. But in Turkey itself, even today it is seen as somewhat indecent and is often attributed to other cultures. So for instance conservative Turks will tell you that these erotic shows originated in Egypt, whereas the Arabs are convinced that the dance was brought to Turkey by the Ottoman occupiers. Belly dance today is primarily put on for the tourist market.

Rock and electronic beats: Catchy guitar sounds are supplied by top rock bands like Duman, Kargo, and Manga or soloists Özlem Tekin, Şebnem Ferah and Teoman. Rashit's music is more punk. Since the Eurovision Song Contest in 2004, God and the world knows that Athena stands for Turkish ska-

punk. Among the country's most popular DJs are Yunus Güvenen, Emre and Soulsonik. Arkın Allen, who lives abroad and is also known as Mercan Dede, pioneered links between Turkish Sufism and contemporary Western electronic music.

Newspapers and magazines

English newspapers and magazines are on sale in all the tourist centres along the Lycian coast, the papers usually being on sale the day after publication. The English-language *Turkish Daily News* prints background information and current news — politics, economics, sport and culture.

A new English-language daily newspaper, *Zaman*, has appeared. It is very conservative (Islamic) editorially; if any Western-thinking Turks see you reading it, you will be shunned.

Catching up on the news

Opening times

The Islamic day of rest is Friday, but the legal day of rest in Turkey has been **Sunday** since Atatürk's reforms.

Banks: see 'Currency', page 35.
Government offices: Mon.-Fri. 08.30-12.00 and 13.00-17.30; closed Sat./Sun.
Shops: The retail trade has no standard opening times; usually shops open Mon.-Fri. from 09.00-13.00 and from 14.00-19.00 and on Sat. from 09.00-13.00 only. But in tourist centres every day is shopping day. Large shopping centres are also usually open every day until late in the evening.
Post office: Mon.-Fri. 08.00-12.00 and 13.00-17.00; closed Sat./Sun. In larger cities and in some tourist centres post offices are open for certain services (like the telephones) until midnight and from 09.00-19.00 on Sun.
Museums: Usually closed Mon., but see individual entries.
Restaurants: Usually open daily from 11.00 until at least 23.00. But small *lokantas* often close early in the evening.

Police

You'll see a lot of police about. Since they are very badly paid, they are usually bad tempered — except in their dealings with tourists, when they are generally very pleasant and courteous. In addition to the police (with blue uniforms) there are tourist police in the major resorts, many of whom speak some English. Yet another police force is the *jandarma*, a military unit in green uniforms, who ensure public order and security.

Post offices

Post offices (and post boxes) are instantly recognisable by their yellow signs with the three black letters PTT. The main post office (*merkez postane*) in larger cities is usually located near the main square or the bank and/or shopping district. A **postcard** takes about a week to arrive in the UK. Post offices usually have **telephones** (see page 50).

Prices

Compared with the UK, Turkey is an inexpensive destination. Although prices rocketed with the introduction of the YTL in 2005 (and are of course higher in tourist centres than in the rest of the country), Turkey still offers extraordinary value for money. According to economists, the YTL was substantially over-valued, and no one was surprised when it suddenly dropped about 20% in value in 2006. In 2008 exchange rates were fluctuating dramatically. What a holiday will cost you depends on your requirements, but there is something for virtually every budget. Living very simply, for instance in a *pansiyon* with breakfast provided, picnic lunch and one restaurant meal, you could get by on well under £25 a day, including bus or *dolmuş* travel.

Shopping and bargaining

Leather goods, carpets, gold jewellery, ceramics, tea, spices, onyx, and all the other purchases that hint of the Orient are among the most popular souvenirs. Not forgetting T-shirts, jackets and trousers from the top designer labels — these are all imitations

Buying Turkish carpets

Turkey is well known for its low-priced carpets. But you have to know what you're doing and exactly what you want. Most tourists are talked into buying something on the spot — usually overpriced, too large, too small, or in unsuitable colours.

To negotiate a good price you must be able to distinguish high-quality workmanship from inferior goods. Forget everything you've ever heard about settling on one-third the asking price to guarantee a bargain; *everyone* gets two-thirds off after the tenth tea. The dealers know all about this rule of thumb, so who's to say that they don't start with a price magnified a hundredfold?

If you know next to nothing about carpets, by all means buy a small, cheap one as a souvenir (when you consign it to the loft the moths will be happy) — or go to a specialist back home, put up some security, and take a carpet home to try out.

If you *must* buy a carpet in Turkey, go with the advice of an expert: check the thickness of the knots and the number of knots per sq cm. Flex the carpet in natural light, dividing the pile with your fingers to make sure the colour goes straight through. Be careful not to burn a hole in the carpet with the infamous cigarette lighter test, or you'll fall straight through. Be sure to ask if the carpet can fly and, if not, immediately ask for a 50% discount. If you heed all this advice, the dealer won't take you for a fool. One more thing: *never* accept a dealer's offer to post your carpet home for you!

Carpet shop in Kaş. Some tips for buying hand-knotted Turkish carpets are in the panel opposite … forewarned is forearmed.

of course, but at least they fulfil their purpose: you can at least wear them. On the other hand, take care with the deceptively packaged top-name perfumes, which are just ghastly.

It's best to buy from boutiques and shopping centres in the larger cities, where items are priced and you can compare prices. Where there are **no fixed prices**, you must **bargain**. To bargain well, you must be able to estimate value and authenticity. Without wishing to get the better of you, unfortunately just about all Turkish dealers are as sly as foxes (like the waiters mentioned earlier). So don't let them sell you artificial leather as fine napa

What Turkish names can mean

Imagine your butcher being called Etyemez ('he does not eat meat') or the drinks salesman Eck Suiçmez ('he does not drink water'). This can happen in Turkey.

The many strange, composite surnames go back to a law passed in 1934. In the course of Atatürk's reforms the Turks, who until that time had no surnames, had to give themselves one. Some could select a name, others were appointed one. Some made perhaps a suitable choice for their circumstances at that time, but didn't consider the legacy that would be left to their sons and daughters. And so the piano player at the hotel bar may be called Parmaksız ('without fingers')...

Unfortunately, today only the choice of first names remains. But these are in no way lacking in imagination either: the joy felt at the birth of a first child may be expressed by the name Devletgeldi ('the luck came') or Gündoğu ('the sun rose'). On the other hand, sometimes when the family is too large, they hope to be able to stop by naming the last-born (whether a boy or girl) Yeter ('this one's enough') or Dursun ('it ought to stop').

lambskin and only believe a fraction of what you are told. If you know in advance that you will be interested in buying gold jewellery or carpets, check the value of what you want to buy in your own country before you leave.

Turkish **weekly markets** with stalls selling everything from vegetables and cheese to clothing and shoes are called *pazar*; **fixed markets**, like those at the bazaar in Antalya or the market quarter, with proper shops, are *çarşi*.

VAT: If you buy anything to the value of around £60 or more from shops or boutiques with a tax-free symbol in the shop window, you can get the VAT of 8% refunded in the airport departure lounge at so-called 'Cash Refund Offices' (in Antalya airport for example the counter is in the check-in hall). To claim the refund you need a completed tax-free receipt from the seller.

Sites and museums

Some of the most famous ancient sites in the world are to be found in the area covered by this book and the *Antalya to Demre* and *Bodrum to Marmaris* guides. You will also come upon a multitude of other sites, all indicated by brown signs. The most important of these are described, usually with accompanying site plans. Some of the walks explore even lesser-known (but nonetheless interesting) sites — and you won't have to pay an entrance fee, since they are not 'commercialised'.

The **entrance prices** for ancient sites and museums are not uniform and are updated annually. Once in a while you find extreme jumps in price of 30-50% (up or down). However, as a rule of thumb, an entrance fee of up to £9 is demanded for the more expensive ones. At time of writing only rarely were **concessions** available for students (with ISC) or seniors — this may change in future. **Photography** or filming (video) occasionally costs

Obelisk at Xanthos, with the Harpy Monument and pillar tomb in the background

extra and then usually *quite a bit extra* (up to £6.50!). On the other hand there is a multitude of sites offering free entrance.

A word to the wise: often self-appointed 'guides' try to take money from tourists. Don't let yourself be taken in; only officially-authorised guides can hand over an entrance ticket!

Sport and leisure

In places where the Turks themselves holiday, the sports on offer generally amount to nothing — after all, the precious holiday weeks are taken for recovery, which means lazing about. In the international tourist centres however, the trend is towards the European style of active holidays. More and more tour operators offer leisure and sports programmes in addition to the obligatory excursions to touristic highlights. Naturally water sports dominate along the coast.

Diving: You can snorkel with mask and fins almost anywhere along the coast, but underwater hunting with tanks is forbidden — as is removing any historical and/or antique articles that you may find. Kaş is the main diving centre.

Golf: There are plenty of opportunities for golfing in the Kaş to Dalyan area. Belek, about 45km east of Antalya, is the golfing centre of Turkey, with championship courses (covered in detail in the *Antalya to Demre* guide).

Kayaking/Rafting: Various tour companies offer kayaking and rafting, especially in the Dalaman River between Dalyan and Fethiye — usually only in early summer. Sea kayaking is very popular around the Kaş area, especially for day-trips to the Kekova area (or you can camp out for a few nights; see 'Kekova Aktif' on page 9).

Paragliding: Baba Dağı (1969m),

Fethiye — a popular yachting centre

above the Ölüdeniz lagoon, is a meeting place for international gliders (see page 143). Tandem flights are offered, but to fly alone, you will have to have the relevant experience. There is also paragliding at Assas Dağı near Kaş (see pages 70-71).

Riding: Most of the larger tourist centres have riding stables offering treks in the highlands; you can usually book through local tour companies.

Sailing: see page 19.

Surfing: In the tourist centres surfing schools offer courses and organise board rentals. But no experts surf in the Kaş to Dalyan area; the surf's better on the Bodrum Peninsula.

Tennis: Many of the larger hotels have tennis courts, at which non-guests can also pay to play.

Walking: One of the best ways to see Lycia; see pages 21-24.

Water sports: In the international resorts on the coast, various water-based activities are offered — water skiing, banana- and speed-boating, paragliding off a boat, jet skiing, etc. The organ-isers are usually on the beaches.

Telephone

Making calls with a mobile phone is problem-free in nearly the entire area, but expensive.

Those who don't have a mobile or want to save money should make calls using a card phone. You can telephone from post offices (you will be assigned a booth and pay at the counter when the call is completed), from kiosks or from shops with the sign *kontörlü telefon* (telephone counter).

International dialling codes: for the UK first dial 00 44, for the USA 00 1, for the Irish Republic 00 353. This is followed by the local code (without the initial zero, if there is one), then the number.

Calls to Turkey: From outside the country dial 00-90, then the local code (without the initial zero), then the number.

Telephone cards *(telefon kartı)* are available from post offices, kiosks and small roadside stands. A good choice for international calls is the Arakart (www. arakart.com.tr): 250 units for example (15 YTL) allows you to phone the UK for 83 minutes.

Internet: Many hotels and guest houses now offer wireless internet connections, whereby you can call free using Skype (www.skype.com).

Beware of making calls from your hotel room; these are often charged at extremely high rates. Better to make a brief call and ask to be called back (directly to your hotel room).

Emergency numbers
Police ℂ 155
Tourist police ℂ 0242 2470336 (Antalya)
Traffic police ℂ 154
Jandarma (see page 46) **ℂ** 156
Ambulance ℂ 112
Fire brigade ℂ 110
Forest fire watch ℂ 177

The *hamam* — cleansing body and soul

The saying goes that the Ottoman past lives on in the *hamams*, the traditional Turkish communal steam baths which cater for all classes. Once inside, you're in a different world … enveloped by hot, moist air and the smell of soap, relaxing under the spell of splashing water and the murmurings of shining naked bodies lying on a huge marble slab.

The *hamam* is divided into three areas. The entrance hall *(came-kân)*, usually with a decorative fountain, is surrounded by the reception and changing rooms. On entering, you will be given a small robe *(peştamal)* and sandals. While it's usual for men to wear a towel around the loins and for women to bathe naked, you can bring a swimsuit if you prefer.

After changing you move through a passageway *(soğukluk)* into the main part of the *hamam*, the steam room *(hararet)*. The huge marble slab in the centre, which is warmed from below, is the *göbek taşı* (navel stone).

First you are expected to wash all over at the basins along the wall, then rise thoroughly (taking care to leave no suds behind, in case the water is used for ritual washing at the mosque). Then you lie on the marble slab, first to sweat for 15 minutes or so, and then to be massaged.

Women are usually massaged by a hefty masseuse, men by wiry muscle-men. Before the massage begins, the *tellaks* soap you down, then use a very rough flannel for exfoliation (a procedure called the *kese*). By this time your limbs are soft and rubbery, ready for the massage. Be warned: you will be pulled, twisted, kneaded and pummelled like a lump of dough; the massage is intended to loosen tight muscles and joints. After-wards you will feel totally drained, totally relaxed.

Most *hamams* have separate sections for men *(erkekler)* and women *(kadınlar)*. At smaller baths men and women bathe at different times or on different days, but in tourist centres mixed bathing is sometimes offered.

Time

Turkey is on Eastern European Time, two hours ahead of Greenwich Mean Time, in both summer and winter (clocks go forward or back on the same days). At noon in Turkey, it's 10am in the UK, 5am in New York.

Toilets

Men's toilets have the label 'Bay', women's 'Bayan'. In tourist centres the facilities are usually up to European standards; otherwise is it not uncommon to find the stand-up 'hole in the floor', and no paper will be provided. *Take your own!* If a small bucket is provided in the toilet cubicle, please throw any paper in there and do not try to flush it away — the old-style thin sewage pipes simply cannot cope (and besides, toilet paper in the cesspits delays decomposition).

Naturally there are toilets in museums and at sites (small charge), and in restaurants. Otherwise you can usually find public toilets near a mosque.

Travel documents

Travelling from the UK or any English-speaking country you will need a **passport** and a **visa**. Package tour operators will arrange visas for you, otherwise you can buy one on the spot *for cash* at the airport or border when you enter Turkey.

While not strictly required, it is suggested that you also have a **ticket** for return or onward travel.

At time of writing you do not need any **inoculations**, but see page 39. Private **health insurance** is strongly recommended; see 'Medical care', page 44; **travel insurance** is mandatory.

If you plan to hire a car, you must have your **driver's licence**; if you are driving to Turkey in your own car, see page 13.

Visiting or business cards
Turks seem to love them, and will sometimes honour you by handing you their card, or will ask for yours. Before a Turk hands you his card, he will usually make a squiggle on the back, thus 'invalidating' the card. This is because in the past people could go into a restaurant or shop, and it was understood that the bill would be settled by the person named on the card.

Turkish

In all the tourist centres you should be able to communicate in English with no difficulty. But in the countryside you may have problems if you don't know at least a few words of Turkish, since many schools there teach no foreign languages at all.

Turkish is a very logical language and, once you have mastered a few of the rules you can progress quite rapidly, especially with pronunciation. A number of the letters in the Turkish language are unfamiliar to English speakers, but are easy to pronounce; one or two 'normal' letters are pronounced differently. **In Turkish, *usually* the first syllable is stressed.**

C/c	pronounced like the 'j' in 'jet'; *cami* (mosque) is pronounced **dj**amee
Ç/ç	pronounced 'ch'; *çam* (pine) is pronounced **ch**am
Ğ/ğ	just elongates the previous vowel; *dağ* (mountain) is pronounced **daah**
İ/i	pronounced 'ee'; *iki* (two) is pronounced ee**kee**
I/ı	pronounced 'eh'; *altı* (six) is pronounced al**teh**
Ö/ö	pronounced like the 'ea' in 'learn'; *köprü* (bridge) is pronounced kurh**prew**
Ş/ş	pronounced 'sh'; *şeker* (sugar) is pronounced **sh**eker
Ü/ü	pronounced like the 'u' in 'lure'; *köprü* (bridge) is pronounced kurh**prew**

Basic words and phrases

Evet/hayır	Yes/No
Lütfen	Please
Teşekkür ederim	Thank you
Affedersiniz	Excuse me
Merhaba	Hello
Allaha ısmarladık (said by the person leaving)	Goodbye
Güle güle (said by the person staying)	Goodbye
Hoşça kal	So long, cheers
Günaydın	Good morning

İyi günler (as a greeting or when leaving)	Good day
İyi akşamlar	Good evening
İyi geceler	Good night
Nasılsın?	How are you (singular)?
Nasılsınız?	How are you (plural)?
İyiyim	I'm fine.
... var mı?	Do you have...?
Saat kaç?	What time is it?
Büyük/küçük	Big/little
İyi/kötü	Good/bad

In towns

Tren istasyonu	Railway station
Garaj/otogar	Bus station
Havalimanı/ havaalanı	Airport
İskele	Ferry dock
Saray	Palace
Sokak	Alley
Cadde	Road
Meydan	Square
Cami	Mosque
Hisar	Fort
Kule	Tower
Kilise	Church
Müze	Museum
Banka	Bank
Hastane	Hospital
Köprü	Bridge
Ada	Island

Modern Turkish

Originally Turkish contained many Arabic and Persian words written in Arabic script. Despite Atatürk's language reforms (the Roman alphabet has been used since 1928), these influences remain. In his attempts to make the language more 'Turkish', the old words had to be transliterated into the Roman alphabet, leading to some inconsistencies that remain today.

Kütüphane	Library
Kitabevi	Bookshop
Eczane	Chemist
Bakkal	Grocer
Süpermarket	Supermarket
Pazar	Weekly market
Çarşı	Market
Postane	Post
Seyahat acentası	Travel agency

Directions/getting around

Nerede ... ?	Where is ... ?
Ne zaman?	When?
Sağ/sol	Right/left
Doğru	Straight ahead
Otobüs	Bus
Tren	Train
Araba	Car
Taksi	Taxi
Vapur	Ferry
Yaya	On foot
Bilet	Ticket
Varış	Arrival
Kalkış	Departure
Giriş	Entrance
Çıkış	Exit
Tuvalet	Toilets
Bay/Bayan	Men's/Ladies'
Açık/kapalı	Open/closed
Polis	Police
Girilmez	No entry

Numbers

Bir	1	*On sekiz*	18
İki	2	*On dokuz*	19
Üç	3	*Yirmi*	20
Dört	4	*Yirmi bir*	21
Beş	5	*Otuz*	30
Altı	6	*Kırk*	40
Yedi	7	*Elli*	50
Sekiz	8	*Altmış*	60
Dokuz	9	*Yetmiş*	70
On	10	*Seksen*	80
On bir	11	*Doksan*	90
On iki	12	*Yüz*	100
On üç	13	*İki yüz*	200
On dört	14	*Bin*	1,000
On beş	15	*On bin*	10,000
On altı	16	*Bir milyon*	1,000,000
On yedi	17		

Eating and drinking — general

Şerefe!	Cheers!
Yemek listesi	Menu
Bunu ısmar-lamadım	I didn't order that
Hesap, lütfen	The bill, please
Kahvaltı	Breakfast
Öğle yemeği	Lunch
Akşam yemeği	Dinner
Tabak/çatal	Plate/fork
Bıçak/kaşık	Knife/spoon

Breakfast

Beyaz peynir	Sheep's cheese
Bal	Honey
Reçel	Marmalade
Ekmek/tereyağı	Bread/butter
Yumurta	Egg
Seker/tuz	Sugar/salt

Drinks

Çay/kahve	Tea/coffee
Türk kahvesi	Turkish mocca
Neskafe	Instant coffee
Süt	Milk
Meşrubat	Non-alcoholic
Su	Water
Soda	Sparkling water
Meyve suyu	Fruit juice
Ayran	Drink made of yogurt, water and salt
İçki	Alcoholic drink
Bira	Beer
Fıçı bira	Draught beer
Şarap	Wine
Beyaz şarap	White wine
Kırmızı şarap	red wine
Viski/votka	Whisky/vodka

Starters

Meze	Turkish starters
Ezme	Vegetable or yogurt cream
Haydari	Yogurt dip with mint and garlic
Humus	Hummus
Patlıcan salatası	Aubergine salad
Zeytinyağlılar	Cold vegetables in olive oil (various types)
Piyaz	Salad of beans, olive oil and lemon
Sigara böreği	Elongated fried pastry filled with sheep's cheese
Çerkes tavuğu	Chicken in walnut sauce
Beyin salatası	Salad of calves brains
Çiğ köfte	raw meatballs
Çorba	soup
Mercimek çorbası	Lentil soup
Yayla çorbası	Yogurt soup with mint and lemon
Domates çorbası	Tomato soup
Tavuk çorbası	Chicken soup
İşkembe çorbası	Entrail soup

Main courses

Dolma	Stuffed vegetables
Yaprak dolması	— vine leaves
Biber dolması	— peppers
Patlıcan dolması	— aubergines
Kabak dolması	— zucchini
İmam bayıldı	Baked aubergine with onions and tomatoes (literally 'the iman fainted')
Güveç	Braised vegetables, often with bits of meat
Köfte	Meatballs
Hindi	Turkey
Tavuk	Chicken
Piliç	Small chicken
Sığır/dana	Beef/veal
Kuzu	Lamb
Pirzola	Cutlet
Karışık ızgara	Mixed grill
Şiş kebap	Skewer
Adana kebap	Peppered mince kebap
Bursa kebap	Döner kebab/tomato sauce and yogurt

Tas kebap	Braised lamb
Arnavut ciğeri	Pieces of liver

Fish and seafood

Alabalık	Trout
Balık	Fish
Barbunya	Mullet
Levrek	Sea bass
Lüfer	Blue bass
Kılıç	Sword fish
Sardalya	Sardines
Kalkan	Turbot
Hamsi	Anchovy
Uskumru	Mackerel
Dil balığı	Sole
Midye/yengeç	Mussels/crabs

Vegetables and side dishes

Sebze	Vegetables
Bamya	Okra
Kuru fazulye	Dried beans
Taze fazulye	Green beans
Bezelye	Peas
Havuç	Carrots
Ispanak	Spinach
Karnıbahar	Cauliflower
Lahana	Cabbage
Domates	Tomatoes
Zeytin	Olives
Soğan	Onions
Salatalık	Cucumbers
Sarmısak	Garlic
Salata	Salad
Çoban salatası	Mixed salad with sheep's cheese
Yeşil salata	Green salad
Cacık	Yogurt/cucumber/garlic
Makarna	Noodles
Patates	Potatoes
Pilav	Rice
Bulgur	Cracked wheat
Yoğurt	Yogurt

Fruit

Meyve	Fruit
Armut/elma	Pear/apple
Karpuz	Watermelon
Kavun	Honeydew
Üzüm	Grapes
Muz	Banana
Portakal/limon	Orange/lemon
Çilek	Strawberries
İncir/kiraz	Figs/cherries
Şeftali/kayısı	Peach/apricots
Nar	Pomegranate

Desserts, sweet

Tatlı	Any sweet
Sütlaç	Rice pudding
Lokum	Turkish delight
Dondurma	Ice cream
Kek	Cake
Pasta	Gâteau

Snacks

Börek	Stuffed filo pastry
Gözleme	'Turkish pan cake' (filled)
Lahmacun	Turkish pizza
Simit	Sesame rings
Turşu	Pickled vegetables

Women

Thanks to the reforms of Atatürk in the 1920s (and Turkey's ambitions to join the EU), the position of women is nothing like that in most Islamic countries. Nevertheless there is a large discrepancy between their legal rights and reality in a country so long dominated by men. Naturally the divide is greatest between town and country. The increased literacy rate is mainly due to the education of women. On the Mediterranean coast and in the towns, over 50% of the female workforce are educated beyond the compulsory eight years (a third of all graduates are women), but in the countryside the figure falls to 5%, and one woman in three is illiterate. Interestingly, more women work at the Istanbul stock exchange than men, a quarter of the country's lawyers are women, and a third of the doctors…

History

From about 150,000 BC (palaeolithic): Nomadic hunter/gatherers roam across the Turkish Mediterranean coast according to finds from caves like the Karain Cave near Antalya.

8,000-5500 BC (neolithic): The cave paintings at Beldibi (also west of Antalya) date from this period. Inland there are town-like settlements which today rank among the oldest 'cities' in the world. Loam is used in the building of dwellings. With the establishing of settlements, agriculture and cattle breeding also begin. Pottery is developed at about the same time — during excavations close to Konya (about 150km northeast of Antalya as the crow flies), archaeologists discovered small sculptures of full-breasted goddesses, symbols of fertility.

5500-3200 BC (chalcolithic): More finely-worked pottery and simple tools come into use, wrought from copper (found at the Hacılar excavations near Burdur, also some 150km north of Antalya).

3200-2000 BC: The Early Bronze Age sees the spread of spinning and weaving mills, as well as bronze jewellery work. Troy is founded, the oldest city on the Turkish coast. Traders from Assur (on the Tigris in what is today northern Iraq) meet with the central and eastern Anatolians, bringing them into contact with writing.

2000-1200 BC: The Hittites cross the Caucasus, and central Anatolia becomes part of the 'Old Kingdom', from which the 'Great Kingdom' is later formed.

Hattussas (some 170km east of Ankara) is made the capital. At the same time Mycenaeans expand their rule over the Aegean as far as Minoan Crete. Troy develops into a prosperous trading centre.

Around 1200 BC: The so-called 'Sea People', about whom little is known, invade from the north via Thrace. Among them are the Phrygians, who play a substantial role in the destruction of Troy and also put an end to the supremacy of the Hittites and Mycenaeans.

1200-700 BC: After the fall of Troy, Greek tribes (led by the seers Mopsos, Kalchas and Amphilochos) migrate from the west coast through Asia Minor to the south coast and found several cities, including Perge and Sillyon — or so ancient sources would lead us to believe, but these are now disputed. What is not in dispute is that, starting from about the 11th century BC, there is an increase in Greek colonisation (Aeolian, Ionian and Dorian) on the Mediterranean coast of Asia Minor. They come into direct competition with the local tribes (Lelegians, Carians, Lycians, and Lydians). By the 9th century BC many of these Greek settlements have grown into substantial ports.

690-550 BC: The Lydians found a large kingdom in the west of Asia Minor, with Sardis as its capital (about 90km east of İzmir); their king, Croesus, becomes legendary. They also conquer further parts of the south coast. Art, culture and science begin to flourish in the cities.

From 545 BC: Under Cyrus the Great, the Persians penetrate as far as western Anatolia and destroy the Lydian Kingdom. They use satraps (colonial governors) for the administration of Asia Minor. Regular rebellions against the Persians follow.

From 479 BC: The Persians withdraw from the Aegean coast. Cities and small towns come and go.

334-333 BC. Alexander the Great conquers Asia Minor; he spends the winter in Phaselis (south of Antalya). This is the beginning of the Hellenistic period, which lasts until the era of the Roman Caesars and brings enormous cultural development.

From 323 BC: After Alexander's death the Macedonian Kingdom disintegrates; its army leaders divide it among themselves. The most important of these Diadochian realms are those of Ptolemy (in Egypt), incorporating Lycia and other parts of the south coast, the Attalid Kingdom of Pergamon in western Anatolia, and the Seleucid Empire — the largest part of Alexander's former kingdom, with Antioch (modern Antakya) as the capital.

197 BC: Under Antiochus III (the Great) the Seleucids conquer Lycia.

190 BC: The Attalids, with the support of Rome and Rhodes, defeat the Seleucids in the battle of Magnesia (today's Manisa). Nearly the whole Seleucid Empire falls to the Kingdom of Pergamon, which is allied with Rome. Only Lycia goes to Rhodes.

Harpy Monument and pillar tomb behind the theatre at Xanthos, one of the key cities in the Lycian League

From 167 BC: The Lycian cities separate from Rhodes and form a federation, retaining their independence for about two centuries, thanks to skillful, Rome-friendly diplomacy.

From 133 BC: On the death of Attalus III, the kingdom of Pergamon passes to Rome and becomes the Roman province of Asia. Several cities on the south coast ignore Roman law, however, and indulge in piracy.

63-67 BC: The Roman Commander Pompey (the Great) brings the piracy to an end. Four years later he creates the Roman province of Syria.

42 BC: With Caesar's murder, the eastern part of the Roman Empire falls to Mark Antony.

31 BC: Octavian (later Emperor Augustus) is victorious over Mark Antony's fleet in the battle of Actium. Beginning of the 'Pax Romana', lasting nearly 250 years. Roman culture penetrates all cities in Asia Minor. Temples, boulevards, theatres, aqueducts and the like still bear witness today to the glory of the age.

43 AD: Lycia is merged with Pamphylia into a Roman province, but the Lycian League continues to exist under the Romans.

45-60 AD: St. Paul the Apostle stops off in different cities on the Lycian coast during his missionary journeys. The first Christian communities are formed.

Around 290: A child is born in Patara, who later becomes world-famous as St. Nicholas.

330: Emperor Constantine (the Great) names the former Byzantium (Istanbul today) Nea Roma (New Rome) and makes it the new capital of the Roman Empire. Soon after his death, Constantinople becomes the generally accepted name.

380: Christianity becomes the state religion; all pagan cults are forbidden.

395: The final division of the Roman Empire into west and east. The latter, later known as the Byzantine Empire, becomes the heartland of Christianity, with Roman law and Greek as the language.

527-565: Under Emperor Justinian I, Byzantium expands and blooms. It extends from southern Italy over the Balkan Peninsula and the whole of Asia Minor to the edge of the Iranian highlands. All building activity is concentrated in Constantinople. The coastal towns play a subordinate role from now on, even though many of them are made diocesan towns.

622: Mohammed and his followers emigrate to Medina (the *Hijra*, or 'Flight'); this is later designated the first year of the Islamic calendar.

From 636: Eastern Byzantium is conquered by the Arabs. Trained by Syrian sailors, seaborne invaders plunder the Byzantine coastal towns. Coastal fortresses are rebuilt or strengthened for protection — often using ancient stonework for the building materials.

860: Arabs occupy Antalya.

1054: Schism of the Roman Catholic and the Greek Orthodox churches.

From 1071: Seljuk Muslims penetrate west from the Kirgistan steppes and attack Byzantine troops in the battle of Manzikert. They bring Islam with them, and spread throughout central Anatolia, making Konya their capital and holding the remnants of the Byzantine Empire in fear.

From 1096: Help comes to Byzantium from the Occident: the Crusades begin, to free the lost holy cities from Islamic rule.

1204-1261: The Fourth Crusade is organised against Constantinople itself, with the intention of reviving the Roman Catholic faith. After taking the city, the

Knights establish a Latin (Roman Catholic) Empire. The Greek Byzantines withdraw to Nicea (İznik); it is not until 1261 that, under Michael VIII Palaeologos, the Greeks take Constantinople back from the Latins.

1226: The Seljuks conquer further parts of the coastal region. Venetians and Genoese receive permission to establish future trade.

From 1243: The Seljuk Sultanate is crushed by the Mongols. In its place several small principalities are established in Anatolia by Turkmen dynasties.

From 1309: The Order of Knights of St. John found a sovereign state on Rhodes; in the following years they establish various fortresses in the Aegean.

1326: Osman I (1281-1326), army leader and chieftain of a Turkmen tribe, conquers the west Anatolian city of Bursa, later called the cradle of the Ottoman Empire. Since Mongolian armies control the east, Osman's successors look to the north and west.

1354: Gallipoli is conquered by the Ottomans, providing them with their first foothold in Europe.

1402-1406: The Mongolian ruler Timur Lenk (1365-1405; also known as Tamerlane) makes a short and bloody appearance in Anatolia, devastating many cities. This however has little effect on the ascent of the Ottoman Empire.

1453: The Ottomans conquer Constantinople, the only remaining stronghold of the

---

Sultanate of Women

Süleyman the Magnificent (1520-1566) and his main wife Roxelane initiated the so-called 'Sultanate of Women' — a transfer of power from men to women and an explanation for the slow decline of the Ottoman Empire lasting over three centuries.

With her intrigues and murderous plots, Roxelane brought her own son Selim II (1566-1574) to the throne. He went down in history as 'Selim the Sot'. Even before he slipped and drowned in the bathtub, the Ottoman Empire lost its entire fleet.

Selim II had five sons, four of whom were murdered by his wife Nurbanu, so that her own offspring could be crowned Sultan Murat III (1574-1595). Like so many sultans, he proved to be more active in the harem than in politics. This rewarded him with over 100 children, of whom his wife Safiye contrived to have 19 murdered, so that their son took the throne as Sultan Mehmet III (1595-1603)…

One could go on and on about the history of female influence on the successors to the Ottoman throne. And the fact that the budding sultans grew up in the harems, pampered and spoilt, in a world completely out of touch with reality. Flattered by courtiers scheming to see their own interests satisfied, the regents were for the most part incapable of acting for themselves. Many were not even strong enough to govern to the natural end of their lives. They were either strangled, poisoned or so weak-willed that they were driven out of office.

Byzantine Empire, thereby wiping it off the map. From now on Constantiniya (Istanbul since 1930), is capital of the Ottoman Ottoman Empire, and its sphere of influence grows steadily. Less than 20 years later the Ottomans take the Turkish south coast.

1517: Selim I (1512-1520) conquers Syria and Egypt, thus bringing the Caliphate to the Bosphorus.

1520-1566: Süleyman I, known as the Magnificent, conquers Bagdad, Belgrade, Rhodes, Hungary, Georgia, Azerbajan and parts of North Africa. In 1529 he besieges Vienna for the first time. He leads the Ottomans to the zenith of their powers, when it takes 75 minutes for the sun to set over their Empire. Süleyman and his successors have little interest in the development of Asia Minor's coastal towns.

From 1683: Defeat after the second siege of Vienna means the end of expansion and heralds the gradual decline of the Ottoman Empire. There are repeated flashes of unrest on the domestic front.

From 1808: Under Mahmut II (1808-1839) the first attempts take place to gradually reform the Empire. He eliminates the Janissaries (an elite military unit who resist all progressive currents), probably by the ruse of inciting them to revolt, leading to their massacre or exile. He outlaws the turban and introduces the fez in its place.

1853-1856: The Crimean War; the alliance of the UK, France, Sardinia and the Ottoman

Empire recaptures the Russian-occupied territories. Florence Nightingale gains fame for her nursing work in Istanbul.

1875: The 'Sick Man of the Bosphorus' receives the bill for its failure to join the Industrial Revolution and its many expensive wars: France and England cancel all credit; the consequence is national bankruptcy.

1908: At the start of the Young Turk movement, officers force the resignation of Sultan Abdül Hamit II in favour of his brother. True power now lies in the hands of the military.

1912-13: The First Balkan War; the Ottoman Empire loses its remaining European territories.

1914-1918: During the First World War the Turks side with Germany and lose. The winners divide the spoils: Greek troops march on Ankara; Italy occupies the coastal strip around Antalya; France occupies Cilicia; English troops control the Bosphorus. The Ottoman Empire now only consists of central Anatolia.

1919-20: Istanbul is forced to accept the Treaty of Sèvres on behalf of the Ottoman Empire, however the nationalists do not. April 1920 sees the first meeting of the Grand National Assembly in Ankara and the formation of a new government under Mustafa Kemal, later Atatürk (see panel opposite). Military resistance is organised.

1921-22: Kemal's troops strike the Greek army at the Sakarya River. The Italians and French retreat.

1923: With the Treaty of Lausanne the Allies recognise the

Atatürk, father of the Turks

Atatürk's likeness greets you in every office, shop and restaurant; he bids you goodbye from every lira you hand out. He excites the imagination of Turkish sculptors, too — because with the exception of Atatürk, public statues are rarely commissioned. Hardly any other statesman is assigned such cult status.

As Mustafa Kemal (born around 1881) he was elected the first President of the new Republic of Turkey in 1923. He secularised and Europeanised the new state in an enormous act of will. For his services to the country, in 1934 Parliament gave him the name Atatürk, 'Father of the Turks'. Four years later he died in Istanbul from cirrhosis of the liver. His remains rest in the Atatürk Mausoleum in Ankara.

independence and sovereignty of the new Turkey. In Ankara, the new capital, the National Assembly proclaims the Republic and selects Mustafa Kemal as President. In the same year, the Norwegian Fritjof Nansen, working on behalf of the League of Nations, suggests a population exchange between Greeks and Turks. Ankara agrees immediately. This effectively ends the 3000 years' history of the Greeks in Asia Minor (see panel on page 146).

1924: A new constitution comes into force, which among other things incorporates the separation of state and religion. Islamic Sharia law is replaced by Swiss civil law, Italian criminal law and German commercial law.

1925-1938: Up until Atatürk's death numerous reforms are brought in to Europeanise Turkey: education and writing reform (transition from Arabic script to the Roman alphabet), the introduction of surnames, changing of the rest day from Friday to Sunday, etc.

1945: Having remained neutral for most of the Second World War, Turkey declares war on

Germany. In the same year it becomes a founding member of the United Nations.
1952: Turkey joins NATO.

From 1960: Long periods of political and social unrest, with several interventions by the military. 1960: Kemalistic officers stage a *coup d'état* and allow the execution of the Prime Minister Adnan Menderes. 1971: The cabinet is forced to resign. 1980: The military take power again and dissolve Parliament. The military sees itself as the guardian of Laicism (see page 42) and of Atatürk's legacy. It stands in clear opposition to Islamic fundamentalism and radical left-wing groups.

1974: Turkish troops occupy northern Cyprus.

1984-1999: The Kurdish fight for autonomy claims roughly 25,000 victims in the east and southeast. The situation eases in February 1999 with the arrest of Kurdish Workers' Party boss Abdullah Öcalan; a truce is agreed.

1999: A devastating earthquake in northwest Turkey kills 18,000.

From 2002: The AKP are clear winners in the elections; many small parties lose seats due to a clause requiring a 10% minimum threshhold for a party to gain entry to Parliament. Party leader Recep Tayyip Erdoğan becomes the head of government a year later, and there is a full-on push for much-needed reforms. Laws are passed to meet the Copenhagen criteria for EU membership. But Islamic extremists do not want to see a successful democracy in an Islamic land: to destabilise the country and make

Europe fear Turkish EU membership, a Turkish terrorist cell with supposed Al-Qaida connections commits several atrocities. The bloodiest shake Istanbul in November 2003: explosions at two synagogues, the HSBC Bank and the British Consulate kill 64 (including the Consul) and wound 750.

From 2005: Having ended their five-year armistice in 2004, the PKK brings more terror. Splinter groups cause atrocities in several resorts, including Marmaris.

2006: The long-awaited EU negotiations begin. But any joy in finally getting to the table is quickly swept aside by the unwelcoming attitude of the EU member states. EU euphoria in Turkey decreases correspondingly: in 2004, 70% of the population were in favour of joining, by 2006 the figure is down to only 30%. Orhan Pamuk becomes the first Turk to win a Nobel Prize; his novels typically deal with the clashes of identity between East and West.

2007: Gül, a member of the conservative AKP, becomes President. The fact that his wife wears a headscarf almost precipitates a military coup

2008: Turkey reaches the semi-finals in the European World Cup. In Istanbul, a bomb attack by the PKK leaves 17 dead, and a terrorist shooting in front of the US Consulate 6 dead.

Outlook: In 2010 Istanbul will be European Culture Capital. EU membership is not expected before 2015: the measuring stick for Turkey has been set higher than for any other EU aspirant.

1 KAŞ

Accommodation/camping • Food and drink • Nightlife • Beaches and diving • Sights • Practicalities A-Z

Area code: (0242

Information: the official Tourist Office is in the main square at Cumhuriyet Meydanı 7. The competent and helpful staff are also responsible for Kalkan and Patara. Open all year round, in season daily from 08.30-12.00 and 13.00-18.30, from Oct.-May open Mon.-Fri. from 08.30-12.00 and 13.00-17.30. (8361238, (8361695.

Connections: Buses almost every half hour to Antalya (4 hours; £6). (Buses from Antalya to the airport leave from in front of the THY office at Konyaaltı Cad. 24. The operator is Havaş; price £5.) For information about Dalaman airport, see page 171. See also Bougainville Travel on page 70 for airport services. There are also buses to Fethiye (2h30min; £5), Pamukkale (with transfer in Denizli, 8 hours), Selçuk (with transfer in Aydın, 9 hours), and Marmaris (transfer in Gökova, 4 hours). The **bus station** is 700m inland from the port, close to the coastal road.

Dolmuş: Depending on the season, these leave from the bus station approximately hourly to Kalkan (£1.20), Kaputaş (£1.20) and Patara (£2.80); daily at 10.00 to Saklıkent (return £9), Myra and Kekova (return £9). *Dolmuşes* to the Çukurbağ Peninsula, Big Pebble Beach and the Olympos campsite on the way to Kalkan leave from the port.

Taxi: The taxi rank is at the port.

Water *dolmuşes:* These sail to the local islands. No connections to Kastellórizo; you must book a boat trip (see 'Travel', page 73).

Walks: 1-7 (8-10 are nearby)

K aş sits in a delightful bay, framed by two peninsulas; the white façades of its Greek houses glisten in the sun — as do the sparkling souvenirs and brightly coloured carpets.

At the beginning of the 1990s Kaş was only a place for those 'in the know'. Today it's among the established holiday destinations on the Lycian coast, its population of some 8000 or so inhabitants swelling to 16,000 in summer. During the day boat trips to the surrounding beaches and islands are popular; in the evening there's plenty of action late into the night.

British and Germans make up the bulk of visitors — among them divers, since Kaş is the top diving area in the region (see page 68). But Kaş also attracts the 'un-packaged' tourists, from the yachting crowd to back-packers. Restaurant prices have been rising steadily to take advantage of the relative wealth of most tourists, but there are still a few cheaper *lokantas* and some good accommodation to be found for relatively little money.

Fortunately Kaş has avoided down-market tourism; this is probably due to the fact that it has no vast beaches or the accompanying low- to mid-range hotels and so only merits a marginal reference in most tour operators' brochures.

Kaş was Antiphellos in ancient times. During the Roman era the town exported sponges and wood. Under Byzantine rule, Antiphellos was a bishopric. Then it suffered the same fate as numerous other places on the coast: repeated assaults by the Arabs caused Antiphellos to dwindle to an insignificant fishing village. Up until 1923 (by which time it was called Kaş) the population was mostly Greek, and buildings dating from that time still shape the charming centre around the port.

Owing to the favourable climate, citrus fruits, rubber trees and palms prosper in Kaş, and so do lavish villas and hotels. The small town is growing by leaps and bounds. Since the bay blocks expansion to the south, it simply reaches for the sky on the surrounding hillsides. Reality makes a mockery of the town's once-official proclamation that the bay would not be concreted over and that its ecological equilibrium would always be protected. Even the Çukurbağ Peninsula which stretches southwest into the bay, where not too long ago there was only a handful of houses, is slowly developing into its own postal address. Despite all this, Kaş — in contrast to Fethiye, Kemer or Marmaris — is still basically a cosy, easily manageable resort with charm.

Accommodation/camping
(see plan on pages 66-67)

The town has some 6000 guest beds. There's a huge amount of accommodation above Küçük Çakıl Plajı; if you start from the second row of buildings behind the beach there are plenty of inexpensive places to stay, including well-kept mid-range hotels. Nearly all have a roof terrace with wonderful views, so just be sure that a room with sea view is still available before checking in. There is so much competition that in low season you should be able to negotiate a good discount. And remember that the higher uphill you stay, the less you will be plagued by mosquitoes. Many small stylish boutique hotels have opened in recent years on the Çukurbağ Peninsula, west of the centre.

Hotel Villa Tamara (5), on the Çukurbağ Peninsula. Natural stone buildings with 19 large rooms and 11 suites (all indivi-dually and tastefully decorated and reached via an atrium). Small library. But the real hit here is the lovely pool area with magical sea views. Very popular with honeymooners. Doubles £90. Çukurbağ Yarımadası, (8363273, (8362112, www. hoteltamara.com.tr.

Hotel Hadrian (9), a comfortable small club-style hotel on the Çukurbağ Peninsula; 14 pretty rooms with balconies, most with a delightful sea view. Lots of flowers, large sea-water pool. German/Turkish management and mostly German guests (but with 5-star web reviews from English-speaking clients). Double room with H/B from £90, single from £60. (8362856, www.hotel-hadrian.de. The **Hotel Aquarius (9)** next door is also highly recommended.

Otel Sonne (11), small hotel with 12 neatly furnished, very clean rooms with tiled floors, air-conditioning, telephone, and most with small balcony. Roof terrace with oriental-style seating nooks. Tours can be organised for guests. Double room with breakfast from £35. Yeni Cami Yanı 6, (8361528, www.sonneotel.com.

Hotel Begonvil (23), on the second street in from Küçük Çakıl Plajı. Run by Swiss of Turkish descent. 15 spotless rooms with tiled floors. Lovely breakfast terrace, good choice of international newspapers and books. Very good value for money: double room with breakfast £40. Highly praised by readers. Koza Sok. 13, (8363079, www.hotelbegonvil. com.

Lale Pansiyon (21), a well-established house near Küçük Çakıl Plajı. Saniye, the friendly owner, has lived in Switzerland. Clean rooms with tiled floors, many with sea views. They can arrange tours. Double room £35. Küçük Çakıl Mah., (8361575, www.lalepension.com.

Aphrodite Pension (2), 150m above the bus station. Friendly family-run business in a relatively quiet spot with a view over Kaş. All 27 rooms with shower/WC, small balcony and usually a fine view. Very clean and well kept. Praised by readers. Double room £28, single £18. Yaka Mah., (8361216, (8361449.

Kaptan Pansiyon (13), at Hastane Cad. 68. Readers really like the friendly family, the good breakfasts and the wonderful roof terrace where the boss some-times grills fish for dinner. 14 spotless rooms with tiled floors, several of them with sea view. Double room with breakfast £25. (0535/9293148 (mobile).

Meltem Pansiyon (6), one of several places to stay in the same neighbourhood. Small or large rooms, with and without balconies, the loveliest on the second floor. Nice roof terrace with hammocks, where there are sometimes barbecues. Note: the place changes hands often! Doubles £29. Meltem Sok., 55. (8361855, www.kasmeltem pansion.com.

Camping: **Kaş Camping (22)**, relatively small but attractive site in an olive grove. Terraces on the hillside, with nicely laid out access to the rocky coast and bathing platform. Small restau-rant with a super view. 8 clean bungalows — either in 'dog-house' style with no bath or in tasteful 'luxury' style with bath and air-conditioning. Diving centre. Bungalow for 2 people £18-45, depending on the style. 2 people with camper van £13. On the coast, past the theatre. (8361050, (8363679, www.kascamping.com.

There are other campsites on the road to Kalkan but, being just off the main road, they are quite noisy. One of these, **Olympos Mocamp (1)**, 2,5km out of town towards Kalkan, is staffed and has cooking facilities, hot water showers and a restaurant. They also rent 10 wooden bungalows with fridges and climate control (£28 for 2 people). There is a small pebble beach on the far side of the road. 2 people with camper van £12. (8362252, www.kasolympos.com.

Outside Kaş is **Don Quijote** — a hot tip, but not for everyone. It's in an isolated position on Liman-ağzı Bay and only accessible by boat or a long walk (see the map on pages 78-79). It's totally peaceful and idyllic before 10.00 and after 18.00 (when the tour boats from Kaş aren't at the beach). The bar behind the beach rents 6 simple but nice rooms, all with mosquito netting, climate control, and little verandah. They're divided between two single-story blue and white buildings drenched in flowers and palm trees. There's a restaurant, too (fish dishes about £7). For guests there's a free boat service to Kaş until midnight. Only open from mid-May till end Oct. Reservations on (0536 5244957 (mobile); ask for Ali.

Food and drink

(see plan above)

Restaurant prices are somewhat higher in Kaş, as they are in Kalkan. You can find good, inexpensive places for *pide* and kebabs on Atatürk Bul., heading out of town, and there are several pleasant cafés for breakfast near the post office on Bahçe Sok. A few recommendations follow.

Chez Evy (8), French-run. International cooking with a heavy

Fethiye, Çukurbağ,

Fethiy

Çukurbağ Peninsula
not drawn to scale

Aquapark

Beyhan

Çukurbağ
Peninsula

Cenk

Demokrasi

C

Dolphin Park

Süleyman

Yücesan

Theatre

Yaşar Yarıcı Cad

22 Λ

Nightlife
3 Kapadokya Restaurant
10 Red Point Bar
16 Queen Bar and Mavi Bar
20 Meis Bar

Shopping
14 Erdem Market

French accent — served either in the leafy little garden or the very dainty inside dining room. From salade Niçoise and crêpes to wild boar. Main course from £12-18. Terzi Sok. 2, (8361253.

Mercan (18) has for years been the best fish restaurant in Kaş. In a lovely situation on the seafront promenade, with a nice terrace overlooking the port. You can watch your fish being grilled. The freshest ingredients, but a meal with entrée is fairly pricey. Mains £6-17. (8361209.

Lola Restaurant (16), well-run local in the main square in front of the port — a readers' tip. Inter-

F ood and drink

4 Hanımeli Restaurant
7 Café Merhaba
8 Chez Evy
12 Bahçe
15 İkbâl and Karavan
16 Natur-el and Lola Restaurant
17 Sardunya Paşabahçesi Restaurant
18 Mercan
19 Bi Lokma Mama's Kitchen
24 Memed'im Yeri

A ccommodation

1 Olympos Mocamp
2 Aphrodite Pension
5 Hotel Villa Tamara
6 Meltem Pansiyon
9 Hotel Hadrian and Hotel Aquarius
11 Otel Sonne
13 Kaptan Pansiyon
21 Lale Pansiyon
22 Kaş Camping
23 Hotel Begonvil

national And Turkish dishes: kebabs, good steaks, pasta. Main courses £3-12. Cumhuriyet Meydanı, (8362186.

Bahçe (12), in a shady little garden with wicker furniture, has the best starters in Kaş. And if you still have any appetite left, they have good *adana* and *urfa* kebabs. Meze about £1.80, main courses £4-8.50. Anıt Mezar Karşısı 31, (8362370.

İkbâl (15), nice garden restaurant. Cooking with a Cypriot influence (the owner comes from Cyprus). Prices in the higher mid-range. Süleyman Sandıkçı Sok. 6, (8363193. The **Karavan**

(15) next door is also good. **Natur-el (16)**, 'very friendly management and very good food' say readers. It's near the Queen Bar (on the port side). Among the specialities are different *mantı* (Turkish ravioli) and the sticky sweet *aşure*. Naturally it's all organic. Mains £4-7.50. Gürsoy Sok. 6, (8362834. **Sardunya Paşabahçesi Restaurant (17)**, recommended by many readers. Cosy garden restaurant with sea view. Good *meze*; specialities include *saç kavurma* (a casserole) and different variations on *güveç*. Mains £3.50-6.50. Hastane Cad., (8363180.

Bi Lokma Mama's Kitchen (19) is another garden restaurant, this time overlooking the port. Popular with locals because of the good home-cooked dishes. Family atmosphere; they take a lot of trouble. Hükümet Cad. 2, (8363942.

Hanımeli Restaurant (4), is a readers' tip. You will be greeted by the Şahins and served really excellent Turkish food. Put your own menu together in the open kitchen. Nice inside room and a simple area outside. Some evenings Celal Şahin plays the guitar. Efficient service, fair prices. *Meze* £1.10-1.50, main courses £2.50-£4. Çukurbağlı Sok. 3, (8362818.

Café Merhaba (7), near the post office. Friendly café with delicious home-baked cakes (including organic).

Memed'in Yeri (24), at Büyük Çakil Plajı, is a simple bar/restaurant with film and concert posters on the walls; appreciated by the locals because of the tasty home-cooking.

Nightlife

Most of the nightlife centres on the area at and behind the port — and can last till 3am.

One of the most popular venues is the **Queen Bar (16)**, with dancing on the first floor and a roof terrace above. **Mavi Bar (16)**, nearby, is *the* 'in' place for the diving fraternity, where they drink expensive beers perched on wonky bar stools and listen to loud music like Dire Straits and Bob Marley.

Another divers' favourite is the **Red Point Bar (10)** on Süleyman Topçu Cad. Nice interior, good music, tables in the alley outside.

Only open in the evenings.
The **Meis Bar (20)**, at the port near the taxi rank, usually has live Turkish music. Cosy interior, terrace outside. Friendly service and free entry (so the drinks cost a bit more).

The **Kapadokya Restaurant (3)** on Atatürk Bul. has cheap beer and attacts both Turks and tourists; the food is just secondary. Large terrace.

Beaches and diving

The nearest swimming spot is **Küçük Çakıl Plajı** just east of the port, with a well-maintained terraced lido with bar and sunshade rental — and a few metres of beach. West of the port, below Hastane Cad., various beach clubs have sun-loungers on concrete terraces, and you climb over rocks to get into the sea. There are good beaches outside town. **Büyük Çakıl Plajı** (better known and aptly described as **Big Pebble Beach**) lies about 20 minutes to the east on foot (also accessible by *dolmuş* from the port 4 times a day in summer). **Liman Ağzı** is a double bay with 4 narrow pebble/rocky beaches: Nuris, Don Quijote, Otağ and Bilal. All have loungers and bars. Most easily reached by (irregular) water *dolmuş* in about 20 minutes (£3.50); on foot it takes about two hours from Kaş (see Walks 2 and 3). But the most beautiful beach within reasonable distance is **Kaputaş Plajı** between Kaş and Kalkan (see page 113). Boat trips also offer sailings to the different bays in the area (see 'Boat trips' opposite).

Diving: Kaş is an ideal area for diving. The water is warm and clear, and there are a lot of fish — to say nothing of two underwater caves, reefs, amphorae, and a plane wreck from World War II. The newest sight is a sunken copy of a ship wrecked near Ulu Burun some 3300 years ago (the original model is in Bodrum's museum). They are even planning to create an underwater archaeological park.

Diving with rented equipment costs on average £20-25; for a beginner's course allow £230-280. There are a good dozen diving centres in Kaş, among them:
Barakuda Diving Centre, on the road to Küçük Çakıl Plajı. Well-known diving school, recommended by readers. ℂ/℡ 8362996, www.barakuda-kas.de.
Likya Diving, in the hotel of the same name above Küçük Çakıl Plajı; established for many years. ℂ 8361270, www.likyadiving.de
Kaş Diving, in the Hotel Ferah, ℂ 8364045, www.kas-diving.com.
Note: Diving, snorkelling or swimming above the underwater ruins at Kekova are forbidden.
Aquapark: The aquapark on the Çukurbağ Peninsula has a giant slide and everything else you would expect. Open mid-May until the beginning of October, easily reached by shuttle from Kaş centre; entry fee £9.50.

Sights

Sarcophagi are scattered over the entire area, but most of them are badly damaged. The most beautiful old sarcophagus is right in the town centre on Uzun Çarşı Cad. — the famous '**Lion's Tomb**' shown below. Over 4m high, it is carved from a single block and has an eight-line Lycian inscription. There are also

> **Boat trips to Kastellórizo**
> Day trips to the nearby Greek island of Kastellórizo (Walk 1) are highly recommended. The crossing only takes 15 minutes and costs about £20 per person. Reservations in travel agencies or at the port with Kahramanlar (see 'Organised tours' below).

some remains of the old town wall still visible at the port. The ancient **theatre** of Antiphellos, dating from the 1st century BC, with 25 rows of seats, while rather small, is very well preserved and well worth a visit — not least because of the beautiful views of the bay, the sea and the nearby island of Kastellórizo (there is no fly tower to obstruct the panorama).

The magnificent 4th century BC Lion's Tomb in the centre of Kaş; you pass it just at the start of Walk 6.

Kaş — the port

Practicalities A-Z

Boat trips: There are quite a few options. No matter where you book, a trip usually costs about £17. Popular trips include the **Bay of Kaputaş** (see page 113), the grottos or … just into the blue. Depending on the size of the boat, a trip to Kekova takes about 1h30min-2h. There are also glass-bottomed boats which are particularly good for seeing the underground ruins.

Car hire: You can hire a car through travel agencies or use a local company like **Ali Baba Rent a Car** near the mosque. Cars start from £32 including insurance, jeeps start from £50. ℂ 8362501, Kasalibaba@hotmail.com.

Dolphinpark: This is on the way to the Çukurbağ Peninsula. Two dolphins (Misha and Tom) help with therapy for disabled children. 'Just looking' £2, photography £4.50, swimming with the dolphins (7-8 minutes) £50. Open daily 09.00-19.00. www.dolphinparkkas.com.

Doctors and dentists, English-speaking: English-speaking staff at the town's small hospital, **Devlet Hastanesi**, on Hastane Cad., the road to the Çukurbağ Peninsula. ℂ 8361185.

Events: The **International Kaş Lycia Culture and Art Festival** takes place at the beginning of September — an international festival of folkloric music.

Launderette: Sky Laundry, at the port next to the showers. A full wash and dry £7.50. **Rose Laundry** on Süleyman Topçu Sok., is somewhat cheaper.

Newspapers: English-language papers are sold at several places, for instance at the **Erdem Market (15)** at the mini-palm roundabout on the way to the port.

Organised tours: There are numerous agencies with hundreds of offers. Three examples: **Bougainville Travel Tours**, a travel agency, focuses on active holidays: mountain biking (£30), kayaking near Kekova (£25), etc. They also have an **airport service to Dalaman** (£75 for 1-4 people) **or Antalya** (£85). Çukurbağlı Cad., ℂ 8363737, www.bougainville-turkey.com. Among the trips on offer from **Kahramanlar** at the port are tours to mountain villages where you can experience real Turkish hospitality (£20 including lunch), coach trips to Xanthos and the Saklıkent Gorge (£20) or to Myra and Arykanda (£25). (8361062, kahramanlary@tnn.net.

Paragliding: Tandem flights starting from the top of Assas Dağı (about 1000m) last between 25-45 minutes, depending on the thermals, and cost £90. Try **Sky Paragliding**, at the port, Liman Sok. 10/A, (8363291, www. skyparagliding.com, or **Nautilus**, Terzi Sok., (8364115, www. nautilusparagliding.com.

Police: The station is east of the port (close to the Hükümet Cad.). (8361024.

Post: The post office is in the centre on Bahçe Sok.

Shopping and souvenirs: All the usual touristic things are on offer, from jewellery to carpets to meerschaum pipes. Everything is displayed with some style in the shopping lanes behind the main square, in particular on Uzun Çarşı Cad. Every Friday there is a large **fruit and vegetable market** behind the bus station.

Travel Agencies: Bougainville Travel Tours (mentioned under 'Organised tours' above) also sells flight tickets.

Two-wheel hire: You can rent **scooters** from Ali Baba (see 'Car hire' above) starting from £17 a day.

Yacht charter: Day trips, three-day trips, and week-long trips are all on offer. One week with crew, including food, on **Kahra-manlar's** 24m-long *gulet* (see 'Organised tours') costs £350 per person, based on 8 people minimum. For a two-day package allow £90.

Day trip to the Greek island of Kastellórizo

Area code: (00 30 (the international code for Greece)

Connections: see 'Travel' on page 73
Walks: Walk 1

'Europe begins here' is what it says on a large board at the port in Megísti, the only town on the small Greek island of Kastellórizo 7km off the Turkish coast. If you want to turn your back on Asia for a day, catch a tour boat from Kaş; you'll be there in just 15 minutes. You can take in Walk 1 and still have plenty of time for a slap-up lunch.

Megísti has only about 450 inhabitants, and that's in the summer. Along the promenade in the port, most of the houses have newly done-up façades and even those one street back are being restored — but fragile ruins border their back gardens. Above this there's a wide band of houses overgrown with flowers and greenery. The only road leads to the island's small airport. The rest of Kastellórizo is a maze of old goats' paths, ideal for walking. You hardly ever see any young people here outside summer — they are off working far from home.

Until World War II some 10,000 people still lived on Kastellórizo (called 'Meis' by the Turks). But three factors conspired to destroy the island: an earthquake (1926), German and Italian bombardments (1943), and a devastating fire (1944). Thus Kastellórizo experienced emigration on a scale unknown on virtually any other Greek island. Since only a handful of people live on the island all year round, Athens is making great efforts to encourage repopulation — every family has received a sewing machine and refrigerator; an airport and desalination plant have been built; the telephone network has been improved; taxes have been lowered. So the old men can relax and sit, day in, day out, in front of the tavernas at the port, looking out to sea and the Turkish coast.

Most of the emigrants went to Australia. Today many are returning — at least on holiday. On mild nights they join other tourists and locals at the horseshoe-shaped port. Today the island is also becoming popular with the Aegean yachting fraternity.

Accommodation

There are only about 200 guest beds on the island; in high season all accommodation is usually fully booked; in winter everything shuts down!

Kastellórizo Hotel, modern, 20 rooms with sea views and air-conditioning. Bar, pool, mini-market. Apartments £100-125. ℂ 22460-49044, www. kastellorizohotel.gr.

Pension Mediterranea, at the western end of the port. 7 rooms with fridge and ventilation, 3 of them with sea view. Very peaceful. Doubles £50. ℂ 22460-49007.

Pension Caretta is a lovingly restored old house, thanks to brothers Damian and Jimmy. Simple, clean double room with bath, depending on the season, from £20-30. ℂ/℡ 22460-49028.

Villa Kaserma, also to the west but somewhat higher up, has a wonderful view over the port. Simple rooms with fridge.

Doubles £20-30. ℂ 22460 49370, ℡ 22460 49365.

Food and drink

The port tavernas are famous for their fish; two recommendations: **To Mikro Parisi**: the owner, Jorgo, has been getting his own fish from the sea since 1974. The speciality is fish soup, but the swordfish, *barbournia* and prawns are equally good.

Akrothalassi is a pleasant taverna at the southwestern side of the port, also popular with the locals. Very good grills and fish; huge portions.

Sights

The **museum** (open daily except Mon. from 07.00-14.30, admission free), with its exhibitions about the small island's history, is above the mosque with the slender minaret you see at the far end of the port. The displays include diving equipment, amphorae, ceramic bowls, wall frescoes, pieces of jewellery, and coins. There is a wonderful panoramic view over the bay from the ruined 14th-century **Crusader fortress** above the southern port (Mandráki). The local reddish rock used in the building also gave the island its name: **Castello Rosso** (Kastellórizo, or Red Castle). The island's main attraction is located on the east coast: the **cave of Fokalia**, also known as the **Blue Grotto** or simply as **Grotta**. It can only be reached by boat (£7.50 per person) and, since the entrance is only a metre high, only with a calm sea. Once inside, the boat curves round into a large cavern above water gleaming with blue light. A unique experience!

Walk 1: Kastellórizo

Time: 3h
Grade: moderate; short, but with a stiff climb up to the plateau, and other steps (overall ups and downs about 150m). *No shade.*
Equipment: see pages 23-24.
Travel: 🚢 daily boat trips from Kaş harbour to Kastellórizo, crossing time 15min (7km). It's a good idea to give your passport to the captain or agency the night before you sail, so as not to delay the departure. There is a bank and ATM machine on the island if you wish to change money.
Shorter walk: Mandráki Harbour (time immaterial; easy). Follow the walk to the main square, then walk down to Mandráki Harbour and round the front of the castle. There are plenty of places to swim, or you could visit the museum, climb to the castle and photograph the houses lining the harbour front.

A boat trip across the Bay of Kaş to the Greek Island of Kastellórizo — 'Megísti' to the locals and 'Meis' to their Turkish neighbours — is a 'must'. The island is the furthest east of the Dodecanese chain, of which Rhodes is the main island. The idyllic sheltered harbour enjoys a relaxed, slow pace of life, with cafés and restaurants lining the quayside fronting the traditional whitewashed buildings with their colourful balconies and shuttered windows. In the few shops, there are black and white postcards on sale — old prints showing a bustling harbour full of steamships and seaplanes before the island was crushed by the devastation of the Second World War. The Kastellórizans were a seafaring nation, trading all over the eastern Mediterranean from ancient times, and the sheltered harbour was an important safe haven for shipping on route to and from the Near East.

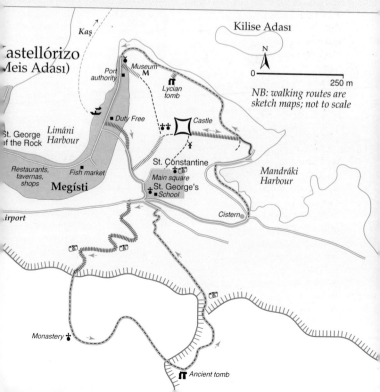

This walk takes in the architectural beauty of the place; the churches and monastery date back to the 18th century, and the ruined castle was fought over since Byzantine times. Climbing the cliff up a whitewashed staircase to the monastery of St. George on the plateau, there are fantastic views over the town and the coastal mountains of Lycia. Then you descend to Mandráki Harbour and continue round the castle rock to the main harbour, where the fishermen assemble, mending their nets by the brightly coloured boats and selling their catch in the covered market. You can enjoy a seafood lunch here at one of the quayside restaurants and swim in the sheltered turquoise waters, before returning by boat to Kaş.

Start the walk at the **quayside**: facing the duty-free shop, turn right and walk along the quay to the dolphin sculptures, then turn left up the steps lined by eucalyptus trees, joining the road up to the **main square**. Explore the area with its splendid architecture. The two main churches on the island are **St. George's** and the cathedral church of **St. Constantine** — the latter with gothic arches and columns which, according to tradition, the islanders had brought from the temple of Apollo at Patara. The **school-house** is also a listed building, and there is a bust of the legendary 'Lady of Ro', Despina Achladiotu (1898-1982). She was the last inhabitant on the smaller island to the west, and kept the Greek flag flying on this isolated outpost, making her a symbol of heroic patriotism.

Turn right round the front of

St. George's and climb the road up the hillside for a short way. Then take the **whitewashed steps** winding up the cliff on your left. The view gets better as you gain height. On a beautiful day in January, purple crown anemones, *Anemone coronaria*, speckle the ground, and spring mandrake, *Mandragora officinarum*, with its greenish-silver flowers, grows through gaps in the stone path. The root of the latter contains mildly poisonous alkaloids, associated with witchcraft and supposedly possessing magical and aphrodisiac properties because of its resemblance to a human being. The plant is said to scream if pulled from the ground!

The staircase ascends rapidly, with fine views over the two harbours and whitewashed houses with tastefully coloured woodwork. Looking across the bay, Kaş is seen nestled below the coastal slopes, with barren scars marking the sites of new development. Continue up through the gate. Arum lilies dot the way, and the aromatic scents of thyme and oregano linger in the air. Then the vegetation thins, giving way to rocky cliff as you near the **top of the plateau (1h15min)**.

After a well-earned breather, continue on the path heading inland, forking left to a fenced-off building (awaiting restoration). This was once the **monastery of St. George**, housing the crypt of St. Charabamleros. If the gate is open, you can see the early Christian mosaic pavement inside. Continue alongside the fenced garden, full of anemones and a few citrus trees, heading east-northeast across the harsh landscape. Take the left fork towards a solitary pine tree (the path is marked by red dots and the odd arrow). Channels, bowls and circles have been carved into a bare slab of limestone; this was either an olive or grape press. Ruined buildings dot the open ground — some circular and faced with ancient stonework. The path heads north, then swings back right by some ruined houses, with views over another Greek island and Cape Ulu Burun, the site of the world's oldest recovered shipwreck (about 1300 BC) protruding from the mainland.

The path then descends to a walled area with a modern shrine placed in the centre of an **ancient tomb** on the right. Follow the water pipe channel running over the terraces to your left. There is another tomb in the cliff and, further on, past the carob and olive trees, an L-shaped tunnel now used as a goat shelter. The path starts descending near the cliff, before swinging away right to another walled area and an old house with a fine view over Mandráki Harbour. The path cuts left around the cliff face, runs through a gate and zigzags down the slope. You go through another gate, heading left, above the road. Drop to the road, turn left, and then turn right by houses and fig trees; follow the road lined by cypress trees. Turn left by the domed **cistern,** to the seafront at **Mandráki Harbour (2h35min).**

Now walk round the harbour. Brightly painted fishing boats are tied to the quayside, and wooden benches stretch along the shore,

awaiting the budding artist. Turn left on the track leading to the front of the castle, then drop to the paved path. Steps lead up to the meagre remains of the **castle,** which was originally divided into two fortified areas to over-look and protect both harbours. In 1306 Kastellórizo was cap-tured by the Knights of St. John; since then the island has been taken by Eygptians, Neapolitans, Spanish, Venetians, Ottoman Turks, Maltese pirates and Russians — all trying to control the naturally sheltered harbour and important trading routes in the eastern Mediterranean.

From the base of the castle follow the walled path lined with cast-iron lamp posts, circling the fortified rock. Steps lead down to the sea. Other steps lead up to a **Lycian temple tomb** (4th century BC). Continue round the walled walkway to the **main harbour entrance**, where the renovated **mosque** is a legacy from the Turkish Ottoman occupation. Nearby, steps lead up to the local **museum**. Carry on past the Port Authority building and back to the start of the walk by the **duty-free shop (3h).**

From here you can explore the houses fronting the harbour. Cafés edge the quayside, the sea is amazingly clean, and fish can be seen, as well as a loggerhead turtle if you're lucky. Wander through the **fish market** into the narrow whitewashed lanes between houses. On the right side of the harbour is another renovated church dedicated to **St. George**; inside is an interest-ing fresco of an eye surrounded by a sunburst.

Time: 8h30min
Grade: moderate, with many ups and downs; mainly on good paths, tracks and roads. Care is needed in a couple of places — when crossing the rocks after Coban Plajı and the short traverse round the cliff face past Nuris Beach and the Lycian tombs. Overall ascent/descent of about 500m.
Equipment: see pages 23-24; *no* drinking water en route; carry *at least* 2 litres of fluid. Refreshments available at Liman Ağzı.
Travel: the walk starts and finishes in Kaş. There are taxi boats from Liman Ağzı to Kaş, if you want to shorten the walk.

Alternative walks

1 Bayındır — Ufakdere —Liman Ağzı — Kaş (7h40min; grade as main walk). 🚌 Take the local service bus or any bus heading in the Antalya direction up the hill from Kaş to the Bayındır turn-off. From here walk along the road to the centre of Bayındır (3km), then join the main walk at the 1h30min-point (by the walled almond grove and open cisterns).

2 Kaş — Coban Plajı — Liman Ağzı — Kaş (6h; grade as main walk). Follow the main walk to the dirt track forking right down the long valley. Take this track down the centre of the farmed plain, passing old oaks and a large keyhole cistern. The track heads left by walled *tarla* (farmland), then swings right to an old stone farmhouse at the end of the valley. There is a is a grand sarcophagus by the side of the house, with a well-preserved ancient Greek inscription on one side. Go back from the tomb to the end of the plain, then take the stony path rising through vegetation.

As it levels out, views open up over the coast and across to the Greek island of Kastellórizo. The path then drops to a covered cistern. Descend on a footpath through the scrub then, at a fork, turn left on the lower of two small tracks. Follow this to a saddle with a ring of olive trees, where you rejoin the main walk at the 4h30min-point.

3 Kaş — Liman Ağzı — Kaş (5h; grade as main walk). Follow Alternative walk 2 to the house with the sarcophagus and the fork where that walk goes left. Turn *right* here, on the higher tractor track. When this track splits, take the left fork, heading down through olive trees and scrub. The track winds down around the hillside with fine views over the rocky shore and continues through a shepherds' encampment. (I was lucky enough to be invited in for a meal here, finished off with home-made *baklava* and *çay*. Outside in a covered pen were over a hundred goat kids, bleating for their mothers' milk.) The track continues downhill, then swings right to a covered cistern. Pick up the main walk here, just before the 6h40min-point.

4 Bayındır — Ufakdere loop (4h30min by car; grade as main walk, with an ascent of 350m). 🚗 Drive to centre of Bayındır village (7km from Kaş) and park near the open cisterns by the walled almond grove. Follow the main walk from the 1h30min-point round to the saddle at the 4h30min-point. Then use the map to follow Alternative walk 2 (in reverse), rising up the hillside through the long valley. On reaching the dirt road leading up to Bayındır, turn right and walk uphill round the next bend. Where the road swings right, take the worn limestone path on the left, heading up a small canyon. At the top of the narrow gorge the path swings sharp right, then left, now as a walled lane. You emerge on an asphalt road; turn left, back to the centre.

The various routes in this walk explore the rugged landscape east of Kaş, rising up to Bayındır village, a mix of ruined stone houses and new buildings set in open farmland, almond and olive groves. In the past, the villagers of Bayındır used to migrate to their yayla (summer pasture) up on the Elmalı plain when the cisterns dried up and temperatures soared. But now most of the villagers have moved permanently to the summer village to tend their apple orchards, leaving the ruins of old stone houses. Some have been bought and renovated by foreigners; others are throwing up buildings which look out of place in this landscape. The walk descends from this high point down to the rocky shore, with fine coastal vistas and idyllic sheltered coves for swimming and picnicking. Once on the coast, the route joins the Lycian Way (for which I marked and cut the path used for your return to Kaş).

Start the walk in **Kaş** by following **Walk 3** (page 80) as far as the bus stop after Big Pebble Beach. Then continue up the road and, at the first hairpin bend, carry straight on up the dirt track in front of the houses. At the top, turn left back onto the road. The asphalt finishes here; continue on the dirt road, through the dip by an olive grove, and go uphill to the next bend, from where there

is a fine view over Kaş ('eyebrow'), the peninsula from which the town takes its modern name, and across the bay to Kastellórizo. As the road rounds the rim of a fertile valley, you pass a dirt track forking off right down this long valley *(Alternative walks 2-4)*. Continue uphill round the next bend. Where the road swings right, take the path on the left, heading up a small canyon. This worn limestone route was part of an ancient way. At the top of the narrow gorge the path swings sharp right, then left, now as a walled lane between new houses and almond groves. You emerge on an asphalt road in the village of **Bayındır** (**1h30min**). Turn left past traditional stone houses and open farmland, an almond grove and the walled **cemetery**, to reach the centre, where there are big open **cisterns**.

Turn right along the dirt track heading south; the track swings right past more cisterns by old stone houses. Just past the white, modern house, fork left on a walled footpath running above the cultivated land on your left. The path runs straight along the plain, with terraced olive and almond groves running up the hillside. Asphodel and sea squill dot the way until the path emerges back on the road. Follow the road seawards along the valley, past a few farmhouses. The road bends and descends and, when you reach an **olive grove** on your right, look through the trees for a covered cistern and ruined house. Leave the road here, and explore the **house with its attached mill** (**2h35min**) — once the local olive press, where the villagers brought their olives to be pressed for oil. Round the left side of the building there is a shady terrace under a carob tree with fantastic views over the the rocky coast-line. The sheltered cove below is Ufakdere, the first of many swimming stops!

From the house rejoin the road, swinging left. Continue downhill and then take the right turn into **Okçüöldüğü**, a small hamlet above Ufakdere. In late winter and early spring the charcoal burners are busy cutting down the scrubby oaks and strawberry trees to build wooden 'igloos', before burning and producing the charcoal that grills your fresh fish in one of the restaurants overlooking the harbour in Kaş. Continue past the last house and turn left on the walled footpath descending towards the coast. Stay on the main, stony path winding down the hillside, with

a gully on your left. The path zigzags down, crosses a dry stream bed and rises slightly before contouring round the hillside. Watch for a **ruined building** on the opposite bank: at this point take a side-path down into another stream bed. At the bottom the path joins the **Lycian Way**, waymarked with red and white flashes. Continue to the stony beach at **Ufakdere (3h35min)**, turn left, pass the ruined buildings and carry on to the headland topped by a Turkish flag. The sheltered cove is an ideal snorkelling spot; there are many broken amphorae scattered in the underwater crevices of the rocky shore, as well as colourful marine plants and sea life.

To rejoin the path, go to the end of the beach and follow the way-marks up the hillside through scrub. The path picks its way

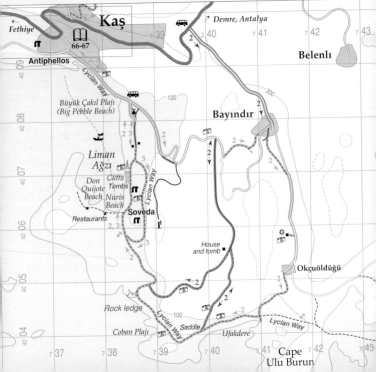

diagonally up the slope to about 70 metres above the jagged shore, then contours around the hillside. Look back for a view of Ufakdere and Cape Ulu Burun, site of a Bronze Age shipwreck (a replica boat is housed is Kaş harbour). In front of you here is a rocky buttress. After the path ascends steeply to a **saddle** on the right-hand side of the buttress, a **ring of olive trees** affords shade for a break (**4h30min**). Continue through the pass, veering slightly right. Through the trees a view opens up across the sea to Kastellórizo's two harbours nestled below the cliffs. Follow the waymarks across the stony ground; the path now drops through denser vegetation as it winds back down to the coast. The stunted trees, taking the brunt of the prevailing southwest wind, grow at an angle. The path leads down to another pebbly beach, **Coban Plajı** (Shepherd's Beach), which unfortunately collects a lot of rubbish from incoming storms. A more sheltered beach lies across the small headland (where goats are normally nearby, munching the prickly vegetation).

Continue northwest along the shore; the path cuts through spiky broom above the rocks. When you come to some large **white boulders**, you have to rock-hop across the sharp-edged limestone, full of drill holes formed by gas bubbles from earlier volcanic activity. The path then ascends back into scrub before contouring and dropping to traverse round the **rock face on a ledge**. You cross a short span with a natural **blowhole** down to your right. Gradually ascending inland through scrub, the path crosses a crest then drops to the edge of a clearing. It then cuts across the plain, heading north-northeast back into trees and rising through olive and carob to a covered **cistern**, where you may meet a friendly shepherdess watering her goats. Go left here along the tractor track, which gradually climbs before dropping and twisting down to open *tarla* (farmland). Continue alongside the cultivated field to the bottom corner of the valley, with a view of Kaş through the gap. Passing through a brushwood barricade, the path continues down to **Nuris Beach** at **Liman Ağzı** (**6h40min**). This is the best beach for swimming, with a fresh-water shower and taverna. From here use the notes for Walk 3 (page 81) to follow the coastal path to **Kaş** (**8h30min**).

Çam Dağı
872

Boğazcık

Kale Tepe

Dinek Tepe

Lycian Way

Walks 8-10

184

1 km

1 mi

N

projection: UTM (35S)
datum: WGS84

Walk 3: Kaş — Liman Ağzı loop

See map on pages 78-79.
Time: 4h
Grade: easy, apart from a vertiginous traverse round the seaside cliff face beyond the Lycian tombs on the return leg (to avoid this, visit the tombs, then retrace your steps, rather than completing the loop). Good paths, although rocky in places.
Equipment: see pages 23-24.
Travel: the walk starts and finishes in Kaş.
Shorter walk: Kaş — Nuris Beach (2h15min; easy). Halve the main walk, taking either the upper or lower route — but remember that the lower route traverses a vertiginous cliff face. Return by ☞: regular taxi boats in season between Kaş harbour and Liman Ağzı.

This loop explores the eastern end of Kaş, going round to the sheltered beaches of Liman Ağzı ('Harbour Mouth'). In spring, tortoises roam the maquis in search of a mate, and porcupine quills can be found along the way. Further along, the ruins of an earlier civilization dot the route, including a hidden fortified citadel which once protected Liman Ağzı (Soveda'a ancient port) from its high vantage point. The walk drops down over worn, fractured limestone to cultivated fields and a small beach where turquoise waters lap the pebbly shore. This tranquil area faces Lycian tombs carved into the rock face. Peregrine falcons dart across the buttressed crags, scanning for prey, and brightly coloured kingfishers fly along the rocky coast. The lower, return path climbs the cliff for closer inspection of the tombs, rises over vertiginous rock steps to a viewpoint, then disappears into the scrub on the return to Kaş.

Start the walk from the main square in Kaş (see plan on pages 66-67): with your back to the **Atatürk statue**, head left up the sea-side road (Hükümet Cad.), past the *jandarma* (military police) and *kaymakamlik* (government offices). The road levels out past the seafront hotels, landscaped with palms, bougainvillea, fragrant jasmine and honeysuckle). Continue up past the forestry commission on a road full of colour — geraniums, lemon and mandarin trees, small pines and a huge Indian bean tree. On your right are helipads and forestry gardens. Once over the rise, views open out over the Bay of Kaş towards Liman Ağzı and Kastellórizo. Behind you is the communications tower on Assas Dağı, launch pad for the paragliders who spiral down to Kaş harbour. The road descends to Büyük Çakıl Plajı (Big Pebble Beach), then rises.

Take the first right turn, opposite the bus stop, towards the houses above the beach. Then, by the turreted but domeless mosque, turn left, past houses. Where the road bends right to some new houses, continue straight ahead on a track. Colonies of the common asphodel, *Asphodelus aestivus*, thrive along here, since the plant is unpalatable to grazing animals; it starts flowering in January. Sand crocuses, *Romulea tempskyana*, with their deep violet, pointed leaves sprout from the rich red soil. The track gradually rises up left by a farmhouse and outbuildings. Continue through the farmyard, then take the path forking right beyond the buildings, into an olive grove. This runs alongside a stone wall, with a field of rock piles on your right (the rocks are collected and piled so that the land can be cultivated).

At a **path junction (1h10min)**, fork left uphill (the right fork is the return route). The path runs through prickly broom and then an animal barricade. You come to a small clearing full of bulbous sea squill (*Urginea maritima*) — its tough leaves wither away before the flower spike appears in July-August. Turn right at a fork and continue through the scrubby oak. After passing a **lidless sarcophagus** on your right, the path forks right. Past a circular stone **cistern,** go right again — to a **viewpoint** overlooking Liman Ağzı, Kaş and the peninsula. Return to the main path, where some channels have been cut into the rock (probably an ancient press for olives or grapes). The scrub circle keeps goats from falling into a deep open cistern. Descending, the path continues through a small clearing with a lone olive tree, from where you can see the communications tower above the buttressed cliffs up to the left. (On the right here, you could climb pathless through scrub to the ancient fortified citadel of Soveda on the ridge.) Carry on along level ground through the clearing, soon sur-rounded by vegetation again. Turn right at the brushwood barricade; the path winds down the cliff on worn limestone to the cultivated fields below. It cuts right through olive trees by a stone pen, then runs alongside the edge of the fields to the bottom corner. You cross over a scrub barricade. Around here you may see charcoal burners

clearing the dense vegetation and cutting the oak and arbutus into small logs to build 'igloos' with air vents. They light a fire inside, then cover the igloo with earth. The wood then smoulders for about six days, the burners keeping watch round the clock to make sure the fires don't die out. They then unearth the charcoal, which is bagged and sold.

The path descends to tiny, pebbly **Nuris Beach** in sheltered **Liman Ağzı (2h15min)**, a good place to swim, with sunbeds and a taverna — try their home-made meatballs *(köfte)*. Continue the walk from the corner of the beach; the path rises above the shoreline through olive trees. When you get up to the cliff, you pass a cavern up on your right, then the path heads left, to clamber up a rocky staircase to the **Lycian tombs**. These are house-tombs, with benches to lay the bodies of the dead inside and slots in the frame to slide open the stone-slab door. There is a Lycian inscription on the roof dating from the 4th century BC. From here the **path traverses the (vertiginous) cliff face** before switching back up to the right — to an electricity **pylon**, an excel-lent viewpoint. On your right here, through the bushes, is a well-preserved sarcophagus. The path continues above the coast through maquis. Past a gap in a stone wall, in a grove of olive and carob trees, the path rises to the right (by a wall), then goes left. Follow the cairns across the field, to rejoin your **outgoing path (3h)**. From here retrace your steps to **Kaş (4h)**.

Time: 7h30min
Grade: moderate-strenuous, depending on the time of year; ascent of about 500m; descent of 1300m. *Only recommended for experienced walkers:* the walk goes above the treeline, to an altitude of 2065m. It is very easy to get lost and also very exposed on the high ridges, as there is *no path* on some sections. *Check the weather report before setting out.*
Equipment: see pages 23-24; warm clothing and waterproofs are essential; walking poles help take the pressure off the knees on the descent.
Travel: 🚌 Elmalı bus from Kaş bus station to Kuruova Beli (Pass); departs 08.00, journey time 1h10min. For the return, there is no bus service to or from Gürsu. When you end the walk, ask at the tea house for a taxi or lift to take you back 8km to the Kaş/Elmalı road. From here hitch-hike or catch a bus back to Kaş or one going towards Demre. If you catch a Demre-bound bus, alight at the main roundabout 11km above Kaş, from where there is a regular town bus service to Kaş.
Alternative walks
1 Kuruova Beli — Bozkaya — Uçoluk Yaylası (6h30min; grade as main walk, but with half the descent). Follow the main walk to the plane tree with the *kösk* and spring (1530m altitude). Continue on the track down the valley, and before losing too much height, cut right to the forestry road by the edge of trees and descend to the main road for a bus at the Uçoluk Yaylasi turn-off.
2 Uçoluk Yaylası — Gürsu (6h30min; fairly easy, with an ascent of under 200m.) Start the walk at the signposted turn-off for Uçoluk Yaylası, about 4km northwest of the village of Gömüce. Walk up the forestry road and drop across the valley, to join the main walk at the plane tree, *kösk* and spring (altitude 1530m). Follow the main walk to the end.
3 Suggestions for motorists.
🚗 Park at Kuruova Pass. Follow the main walk to Bozkaya peak, then retrace your steps to your car. Or do the whole walk, arrange a taxi or lift at Gürsu to take you back to your car. Alternatively, drive up the forestry road to Uçolak Yaylası to do any variation of a shorter walk and enjoy a picnic in the beautiful mountainscape.

I have done this walk in every season, my favourite being a clear sunny day in April, walking in the snow. In late spring, as the snows recede, plant life colours the limestone scree on the elbow below Bozkaya with orange and yellow wild tulips (Tulipa orphanidea), spurge and campanula. A network of open mole tunnels covers the mountainside, half-burrowed through the snow. In autumn, speckled purple colchicums and crocus dot the mountainside, while flocks of cranes fly over on their winter migration to warmer climes.

Start the walk at **Kuruova Beli** (Pass; altitude 1560m). Take the forestry track rising on your right (by the wooden cabin). Go over the barrier and ascend through cedar, pine and juniper forest, with views of Akdağ on your left. Continue up to a **saddle** (1680m), where you turn right on a track down into the next valley. The track levels out across the plain, passing a forester's *kösk* (seating platform) and *shadoof* (a mechanism for raising water from a well, consisting of a pivoted pole with a bucket at one end and counterweight at the other). Woodcutters camp here during the summer months, managing the forest and using their pack mules to porter the cut logs down the mountain. Continue through the open gateway. As the track starts ascending out of the valley, watch for the footpath heading into the forest on the right bank. Take the path up through the trees. Soon the track is again visible on you left. As you pass the last cedar tree, zigzag up onto a higher path, turning right, away from the track. Continue up the path, then skirt the edge of the trees on your right (look around here for fossils of sea life in the limestone scree). Head over left to a **copse** (**1h40min**) and continue through the middle. At the edge of the wood, head left up the slope and up past the treeline. Contour to the right (east), up to the **ridge** (1810m, **2h15min**). From here look east, to see the forestry fire-watch station perched on the summit of Bozkaya.

Traverse to a small green bowl, full of alpine flora after the snows recede in late spring. Take the footpath out of the bowl, rising to the **elbow below Bozkaya** (**3h**). Here views open up, down right over the lush Kasaba valley and up to the Felen ridge, before dropping away to the sea.

From the elbow there is a choice of routes to the summit. Either take the forestry road, which gradually winds its way up to the top, or go straight up the spine of the peak. From the **summit of Bozkaya** (2065m; **3h30min**) there is a magnificent vista over the Lycian hinterland, with all the main peaks in view. The forestry fire-watch station is manned from mid-May to the end of October, reporting any fires back to the Forestry Commission in Kaş.

Descend on the forestry road. From the first bend look down southeast to the village of Gürsu, spread out in farmland — your final destination. To the southwest is Uçolak Yaylası, with Gömüce village below on the main road. Continue down the road, past the elbow. Round the next hairpin you come into cedar forest. At the next bend, descend left through the trees on the footpath in a gully, to meet another, lower track (1600m; **4h30min**). Turn right along the track to a shepherds' encampment, then turn left and drop into the valley. Pick up the path heading right, down the centre of the valley (southwest), passing a spring and fenced corral. The path continues over stony ground, then drops down to a huge **plane tree by a good drinking-water spring** (1530m). A *kösk* is built around the trunk of the tree, taking advantage of the leafy shade out of the hot summer sun.

Fork left and descend into the dip at edge of the forest to pick up an old mule trail. This zigzags down the mountainside, lessening the angle of descent. The trail then heads left (east-northeast), steadily descending through cedar (*Cedarus libanus*), Grecian juniper and Jerusalem sage. Views open up through the clearings over the Kasaba valley and to Alaca Dağ. You pass a cistern and walk on into young regenerating pine trees.

At a **crossroads** (1150m; **6h**) you meet the end of a track: go straight over on the path, twisting through the smaller trees. Dropping to another track, follow it to the left until it bends to the right. Descend left here on a footpath through mature pines. Once down at a crossroads of tracks, head straight across (east) above cultivated land. Continue for 300m — just past the line of pine trees. Then turn right on a footpath winding down through vegetation. At a path junction at a **barbed-wire fence**, turn left and continue alongside the fence. The path goes over trampled barbed wire, passes **two graves**, and descends to a track. Turn left downhill towards Gürsu. You walk under a **wooden aqueduct** carrying water down to the old mill on your right. Turn right in front of the **mill**, then fork left by the houses and follow the track to the asphalt road. Turn left and follow the road, twisting down into the centre of **Gürsu** (740m; **7h30min**). Near the mosque are two teahouses and a market. Past these is a sesame mill on your right, where sesame from the surrounding fields is ground into paste (*pekmez*).

Walk 5: Sinekçi • Semsi • Nisa • Sütleğen

Time: 6h40min
Grade: easy-moderate, mostly on tracks and good footpaths (except for Nisa, where the terrain is very rough in places). There are drinking water springs along the route, and the walk can be done in both early and late summer as the temperatures are cooler than down on the coast — but check the weather report, as the walk is at an average height of 1300 metres.
Equipment: see pages 23-24.
Travel: 🚌 Elmalı bus from Kaş bus station to the Kaş/Sütleğen/Elmalı roundabout outside Sinekçi: departs 08.00, journey time 1h15min; return from Sütleğen's main square on the Kınık bus (every 2 hours); alight at the top of Kalkan and take the next coastal bus back to Kaş.
Alternative walks
1 Sinekçi — Sütleğen (4h; easy). Follow the main walk until you drop down to the school. From here turn right and walk 20 minutes along the road, to the main square in Sütleğen.
2 Sütleğen — Nisa loop (3h; easy, but rough terrain). Start from Sütleğen. Use the map to follow the main walk (in reverse) to the Kumacaz Mosque, Nisa and the school, then turn left and follow the road back to the start.

3 Suggestions for motorists:
🚗 Park near the Sinekçi roundabout for the main walk. From Sütleğen take the Elmalı bus back to the car (15min). Or park in Sütleğen and do Alternative walk 2.

This walk takes you through the diverse landscapes of the Lycian hinterland — valleys of fertile farmland winding up to mountain passes, forests of pine, juniper and cedar overlooked by the snow-streaked slopes of Akdağ (White Mountain; 3024m). While the ruins of Nisa are not as extensive as the major ruined cities near the coast, the stunning views down into Kibris Canyon and the surrounding mountains make for an idyllic setting, and the air has an alpine freshness. Mountain springs irrigate the terraced farmland, where the villagers still use horse and plough to turn the soil before sowing their wheat. Apples are the main produce, along with quince and pear. You will venture through mountain villages, meeting the friendly, hospitable locals, who are likely to invite you to drink çay or offer you apples. The walk finishes in the main square at Sütleğen, a hive of activity, a perfect place to sit outside the teahouse with the village elders … and perhaps help the inquisitive schoolchildren practise their English.

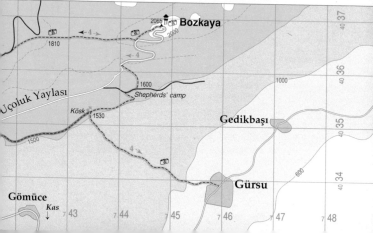

Start the walk at the **roundabout outside Sinekçi** (1260m). Cross the road and take the minor road descending to the right, to a poplar plantation in a dip. Continue straight on, following the road up through **Sinekçi** village. Pass the **cemetery** (with the grave of a young soldier who died fighting terrorists in the mountainous southeast of the country during his national service). Continue uphill past apple orchards, then fork right (by the **mosque** with a large walnut tree on the right). Once round a sharp bend, fork left, up to a **spring** in a wall, then continue straight on along a dirt track lined by blackberry bushes. Turn right at a junction and descend to a bridge, from where you look up the ravine to Akdağ. As the dirt road rises, keep to the higher route at the next junction (although both forks lead to Semsi village). Then take the next left fork and follow this track through farmland and down to **Semsi** (1h15min). The track winds past the **mosque** and on to the village green, with a tree-shaded *kösk* (seating platform). Turn right on the asphalt road. The houses are much larger than those near the coast, the bottom floors being used as storage for the apples picked from mid-September. (The harvest is a big family operation, with every member getting involved.) The road dips then rises to the **cemetery** on the corner. Check the dates on some of the gravestones: 1314-1980 — it must be the fresh mountain air and good clean living! The dates are from two different calendars — 1314 is from the Islamic calendar, which starts in 622, when Mohammed emigrated to Medina.

From the cemetery turn right uphill on a dirt road. The road dips into a wide, open plain. After crossing a stream, turn left up the bank to a **lone juniper on the crest** (1360m). The tree has small berries that ripen dark purple; bite into one, to taste the oil that is used to flavour gin. From here the view stretches to the Susuz Dağlar (Waterless Mountains); below, the valley disappears into the split of the Kibris Canyon. Behind is the mass of Akdağ. Cut back diagonally across the plain to rejoin the road, heading towards the apple and quince orchards. At a house, turn left uphill on a fairly wide road into cedar and pine forest. Fifty metres over the rise (past the small **graveyard**), turn right on a footpath descending through the forest. The path winds down to a forestry road: follow this to the right and then, once around the left bend, turn right on a minor track ascending back into the forest. The track leads to a small clearing, from where you fork right on a footpath winding down the slope. Turn right at a path junction and drop into a fertile valley. You cross an irrigation ditch and walk through a hollow, to a rocky stream bed. Cross this, then take the track ahead up to the clear pool of a natural **spring**.

Walk ahead, then take a footpath on the left down to the concrete channel guiding the snow melt waters into the valley. Cross the channel and ascend through pines, some of which have been scarred where tapped for resin. The path cuts across the track and rejoins it at a higher point. Turn right along the track now, and look back for another view of Akdağ. You pass very stony terraced farmland, cross a saddle (by a leaky water valve chamber) and drop to a road by a **boarding school** in **Sütleğen (3h)**.

Turn right on a track by the left-hand side of the school (by a drinking tap), descending past village houses. Near the end of the track, turn right downhill on a footpath. Go straight over a junction, then turn left at the last house, through a field full of boulders. Take the right fork and descend through the erosion zone to a dirt road. Turn right, rise round the hillside and, at the top of the rise, turn left opposite the walled **cemetery**. The path dips, then forks right and contours round the hillside into the ancient site of **Nisa**.

The first ruins are broken **sarcophagi**. Look below the path for a highly **decorated tomb** with a mother and child sculpted into the stone lid; the now-faceless figures would have had marble insets depicting the tomb's occupants. From here drop to a lower path, turn left, and round the hillside to the small **theatre** (with some 300 seats). Looking over the remnants of the stagehouse is the backdrop of the Sütleğen valley, with its ravines disappearing into the Kibris Canyon. Nisa was strategically positioned to control the pass through to the Xanthos Valley from the Elmalı plain and the more distant Anatolian plateau. Rejoin the path running through Jerusalem sage and scrubby oak. You come to the main street, where white slabs pave the way and stone pediments with ancient Greek inscriptions lie around helter-skelter (upturned by an earthquake). Continue around the hillside, then cut up left to a building with a solitary arch vaulting the outside walls. This could have been the **bath house**, as there is evidence of a hypocaust system supporting the floor and retaining the heat.

From here, drop diagonally right down the hillside across open ground full of pottery shards, to a clump of overhanging rocks. Peer over the edge down into the canyon: you can hear the sound of water 200m below. There are two **caves** in the cliff face here, where Nisa's inhabitants sheltered from earthquakes or hid from advancing armies. Turn south-southeast and continue to the corner of the site, where a ruined **round tower** commands views across the valley. From the tower cut back into the hillside and descend towards Sütleğen alongside the heavy masonry wall. The path passes below the theatre, then rises to where you first entered the site. Descend back to the dirt road (**5h50min**). Turn left and head down to the Kumacaz Mosque (tap with drinking water). Turn right in front of the mosque and rise to a crossroads by an electricity pylon. Go straight over and take the path up the hillside. At a house with open storage underneath, take the left-hand track, down into a dip. Turn right here and climb the hill, past orchards and houses, to the attractive centre of **Sütleğen (6h40min)** — with a spring, a few shops, *lokantas,* tea houses, and a couple of basic *pensions.*

Walk 6: Kaş • Çukurbağ • Phellos • Dereköy • Felen Bridge

Time: 12h15min
Grade: moderate, but long and over very rocky terrain; overall ascent of about 800m. *Not suitable from mid-June to early September, when you should choose one of the shorter, downhill walks.*
Equipment: see pages 23-24.
Travel: the walk begins in Kaş; return by 🚌 from Felen Bridge to Kaş (every two hours).
Alternative or shorter walks
1 Kaş — Çukurbağ — Ağullu (4h45min; moderate, uphill). Follow the main walk to the upper mosque in Çukurbağ, then walk 3km along a road to the Ağullu teahouse on the D400 (frequent buses to Kaş; journey 10min). Or use the map to do this in reverse:
Ağullu — Çukurbağ — Kaş (4h15min; easy, downhill).
2 Kaş to Phellos (6h45min; grade as main walk, uphill). Follow the main walk to explore Phellos. Then descend from the Lycian Way sign down to the track, where you turn right up the hill (the main walk goes left here). Walk down to the forestry fire-watch tower (30min), continue to the asphalt road, and turn right. Descend through Pınarbaşı village (drinking water at the spring under the plane tree in the centre). Continuing downhill, take the left turn at a junction and another left after 2km, to reach the Ağullu tea house on the D400 (6km from the fire-watch tower). Or use the map to reverse this:
Phellos to Kaş (6h; moderate, downhill). Either option could be shortened by finishing/starting at the fire-watch tower, a 14km taxi ride from Kaş (arrange to be collected there in advance).
3 Felen Bridge to Kaş (11h15min; grade as main walk, ascent of about 600m). Start from Felen

Bridge (Elmalı/Gömbe bus from Kaş, first bus 08.00). Use the map to do the main walk in reverse.
4 Suggestions for motorists:
🚗 Part at the fire-watch tower north of Pınarbaşı and walk up the track (20min) to Phellos. Then drive via Dereköy to the Kasaba valley; return to Kaş on the D400.

This walk connects the ancient cities of Antiphellos (the modern-day port of Kaş) to Phellos with its numerous Lycian tombs scattered on the ridge of Mount Felen. You enjoy fantastic views to Kastellórizo and the rugged Lycian shoreline, the alpine vista of the snow-capped Taurus Mountains, and diverse landscapes — from the red earth of the Çukurbağ plain to the lush meadows and spring flowers of the Dereköy valley. Time stands still here: shepherds still water their goats by open cisterns, as their ancestors have done for centuries. Çukurbağ village, with its old stone houses set among almond groves, is a picture-postcard during February when the trees are in blossom. After winter rains, numerous waterfalls spring to life cascading down the cliffs of the Dereköy canyon. Whatever the season, there is a kaleidoscope of colour, all charged by the amazing light of Lycia.

Start the walk in **Kaş** (see plan on pages 66-67): facing the **Atatürk statue** in the main square, head to the right-hand corner and turn right up Uzun Çarşı, passing old Greek houses with bougainvillea draping the traditional wooden balconies. At the top, shaded by a plane tree, is the **Lion's Tomb** shown on page 69, with protruding lion's-head bosses on the Gothic-style lid. Continue up the hill, then turn left along Likya Cad. Beyond the school, turn left along a concrete-

and-cobbled road, passing a staircase on the right (between houses) up to Lycian rock tombs. Take the first right turn, up a steep road past small apartment blocks. At the top, take the footpath that cuts out all the bends of the old road into Kaş. Turn left at the top of the road and continue 100m to the main **D400 highway** (**30min**; the map below starts here). Look up the mountainside now, to see the 'sleeping giant' — the buttresses of the ridge look like the head and shoulder of a slumbering figure.

Cross the highway *carefully*, then take the road heading left up the mountainside. Look immediately for the red and white flashes of the Lycian Way on your right, to find your ongoing path. This ascends the bank, then forks right before zigzagging steadily up the mountain through maquis. Stopping for a breather, you have ever-better views as you climb. If you look up when you cross a small patch of **scree** (**1h**), you can see the line of an old pipe which brought mains water to Kaş. You pass under the head of the 'sleeping giant', with scents of sage and oregano wafting up as you

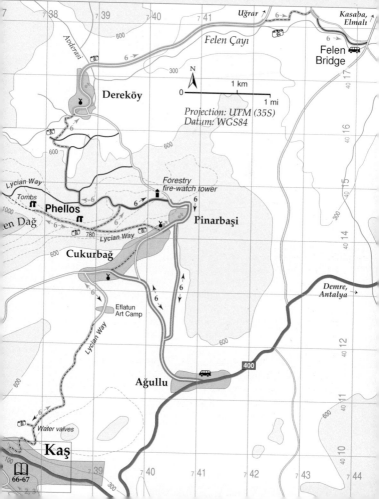

brush pass the vegetation. During spring and summer crickets and grasshoppers spring into action on your approach, and butterflies and thread lacewings (with translucent forewings blotched pale lime and black) flutter past. Near the top of this climb you pass a small cave where goats shelter.

At the **top** (450m; **1h45min**), fork left past the **water valve chambers** for a spectacular view over the Turkish coast. Kaş means 'eyebrow' and, looking over the peninsula, you can see how the town got its modern name. Across the bay, Kastellórizo is suspended somewhere between sky and sea. To the left is Liman Ağzı (Walks 2 and 3), a sheltered haven for shipping. To the right, the mountains rise steeply from the seashore and, if you're lucky, you may spot a Bonelli's eagle soaring on the updraft or paragliders keeping their height in the thermals. Back from the viewpoint, two Lycian **cisterns** and faced stone blocks lie in the vegetation.

Rejoin the path near the water chambers and descend into a large, open plain, following a line of the wild pear trees growing intermittently across the centre. You have now entered a different world, where time stands still; you'll hear goat bells and see shepherds watering their herds at open cisterns. Continue beside a fenced garden on the stony, rich red earth, making for the saddle on the horizon straight ahead. Passing under electricity cables, fork left, then right on a **dirt track/road** (**2h30min**). When this swings left, continue straight ahead on a path. This descends

left and rejoins the dirt track by an open cistern. Turn right and continue along track through a small **hamlet** to **Eflatun Art Camp**. They have a *kösk* (seating platform) and a café; they also exhibit the work of local artists and run painting and ceramic workshops. Continue along the track through village farmland (mainly wheat and barley) and on into **Çukurbağ**, which you enter by old stone houses and almond groves. Turn right at the track junction and continue 50m to the asphalt road and a Lycian Way signpost ('Kaş 8km', 'Phellos 3km'; **3h15min**).

Turn right and walk through Çukurbağ; a short way past the **mosque**, take the footpath on your left that cuts through to another village road. Turn left up the steep hill, passing old stone houses and newly restored ones, until you reach the **upper mosque** (**4h**), with a picturesque drinking-water **spring**. Follow the Lycian Way sign behind the mosque; the path rises, then swings right over conglomerate rock, walled on both sides. As you wind up the hillside, views open up back along the Çukurbağ plain and through the saddle to Kastellórizo. About halfway up the slope the path swings right around a **fenced area** (**4h30min**). Continue up to a Lycian Way signpost planted on the crest of **Felen Dağ** (780m; **5h**). On your right through the vegetation are some sarcophagi; you are now in the ruins of **Phellos**. To explore, back-track 15m, then take the path on your right which contours below the ridge. There are segments of ancient terracing and another huge sarcophagus. Look for a side-path that will take you up to the recently cleared **acropolis**. To the north you have another magnificent view to the Lycian peaks: Akdağ (3024m) on the left and Kızlar Sivrisi (3070m), the highest, on the right, with the Susuz Dağlar between them. Go back down to the path and continue to the end of the site, a walled enclosure with Lycian **house-type tombs** carved out of solid rock (look for the massive bull relief on the side wall dating from the 5th century BC). Then retrace your steps to **Lycian Way signpost (6h15min)**.

Continue north on the Lycian Way path, past more tombs; descend to a track, turn left and wind down the hillside among arbutus and turpentine trees. At a **junction (6h45min)** turn right on another track, *leaving* the Lycian Way. As you descend, the geology changes: notice the interesting strata in the right-hand bank. At the next junction, turn left towards the open valley below; five minutes later turn right, then immediately left onto the plain. Cut right by a small house (an unfinished building at the time of writing) and then go right, across the plain, to a large grey/white **boulder with a tomb (7h20min)**. Skirt the trees on your right, then head left on a track, back to the main track. Turn right and continue through pine forest. Pass a **stone house**, then fork right (the lower track) for 100m, to a sharp bend, where you fork left. Continue down through forest to a rock promontory, then turn right on a track and descend through a dry stream bed to an electricity **pylon**. Turn right

down a track here, then go left and immediately right into open land, heading for a **ruined stone house**. Walk to the right-hand corner of the land, where terraces drop away, to take in the view across the Kasaba plain to the Bey Dağlar. In spring these fields are full of poppies, with snow-capped mountains towering in the distance. Drop down over the terrace to descend a footpath through dense vegetation. Ignore any side-paths and continue down, veering right through pines into a hollow. At a stream bed, fork left on a parallel path and follow this to a small **bridge and road (8h40min)**.

Turn left on the road and walk into **Dereköy** village. Pass the **mosque** (with nearby **spring**) and continue down to the **bridge** (285m; **9h10min**), with a good view upstream to Dereköy canyon. Follow the road through the valley, with the spectacular gorge below on your right. The road gradually descends to farmland by the banks of the **Felen Stream**. After passing the *second* set of **greenhouses (10h 45min)**, the road veers left; 50m further on, fork right on a path heading into forest. The path contours, then crosses a hillock. Go straight on at a path junction, over another hump and through a small eroded area. You can now see the houses of Uğrar. The path skirts the villagers' gardens and greenhouses, then meets an **asphalt road (11h40min)**. Turn right; then, after 50m, take a track on the right to the banks of the Felen. Follow the left bank of the stream to **Felen Bridge** on the Kaş/Kaşaba road (**12h15min**). There is a bus stop to the right.

Walk 7: Dirgenler — Dereağzı loop

The map for the main walk is on page 94.

Time: 4h30min

Grade: easy, apart from the climb up the castle hill (150m), which is steep; mostly on dirt roads and footpaths.

Equipment: see pages 23-24.

Travel: 🚌 from Kaş to Kasaba (Elmalı/Gömbe bus, departs 08.00). From Kasaba take the (infrequent) bus service along the Kasaba plain to the Dirgenler crossroads. Return using the same transport.

Alternative walks

1 Dirgenler to Demre via the Demre Canyon (7h30min; easy, but long — take *plenty* of fluid). Access as main walk; return by bus from Demre. Follow the main walk *past* the marble works and continue on the dirt road through the Demre Canyon. You pass a small ruined church about halfway down. The high cliffs open out lower down, eventually revealing the Demre coastal plain. Cut across to the right-hand side before the end of the canyon. In the cliff at the opening are many Lycian tombs in the rock face. There is a path up to the 'painted tomb', with some still-coloured reliefs. Around the bend in the road you can visit the site of Myra. Once back on the main road, continue to the centre of Demre, where you can visit the restored St. Nicholas church and go on to the bus station.

2 Dereağzı (3h; easy). Follow the main walk just down into the canyon entrance, from where you can look up to the castle and tombs. Then pick up the main walk again, dropping down the bank from the pump station, to continue to the church and walk back to the Dirgenler crossroads.

3 Suggestion for motorists:
🚗 Park at the Dirgenler crossroads (34km from Kaş) for the main walk. It is also possible to drive along the motorable track into the head of the canyon and round to near the church (the main walk in reverse).

Snow-melt waters stream down from the surrounding mountains through the Kasaba valley basin to Dereağzı, the confluence of rivers at the head of the Demre Canyon. This walk explores the area's fertile farmland, following the stony course of the Demre River to the canyon entrance. You climb the fortified hill guarding the ancient route through to Myra and its port, Andriake. There are commanding views over the Lycian mountains and the Kasaba valley from the top of the castle. The walk continues across to a huge church — a wonder of Byzantine architecture and engineering. Through one of its main roof arches you have a view of snow-clad peaks.

Start the walk at the **Dirgenler crossroads**. Turn right (south) on the dirt road and continue through open farmland towards the canyon entrance, **Dereağzı**. Some 50m before the **marble works**, turn right across the ditch at the edge of a *tarla* (cultivated field) and go up the bank full of pine trees, by the edge of a fenced olive grove. At the top, cut left by the **'50' concrete marker**, then turn right over the top of a rise, by the edge of the cultivated land. Drop just below the *tarla* and turn left, contouring round the hillside with views over the plain and the stony river bed. The path descends through trees to a dirt track by an *ambar*. (These grain stores are hand-built and slotted together without nails until the roof is attached. Inside are many compartments for storing different grains. The *ambar* is usually built from cedar, as the smell repels vermin.) Turn right on the track, past small farmhouses, and fork right down to the stony bank of the **Demre River**. Look towards the canyon to see the castle ramparts defending the hill and surrounding area. Turn left along the river bank through oleander. If the water is high, climb the bank and follow the course of the river, meandering through farmland. Drop down the bank to cross a side stream, then take the tractor track up to a ruined building. Turn right up the hillside through a break in the hedge and veer right, contouring round the 'hump'. Descend by the Valonia oak (*Quercus aegilops*). Make your way round the edge of the wheat crop and descend, going round the back of the polytunnel **greenhouse at the base of the fortified hill (1h15min)**.

Ascend by the fenced *tarla* to the top of a first rise, where a water pipe runs down the hillside. Colourful anemones dot the ground among the asphodel. Fork diagonally left to a second water pipe. For a fine view down the canyon, go under this pipe and across to a rocky outcrop. Lycian tombs carved in the cliff face guard the narrow entrance. Go back to the water pipe, from where the path ascends (passing under the pipe two more times), then veers left round a **precipitous edge**. The path then rises diagonally right to the castle walls through Valonia oak. Their acorn cups have recurved scales and are the largest of any Mediterranean species of oak; they are used locally in tanning. Go through the breach in the wall, then zigzag and clamber over the inner citadel walls to reach the **castle summit (2h40min)** and explore the buildings around the ridge. The fantastic view takes in the canyon below and the ancient road through to Myra and the port of Andriake. To the north are the snow-capped ridges of the Susuz Dağlar (Waterless Mountains), to the right, through the gap, is Kızlar Sivrisi, the highest peak in Lycia at 3070m. The nearer mountain is Alaca Dağ (2320m); its cedar-clad slopes run down to the Kasaba valley. The wide fertile plain is surrounded on all sides by mountains with snow-melt streams flowing together at the canyon entrance and continuing to Demre, where they irrigate the

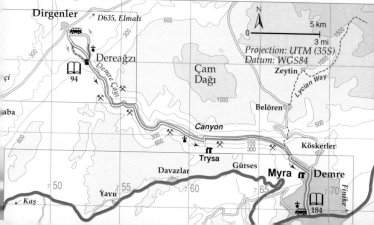

Projection: UTM (35S)
Datum: WGS84
NB: walking routes are
sketch maps; not to scale

Dereağzı: the church and river. The monumental church, built during the 7th-8th century, could be a cathedral. One of the massive arches is still standing; it once supported the drum dome built from clay bricks and lime cement. No restoration work has been done; if the collapsed structures were cleared, it's possible that a precious mosaic floor would be revealed.

orange groves and greenhouses of its fertile coastal plain. Return down the hillside by the same route through Jerusalem sage *(Phlomis lunariifolia)* to the top of the first rise. The water pipes run from a **collection chamber** catching the run-off from the top of the hillside to water the farmland below. Fork right down to the dirt road used by lorries carrying huge blocks of marble quarried from the canyon walls. Go a short way into the **canyon**: the **Lycian tombs** are sited on the cliffs at both sides of the entrance, and worn steps, part of an ancient footpath, lead across the stream.

Walk back to a **pump station** on your right and drop down the bank, to a track following the stony course of the river through oleander and bamboo. Go left up the bank by the **greenhouses**, then turn right up the next bank, past **beehives**. Fork left through the dip, by a massive stone mortar, and walk round the edge of a cultivated field. Continue round the base of the mound for a fantastic view of the church. Turn right past the farm building and continue to the **church (3h30min)**, part of which is now used as a goat pen. The common dragon arum *(Dracunculus vulgaris)*, with its velvet-like leaf and attractive (but foul-smelling) purple spike, grows around the massive walls.

Leave through the back of the church, pick up a track and follow it through a **hamlet** and tall pines. Fork left at a junction, to walk through open farmland (mainly wheat, but broad beans in winter or sesame from late summer). Continue along the dirt road, then fork right to the **Dirgenler junction (4h30min)**.

2 EXCURSIONS EAST OF KAŞ

Demre (Kale) • Myra • Andriake • Kekova and Simena

Area code: (0242
Walks: 7-10 (1-6 are nearby)

Opening times/prices: see
individual attractions.

Demre (Kale), with Myra and Andriake

Information: The Tourist Office on the main square in Kaş is responsible for Demre (see page 63).
Connections: All buses on the D400 coastal road between Antalya and Fethiye stop in Demre (to either Antalya or Fethiye). *Dolmuşes* run to (among others) Finike and Kaş.

Demre (less well known as Kale) is a fairly unappealing little town of about 15,000 inhabitants between Finike and Kaş, covered in more detail in the *Antalya to Demre* guide. On the town's northern outskirts are the ruins of ancient Myra, famous for its impressive Lycian rock tombs ... and as the domain of St. Nicholas. Andriake, to the west of Demre, was Myra's port; today tour boats leave from here for Kekova — one of the top excursions for those based in the area. Three splendid walks await you here, which is why some general information is included.

Accommodation, food and drink

Demre is so far only a day trip destination, with few places to stay. The two-star **Grand Hotel Kekova** is probably best — 40 rooms with worn-out carpeting, but good plumbing and balconies; bar, restaurant. Single room £17, double £28, both with breakfast. Lise Cad. PTT Karşısı 55, signposted from the centre; (8714515, (8715366.
Kent Pansiyon is a family-run place especially suitable for walkers. On the road to Myra, on the left. Garden. Double with bath £18. (8712042, kentpansiyon @hotmail.com.
There are several simple *lokantas* in the centre. **Yüzer Köşk** is a very pleasant restaurant about 10km outside town on the Finike road by the Beymelek Lagoon. Really good fish dishes, as well as freshly caught crabs and prawns. The setting is a plain but lovely terrace out over the water. (0532 5986930 (mobile).

Practicalities A-Z

Boat trips: leave from the port 3km outside Demre, near the ruins of Andriake. Depending on the duration of the tour, prices range from £6.50-£13. They take tourists to the 'sunken cities' and Kekova Island.
Events: Annual **Santa Claus Festival** from 6-8 December (shows, competitions, etc.).

Sights

Church of St. Nicholas: The triple-naved basilica signposted as 'Noel Baba', in whose forerunner Myra's Bishop Nicholas once worked, was a popular place of pilgrimage in the Middle Ages, and the site of several miracles. Don't expect to find the remains of St. Nicholas here: his sarcophagus is thought to have been taken to Bari in Italy, bones and all, in 1087. But some theorists believe that the grave robbers stole the wrong one.

Opening times/prices: May-Oct. daily from 09.00-19:00, Nov.-Apr. 08.00-17.00; entry fee £4..50.

Myra: Founded in the 5th century BC, ancient Myra was one of the prominent cities of the Lycian League. The rock tombs of the so-called '**Sea Necropolis**', dating from the 4th century BC, are fascinating. Carved at eye-level into the side of a sheer cliff are dozens of caves with simple tombs, cells and houses — as well as temple tombs with elaborate façades and fake doors. During the era of the Roman Caesars, Myra was extremely wealthy, as can be seen in parts of the stately **theatre**, where holes built into the terraces once held wooden posts to which awnings could be fastened, so that the spectators were shaded. In and around the theatre lie innumerable architectural fragments. The remains of the **acropolis** above the theatre are meagre.

But an excursion to the **eastern necropolis** *is* worthwhile. From the car park in front of the theatre, either walk or drive back down the approach road and take the first left. Turn left again some 400m further on (between greenhouses; again, this is the first left turn). Entrance to the eastern necropolis is free.

Getting there/opening times/prices: Myra lies about 2km north of Demre's centre. The site is open daily between May and Oct. from 09.00-19.30, between Nov. and Apr. from 08.00-17.00; entry fee £4.50.

Andriake: Myra's old port is 3km west of Demre and also sign-posted as **Çayağzı Bay**. In the year 59, St. Paul the Apostle changed ships here on his way to Rome. Don't miss the ruins of the **granarium** with warehouses (on the left-hand side of the approach road, when coming from Demre). There is a silo consisting of eight sections, which could hold 6000 cubic metres of grain and was built in the year 129 to the order of Emperor Hadrian.

Kekova and Simena

Connections: Most tourists come on boat trips from Andriake, Kaş or Kalkan. The nearest village accessible by road is Üçağız (pop. 500). If you drive there, *ignore* people hitching lifts — they will be touts for the boat tours! No buses from Kaş; in summer 1 a day to/from Demre. A taxi from Kaş to Üçağız costs £17-20, from Demre £13-17. From Üçağız it's just 15 minutes by boat to Simena (£7); on request the boat will take you over to Kekova Island.

The sea between the island of Kekova and the mainland looks more like a lake and is dotted with innumerable islets. On the mainland, facing out to these islets, is Simena, an idyllic village without roads, completely cut off from the outside world, and only accessible by boat or on foot. In the straits in front of it lies the fairy-tale 'Sunken City' (Sualtı Şehir). It was part of Kekova Island, but now lies under water because the whole coast is slowly sinking (about 15cm every 100 years). Kekova, once a gorgeous island, is today uninhabited (and you cannot disembark there), but the sea around it is swamped by boat-trippers, *despite the fact that swimming over the ruins is forbidden.*

By boat you chug in comfort over the foundation walls of some buildings, which are easily visible in the crystal-clear water. Here and there a sarcophagus rises up out of the water. Also eye-catching is the ruin of a **Byzantine church** in the cove of Tersane — only the apse rises above the beach.

Directly opposite **Kekova Island** is the picture-book village of Kaleköy ('Castle Village'), today known as **Simena**. Like a few other places on the Turkish coast, it is reminiscent of an old Greek fishing village in the Aegean. The houses tumble picturesquely down a slope crowned by a Byzantine fortress. The hill itself was settled back in antiquity. Inside the castle walls *(entrance £3.50)* you can still see the remains of a small **theatre** (without stage) chiselled from the rock, which once seated 300 people. A **stone sarcophagus** typical of this area stands at the foot of the castle. Since no public road has ever been built to Simena, the village of just 200 souls has a very special charm — one of the last truly idyllic spots on the Turkish south coast (at least outside the hours of 13.00-15.00, when the boat-trippers come in for lunch).

Üçağız (Teimiussa in antiquity) is today a grouping of restaurants and small *pansiyonlar* with a mosque beside the quay. As in Simena, the boat- and bus-trips determine the rhythm of the place. A few tombs from ancient Teimiussa can still be seen east of the village along the coast.

Accommodation in Üçağız: There are several good guest houses. **Kekova Pansiyon**, newish, right on the sea; 8 large rooms with air-conditioning, wooden floors. Common first-floor balcony. Double room with breakfast £30-40. (0242-8742259, www.kekova pansiyon.com.

Ekin Hotel, 13 rooms, all with bath; clean. Five rooms with small terraces in a sweet-scented garden, others with balconies/ sea view. Kitchen privileges. For two people £12-35. Open all year. (0242-8742064.

Onur Pension, on the sea, with a jetty. Simple, friendly. Rooms with bath/WC. Lovely terrace. Restaurant. Double room with breakfast £35. Highly praised by Sunflower readers. (0242-8742071, www.onurpension.com.

Camping: possible at the Pension Kabay at the village entrance.

Accommodation in Simena: is more expensive than Üçağız. **Kale Pension**, on the sea; lovely terrace. 10 pleasant doubles with air-conditioning, sea view, £60. Very friendly. (0242-8742111, www.kalepansiyon.com.

Ankh Pansiyon, near Kale: 8 nice rooms with stone floors and tra-ditional carpets. Great view from the balcony. (0242-8742171, www.ankhpansion.com.tr.

Mehtap Pension lies further up. 10 rooms with air-conditioning, four of them with sea view. Super terrace. (0242-8742146, www. mehtappansiyon.com.

Food and drink: There are several restaurants with seaside terraces in both Üçağız and Simena, all profiting from the boat trips.

See map on reverse of area map
and photograph on page 9.
Time: 7h30min
Grade: moderate; the rocky
terrain is hard underfoot. The
first half of the walk is mainly
downhill; the route then
undulates around the coast.
Equipment: see pages 23-24.
Travel: 🚌 from Kaş to the
Davazlar junction (Antalya bus;
journey time 35min). Or 🚌 from
Demre bus station (15min). Those
staying in Kekova (Üçağız/
Simena) can take the morning
bus to Demre and change to the
Kaş bus at Demre bus station.
Return from the main D400
above Çayağzı (frequent buses).
Travelling by 🚗, park at Hoyran
and return on the Kaş bus to the
Davazlar junction, walking the
4km back to the car (or park at
Davazlar junction).
Alternative walks
1 Davazlar junction to Kapaklı
(4h; easy). Follow the main walk
to Kapaklı village and catch the
Kekova bus back to the D400 or
to Üçağız.
**2 Davazlar junction — Hoyran
— Kapaklı — Simena — Üçağız**
(9h45min taking the longer
option; grade as main walk).
Follow the main walk to Kapaklı
village, then pick up either Alternative walk 9-1 or 9-2 (page 102),
to finish at Üçağız.
3 Hoyran (3h45min; easy).
Follow the main walk to explore
Hoyran village and ruins and
return to the main road.
4 Suggestions for motorists: If
you are looking for a short scenic
walk, drive to Hoyran village
and explore the ruins (1h30min).
For longer routes, drive to
Kapaklı or Çayağzı and do one of
the other variations.

*This walk explores the central
Lycian hinterland, visiting the little-
known site at Hoyran village, with
its traditional stone houses set amid
almond groves and terraced farmland. Ancient tombs stand out
among the lush vegetation and
meadows full of spring flowers. The
ruins stretch out along the ridge,
and from the idyllic picnic terrace
there is a spectacular view over the
many islands and coastline of the
Kekova region. The route down to
the coast follows the ancient way
connecting the sites of Hoyran and
Istlada with the main port at
Andriake. Past the village of Kapaklı,
the route follows the jagged shoreline
through olive groves and over rocky
terrain to the white pebble beach at
Akdere — another fine picnic spot,
with the chance to swim in the clear
sheltered waters of Gökkaya Bay.
The path continues above the jagged
shoreline and over more rocky
terrain, then crosses a stream on a
rustic footbridge — to emerge on the
golden, palm-fringed sands of
Çayağzı Beach. Andriake is a
birdwatcher's delight, with waders
feeding in the marshes and wetlands
among the ruins of the ancient port.*

Start the walk from the
Davazlar/Hoyran junction on
the main Kaş/Demre highway.
Head southeast down the road
signposted to Hoyran village.
The road descends for 4km,
passing through a small hamlet,
open farmland, and fields of
cultivated sweet marjoram
(*Origanum marjorana*) which is
picked, dried and sold for export
to the west as an organic product.
Maquis cloaks the hillsides
between the fertile hollows and
plains. As you enter the main
village, look out on the right for

the Lycian tomb with animal reliefs on the front and an unusual bell gable (circa 5th century BC). The centre of **Hoyran (1h05min)** is marked by huge plane trees *(Platanus orientalis)* growing by the village cisterns. These open circular reservoirs have ramps for the animals to descend as the water table lowers. (The sealed cisterns held water for human consumption; the mains-water pipe in Hoyran was only connected in 2001.) Continue past the old schoolhouse to 'Hoyran Wedre', a new (2006) tourist complex of country houses built in authentic village style using local stone, cedar doors and traditional patterned shutters. The owner, Süleyman, is very friendly and will give you a guided tour! The houses have open-hearth fireplaces and walls of wattle and daub. If you are looking for a tranquil village setting with stunning views, it's a perfect spot. Continue on the road to the end of the village, by some stone houses. Pass the upturned sarcophagus lid now used as a water trough and, by the last house, turn left along a walled pathway. In the garden you can sometimes see a camel used for portering firewood and other goods. Some of the *yoruk* (nomad) shepherds still use camels to carry their belongings up to the *yayla* (highland pasture) on their summer migration. Follow the path for 50m, then turn right over a step in the wall, following the edge of a terrace. Looking up to your right, you can spot a Lycian tomb in the cliff face. The path twists up ancient, worn stairs through lush vegetation, drops through a gap and turns right. It then forks left, ascending through an ancient **necropolis** full of Lycian **sarcophagi** with their Gothic-style lids. You cross an open area (carpeted with camomile in spring) and come to a **pillar tomb** with the relief of a man (5th century BC). Turn uphill by the sarcophagus with bull's-head bosses protruding from the lid, then sharp left up through sweet laurel to the **rock tombs**. If you look on the side of one of the tombs, there is a carved relief depicting the seated head of the family, receiving the family members who wait in line. On the front of the same tomb are reliefs of a partridge, cockerel and griffon. Continue up through the scrubby oak and bay, squeeze through the gap in the rock, and drop down to the open green terrace for a spectacular view over Kekova Island and the central Lycian coastline. This terrace is an ideal picnic spot (and one of my favourite campsites). Swifts dart about on the updraft, and I once saw a short-toed eagle swoop down and rise with a snake in its talons. Retrace your steps to the **walled footpath by the cultivated stone terraces (2h35min)**, and turn right, descending into the valley. The path is indistinct, so look up to see your direction (east — through to an open clearing). The path snakes down through scrubby oak, levels out, and joins a dirt track. Turn right along the track past a cistern and *tarla* (cultivated land) on your left. Cross the saddle and descend steeply on the rough track. When this track was blasted, the red dots marking the start of your ongoing path were eradicated: look for the path running parallel with the track, on your right, and follow it through rocky scrub to a big oak tree. Once again there are fine views over the coastline, with the villages of Kapaklı and İnişdibi in the valley below.

The path zigzags down the steep slope, sometimes on sections of the ancient mule trail that connected Hoyran with Istlada (modern Kapaklı) and sheltered Gökkaya Bay. At the valley bottom, polytunnel greenhouses have destroyed the path: twist right to skirt round the poly-tunnels and reach the road. Turn left along the road, then go right, to the **mosque** in the centre of **Kapaklı** village (**4h**). There is a water tap and toilet by the side of the mosque.

Continue on the dirt road descending towards the sea. At a fork, head left (southeast) towards the coast. When the road ends, turn right on a footpath winding down through rocky terrain and olive groves to join the **Lycian Way** coastal path. Following the red and white waymarks, take the left fork when the path splits. (The right path heads down towards the sea.) Stay left between the walled *tarla*; the path gradually rises and works it way around the hillside. Views open up over the eastern end of Kekova. Over the hill the path descends past a circular stone cistern to **Çakıl Plajı** (Pebble Beach; **5h35min**). This white-pebble beach is another good place to swim. It's at the mouth of the **Akdere** (White Stream), running down the small valley from the gorge behind.

Cross the beach and pick up the coastal path again, continuing above the rocky shore. At a shepherd's enclosure, walk round the dwellings, past the cistern. Further on, descend, forking right, then left, and drop to the stream. Cross a rustic wooden footbridge to the sandy bank and palm oasis. (The stream meanders up the valley past a temple dedicated to Apollo, but it's not possible to walk there from this end of the valley. Access is from the main road by the tombs of Sura, via an ancient staircase down to the well-preserved temple and Byzantine church.)

Walk along **Çayağzı** (River Mouth) **Beach** (**6h45min**) and cross the bridge to the shops and cafés on the quayside, full of day trippers taking boat tours over Kekova's sunken city.

From here you could just turn left and walk the 3km to the main road (there is a pavement beside the road). But why not have a closer look at the ruins of **Andriake**, Myra's ancient harbour, dominated by a spectacular **granarium** dedicated to the emperor Hadrian who travelled to the region in 131 AD. Turn left along the road, then right through pines, with sand dunes on your left. Ascend the sand and take the path running against the ancient walls. Continue past the covered vaulted cisterns and on to the road. Turn left, then right, and walk on to a **roundabout on the D400** highway (**7h30min**). Buses pass every half hour in both directions — left for Kaş, right for Demre and Antalya. Across the road are the arches of the **nymphaeum** (fountain).

Walk 9: Üçağız • Burç Castle • Gökkaya loop

See map on reverse of area map.

Time: 7h

Grade: moderate; rocky terrain underfoot; undulating throughout, with overall ascents of about 300m. The walk can also be done in reverse allowing more swimming time on the return.

Equipment: see pages 23-24; carry plenty of fluid. Refreshments available at the Smugglers Inn in Gökkaya Bay.

Travel: From Kaş there is no regular bus service, but it is possible to book a return trip with one of the local travel agencies who run tours to Kekova every day (39 km). Otherwise, see 'Connections' on page 96.

Short walk: Üçağız to Simena (2h15min; easy, but with a fair number of steps to climb). This version explores the villages of Üçağız and Kaleköy and their respective ancient sites (Teimiussa and Simena). Follow the main walk around the bay as far as the Lycian Way signpost by the walled cemetery. Continue round the coast by the marsh area (full of egrets and grey herons in spring). Follow the

path up the worn limestone steps to the eastern necropolis below the castle walls. Some of the sarcophagi have sculpted lion's-head bosses protruding from the Gothic-style lids. Continue round the hillside past the tombs and ancient olive trees (possibly planted with the tombs over 2000 years ago). The path runs past the village schoolhouse — rebuilt and financed by the richest businessman in Turkey, Rahmi Koc. Opposite the school is the ticket office for the castle (entry £0.90). Climb the steps to the fortress: to the left is the theatre, carved out of the hillside. The route winds up the side of the theatre on worn steps cut into the rock, to a flagpole at the top. From here there are fantastic views over the battlements to Kekova, Üçağız and the waterfront jetties. The house to the right, built above the Lycian tomb, belongs to Rahmi Koc who sometimes arrives by helicopter and lands at his crazy-paving helipad in the garden. Head to the east side and go through the break in the wall, from where the

The hamlet of Kaleköy (ancient Simena), with its crowning castle

path twists down the hill back to the eastern necropolis. To explore Simena, take the upper path by the ticket booth; this runs below the castle walls and descends past small stone houses dressed in bougainvillea, with lush gardens full of exotic plants. Continue down past Mehtap Pension (a lovely, peaceful place to stay, with wooden terraces looking out across the bay). Down at the water's edge is the partially submerged sarcophagus that displays itself on all the postcards. From here return through the village on the lower paths. Simena is a collection of old stone houses built on top of and in between the ancient structures. There are plenty of waterfront restaurants, and it's possible to take a taxi boat back to Üçağız or even organise a small boat trip over to the sunken city at Kekova Island.

Alternative walks
1 Kapaklı — Gökkaya — Simena — Üçağız (5h30min; moderate; initially downhill, then undulating around the coast). Start from Kapaklı mosque (access by 🚌 or taxi from Demre or Üçağız, see 'Connections', page 96). Take the dirt road heading seawards. After 150m, turn right on a track past the old school. Turn left and descend by a house, then go right, around the greenhouse. Take the footpath through the gap in the wall, heading south through carob trees. Now you pick up the red and white flashes of the Lycian Way and descend into the valley. The ruins of Istlada lie hidden in vegetation of to your left, running down to the sea. The path now runs parallel with a

water pipe, forking right to the valley bottom. Continue along the valley, following the water pipe (south-southwest). The path then forks right (southwest), away from the pipe and across the plain. You come into an enclosed rocky section with very confused waymarking. I think it's easier to veer right here, to the edge of the clearing opposite: skirt to the left of the clearing, then join the main shepherds' path which heads left towards the coast. There is a confusion of paths, most head the same way and eventually rejoin — at which point the path winds down the hillside through rocky terrain. The path improves when you reach a stone wall near a ruined house looking over an inlet of Gökkaya Bay (1h30min). From here use the map to drop round the coast to the Smugglers Inn and follow the main walk in reverse to Üçağız. Burç Castle is a good picnic/swimming stop!

2 Kapaklı to Üçağız (5h45min; moderate; initially downhill, then rising before descending back to the coast; overall ascent about 300m). Follow Alternative walk 1 to the 1h30min-point, then pick up the main walk at the 3h45min-point and follow it to Üçağız (missing out the Smugglers Inn).

3 Üçağız — Gökkaya — Kapaklı — Çayağzı (9h; grade as main walk). Follow the main walk to the ruined house at the 3h45min-point, then use the map to follow the Lycian Way to Kapaklı (Alternative walk 1 in reverse). Turn left past the old school-house, to the mosque (where you can fill water bottles). From here follow Walk 8 from the 4h-point (page 100) to Çayağzı.

4 Suggestions for motorists:

🚗 park at Üçağız for the main walk or Alternative walk 3; park at Kapaklı for Alternative walks 1 or 2. Take a taxi or the evening bus service back to your car (see 'Connections' on page 96).

Kekova is the jewel of Turkey's southern coastline, steeped in history and with many islands and secluded bays. Most people enjoy this paradise by boat or gulet — the traditional sailing vessel built locally at Üçağız and Demre. The villages of Üçağız and Simena are also protected sites, so there are no badly designed concrete apartments to spoil the idyllic setting. To really appreciate the area, stay a night or two in a friendly guest house overlooking the bay — the place is utterly calm and peaceful once the day-trippers have left. The various permutations of this walk are set out so that you can combine walking and boating, exploring the whole area by land and sea. Another excellent way to see the area is by sea kayak — either on a day-trip or camping out (see page 9).

Start out from the main **car park** in **Üçağız** village. Turn right by the public toilets, through the alley, to walk along the shore by the ruins of **Teimiussa**. Continue past your author's Kekova Aktif Sea Kayak Centre (see page 9) and the Kale Alti Pension, then take steps up the side of this guest house, into the ruins. The right fork heads down to the **necropolis** by the shore, full of sarcophagi. The next right fork heads up to the **acropolis**, for a fine view looking down on picturesque Üçağız with its many jetties stretching like fingers out into the bay.

Return through the fortified ruins and drop across to a track by the last of the village houses. Turn right and follow the mains water pipe running along this track. The way gradually rises through rocky terrain, then drops towards the shore and a corner of Üçağız Bay, from where you look across to the battlements of Simena Castle (with the Turkish flag). The track runs past an unkempt, walled cemetery — where I once spotted a Syrian woodpecker *(Dendrocopus medius)* drilling into a telegraph pole. Follow the Lycian Way fingerpost here, towards 'Kapaklı 7km', skirting the **cemetery wall**. Continue along the walled route, lined by eucalyptus and carob trees, with purple anemones dotting the ground. The route goes past the **open cisterns** and village **football pitch**, then across the centre of a plain. The path continues through olives trees, rises, and carries on across another open plain with an ancient ruin on the right.

From the edge of the plain the path heads through rocky vegetation to the next open plain, with a fortification atop the hillside to your right. Head across the plain towards this small fortress, past some open keyhole cisterns (the ramps allow animals to walk down into the cisterns as the water table lowers). At the edge of the plain, *leave* the Lycian Way and take the path down to the small **cove**, an ideal swimming and picnicking spot in summer, popular with day-trippers anchored in the inlet.

From the cove a path (sometimes on worn steps hewn from the rock) takes you up through a

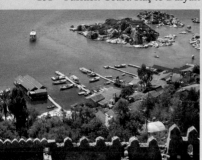

View from Simena Castle battlements

doorway to **Burç Castle**. There is evidence of an ancient settlement down below on the right, with heavy ashlar walls. On the flat terrace inside the battlements, a rusted medieval cannon points out to sea. The view is spectacular: you look out over the eastern end of Kekova across the sea to the Chelidonian Cape on the horizon. Alaca Dağ (2328m) rises inland above the tree line of cedar forest, clad with snow until late spring.

From the castle return over the saddle back into the plain. Head to the far right-hand corner and pick up the Lycian Way again. The path continues through maquis to a narrow inlet in a corner of Gökkaya Bay. It then follows the shore, past a **metal-framed shack** (possibly once used by charcoal burners, now the temporary home of the **Smugglers Inn**. Continue along the coastline to the opening to the bay, from where the path cuts left over a rise by a terraced olive grove. Soon you arrive at the site of the former Smugglers Inn (**3h20min**). This bar/restaurant, popular with the *gulet* crowd, has been dismantled for lack of planning permission. Continue

along the coastal path/Lycian Way to the next inlet, where the path rises to a **ruined stone house** (**3h45min**). Turn left past the house, down to a **fork** in a hollow, where the Lycian Way heads right (northeast).

Go *left* on a path marked by **blue paint flashes**. This climbs gradually northwest, following a line of electricity pylons. From the top, descend towards the village of İnişdibi but, before reaching the village, turn left on a **track** (**4h35min**). Follow this up the hillside, pass some **greenhouses** in a flat area, then continue up and over the saddle. You may spot lumps of calcite crystal, common in limestone terrain, along the track. The track crosses terraced land, passing some square beehives. As you walk through the carob trees, look for your ongoing path — it is faint, but marked by blue paint on the rocks. You round the edge of some cultivated land with a quintessential traditional stone house set in its own small valley. The path heads south up the hillside to a clearing with another stone house. Cross to the right hand-corner of the clearing to pick up the marked path. Start descending, then swing right and ascend out of the dip, through a small pass with views out to sea. Descend through the maquis, cross the middle of a stony clearing, and head back into maquis. The path descends seawards with views over Kekova Island and Simena Castle. It veers right, away from Simena, and gradually descends to the Üçağız/Simena track, thus completing the loop. Turn right and follow the track down into **Üçağız** (**7h**).

See map on reverse of area map.
Time: 4h50min
Grade: moderate, mostly down-hill over rocky terrain, but with a short ascent to the citadel in Apollonia; little shade.
Equipment: see pages 23-24; plenty of fluid.
Travel: 🚕 taxi from Üçağız to Kılınçlı village (9km). There is no regular 🚌 bus service from Kaş to Üçağız, but it is possible to organise transport through one of the local travel agencies who run daily tours to Kekova in the holiday season: in this case you can alight from the tour bus at the Kılınçlı village junction. The walk ends at Ramazan's Yoruk Restaurant, from where a 🚤 taxi boat can be arranged to take you back to Üçağız. (You could even book a boat tour in advance to continue on to Kekova Island via the sunken city and Simena Castle, finishing back in Üçağız.) From Üçağız, the return to Kaş should be arranged in advance with the local travel agency used for the outbound trip.

Alternative walks
1 Kılınçlı — Apollonia — Boğazcık loop (3h; easy-moderate). Follow the main walk to Apollonia and down to the Lycian Way. At the fork, turn right on the Lycian Way. The path climbs through a saddle, round the south side of the fortified hill. It then gradually descends into farmland. When you meet a dirt road (dotted with small, pink-speckled Anatolian orchids), follow it to the right, to the village of Boğazcık. Then take the dirt track across the plain back to Kılınçlı.
2 Kılınçlı — Apollonia — Aperlae — Kılınçlı (7h30min;

moderate, but with an ascent of just under 400m to return). Follow the main walk to Aperlae and return the same way, but keep on the dirt road all the way back to Kılınçlı village.
3 Aperlae — Apollonia — Boğazcık — Kılınçlı (5h15min; moderate, with an ascent of just under 400m). 🚤 Take a boat from Üçağız to Ramazan's Yoruk Restaurant and use the map to do the main walk in reverse, including Boğazcık village in the itinerary and approaching Apollonia from the southwest via the Lycian Way.
4 Aperlae (1h30min; easy). 🚤 Arrange a boat trip from Üçağız to include Aperlae. From Ramazan's jetty, walk across the isthmus plain to the west-facing inlet, explore the ruins of Aperlae and retrace steps to the jetty.
5 Kılınçlı — Apollonia — Aperlae — Üçağız (about 9h; strenuous and long). Follow the main walk to the end. Then continue around the coast on the Lycian Way, sometimes over rough terrain, to the village of Üçağız. *NB: The route is badly waymarked in places.*
6 Suggestions for motorists
🚕 park in Kılınçlı village and do Alternative walk 1 or 2. Or park in Üçağız and take a taxi to Kılınçlı village (9km) from where you can follow the main walk.

This walk explores the western end of the Kekova region, following the ancient way from the fortified hilltop site of Apollonia down to the sunken port of Aperlae. According to old coins found in the area, these two cities, together with Simena, formed a triopolis, enabling them to cast one vote in the Lycian League. There are

Pirate's Cave, Gökkaya Bay

stunning views from Apollonia's
hilltop bastion, and you have the
chance to snorkel over Aperlae's
sunken harbour, where broken
amphorae lie scattered on the seabed.
The walk crosses the Sıçak Yarımadası isthmus to Ramazan's jetty,
before taking a boat to explore this
idyllic region. If you are feeling more
energetic, you can visit the coast by
sea kayak, paddling over the sunken
ruins off Kekova Island or camping
out on one of the many deserted
islands in the area (see page 9).

Start the walk at the **Kılınçlı
junction** on the Kaş/Kekova
road. Kılınçlı looks poorer than
the more prosperous coastal
villages in the area that reap the
benefits of tourism. Follow the
dirt road round the newly renovated mosque (a sharp contrast
to the dilapidated housing). The
road rises out of the village. After
15 minutes the road bends right:
take the footpath off the bend, to
walk round the hillside towards
Apollonia's citadel — the
fortified walls of the site can be
seen defending the top of the hill.
The path veers left over a rise,
then runs down through scrub. It

forks right by an oak tree, then
right again to climb the hillside.
Keep left uphill by the stone wall.
Go over the crest, then turn left,
entering **Apollonia** by the
eastern **necropolis**, full of large
sarcophagi scattered across the
slope leading up to the fortified
citadel. Continue up the spine of
the hillside to the prominent
pillar tomb on top of the house-
type tomb surrounded by
Cyclopean walls. Further up, you
penetrate the **defensive walls** —
goats being the last defenders of
this hilltop bastion. Clamber up
to the **summit (1h)**, to take in the
360° view. To the north is the
ridge of the Susuz Dağları
(Waterless Mountains), snow-
clad through winter, with Alaca
Dağ further to the right. To the
west is Çam Dağı (Pine Mountain), topped by a white forestry
fire-watch station, manned
throughout the hot dry summers.
On the rocky coastline is Cape
Ulu Burun, site of a shipwreck in
the 13th century BC (there's a
replica in the Diving Museum in
Kaş). Below is the farmed plain
around the villages of Kılınçlı
and Boğazcık.

Drop down to the **Byzantine basilica**, then walk round to the small **theatre** with its six rows of seats supported by the hillside. Turn right through the scrubby vegetation and descend past a sarcophagus to the large **vaulted cistern**, part of the city's water supply. Continue around the hillside through the necropolis and back to the pillar tomb, then return on the same path to the bottom of the valley.

Follow the path, walking parallel with the dirt road up on your left. When the path becomes indistinct, start climbing diagonally towards the road, below a vaulted, chambered **mausoleum**. The path runs back to the Lycian Way, crossing the plain near a bend in the road. (*Alternative walk 1 forks right here on the Lycian Way.*) Follow the line of telegraph poles by the side of a stone wall. Ascend from the plain and fork left, following the red and white waymarks, then descend through the rocky limestone to an old circular **stone cistern** by oak and carob trees. The route continues down through a gap in the wall to the left of the telegraph poles and runs over rocky terrain with sage and oregano growing among the scrubby oaks. The path winds down the hillside, swinging left, with views down to the sea. Kekova Island can be seen in the distance. Continue down to a large holm oak (*Quercus ilex*) and ancient **open cistern (2h45min)**, a good, shady place for a short break.

A short way further downhill views open up over the inlet where the sea meets the Sıçak Yarımadası isthmus — your final destination. The path swings right past an ancient doorway protruding from the scrub on your left. As the path begins to level out, turn left by the stone wall and continue to some old stone houses, one of which is occupied during the winter months. Continue south, now on an indistinct path across stony ground, to an **open vaulted cistern** and the upturned lid of a sarcophagus now used as a water trough.

You have now entered the site of **Aperlae**, a fortified port with a sunken ruined harbour. Continue to the walled citadel; the path veers left past a sarcophagus and round the hillside with views down over the old harbour. The quayside can be seen under the clear shallow waters, stretching to an idyllic stone house with a commanding view over the ancient port. Passing tombs, the path zigzags down worn steps hewn from the rock to the ruined buildings on the harbour front. Turn left and follow the path, near the shore, past the 'idyllic stone house' seen earlier. Telegraph poles guide you across the centre of the isthmus connecting the **Sıçak Peninsula** to the mainland. Feral horses and goats wander this plain, watering at the open cisterns.

The path veers left before the end of the plain, rises through olive trees, then drops through a gate to an inlet and **Ramazan's Yoruk Restaurant (4h50min)**. Time to relax and enjoy the home-made food and a swim from the jetty in the clean turquoise waters. You can arrange a taxi boat from here round to the port of Üçağız, perhaps including a tour of Kekova.

3 KALKAN

Accommodation • Food and drink • Beaches • Practicalities A-Z • Sights around Kalkan

Area code: (0242
Information: at the Kaş Tourist Office (see page 63).
Connections: All **buses** running along the coast between Antalya and Fethiye stop in Kalkan. There is a booking office by the *dolmuş* station. Typical journey times and fares: Fethiye (1h30min; £1.90), Dalaman (3 hours; £3), Selçuk (6 hours; £7), Antalya (4h30min; £3.75).

The **Dolmuş Cooperative** provides local transport, with regular services to Kaş (£1), Patara Beach (£1.20) and the Bay of Kaputaş (£0.60).
Taxis are available at the *dolmuş* station: Patara £11.50, Dalaman (airport) £44, Xanthos £22 return, Saklıkent Gorge or Pınara £30 return, Kaş £12.50. Longer trips are negotiable.

Kalkan, with just 3200 inhabitants, is a bijou version of Kaş. The one-time fishing village drops in tiers down to the sea. Restaurants are grouped around the small port, and above them whitewashed little houses draped with bougainvillea nestle into the slopes.

For a long time the *cogniscenti* called Kalkan the 'Porto-fino of Turkey'. But today there is little comparison; St. Ives or Torquay would be nearer the mark, since Kalkan (inhabited exclusively by Greeks until 1922) has become a British enclave. So many British visitors (especially pensioners) have bought summer homes here that there's a standing joke: Kalkan will be the first Turkish town with a British mayor. Unfortunately, an enormous construction boom has been fed by this interest in property, and prices have risen three-fold since 2002. In the bay west of Kalkan's old town, mansions and apartments make up a new settlement called Kalamar, and in the other direction is its counterpart — Kışla. As Kalkan continues to grow at such a tremendous rate, it will be years before all the pieces of this puzzle fall into place.

At least in the old town centre, which rises around the port, peace and tranquillity still reign — despite the fact that it is completely geared to tourism and has a great many pensions and hotels. Kalkan is a very inviting place for a stroll; as you walk past houses decorated with oriels and down to the port there are busy restaurants and cafés to your left, while to the right the sailing crowd dines on their yachts. Bright young things and night owls will be disappointed here; those looking for some peace and quiet will love it. Kalkan is also convenient for trips to the beach at Patara, to Kaş, or to the ruins of Xanthos and Letoon.

Kalkan's harbour

Accommodation
(see plan on page 111)
There are approximately 4500 guest beds. While you can find rooms of all categories in the old centre, remember that the nearer you are to the port, the more you can count on being tortured by mosquitoes. Anyone who books accommodation in the new district of **Kışla** should either choose a comfortable place with a shuttle service to Kalkan or rent their own wheels: you have been warned — to date it's the 'end of the world', with no tavernas or even shops.

Villa Mahal (2), in Kışla, signposted from the road to Kaş. One of those places where reality comes up to the idyll portrayed in the brochure. One of the best places to stay in the area, built on steep cliffs above the sea. 14 tastefully decorated and furnished rooms with fantastic terraces. The only disadvantage is that there are a lot of steps. They run their own boat service to Kalkan and have a private (stony) beach. Double rooms from £150. ℂ 8443268, www.villamahal.com.

Motel Kuluhana (1): first follow signposting to Villa Mahal, from there it's signposted. Small hotel right near the sea, with some bathing platforms. All well-kept rooms have balconies and sea view. Very popular with the Brits. Double rooms from £50. Also 2 apartments for up to 5 people £105. ℂ 8442346, ℂ 8442346, www.villahotelkuluhana.com.

Pension White House (17), in the heart of the old town. Under Turkish/English management and very friendly. 10 well-kept rooms of varying sizes and prices, all with tiled floors and air-conditioning. 4 rooms have balconies. The big attraction is the wonderful roof terrace, where you could sit all day over your (excellent) breakfast. Relatively quiet, despite the location. Recommended by readers. Double rooms £42, singles £22. ℂ 8443738, www.kalkanwhitehouse.co.uk.

Hotel Zinbad (9), large midrange hotel near the port (by the Hotel Pirat). Breakfast terrace with a super view to the mosque and port. Well-kept, exceptionally large rooms for a hotel of this class, all with airconditioning. Bar and restaurant. Double room seaside £55, at the back £35. Open all year. ℂ 8443470, www.zinbadhotel.com.

Pension Türk Evi (3), highly praised by readers, a 9-room guest house run with great care by the Turkish/Norwegian management. Very well kept. Rooms (most with wooden floors) in all different sizes and colours, individually decorated and furnished — sometimes with tasteful antiques; 4 rooms with balconies. A delicious evening meal will be prepared for you on request. Double room with breakfast (depending on size and furnishings) £20-30, singles £17. Not far past the turn-off from the main D400 highway on the left (above the bus station). (8443129, www.kalkanturkevi.com.

Öz Pansiyon (3), just next to Türk Evi. Helpful owner and delightful roof terrace. 11 plain but clean rooms with climate control and carpeted floors. Always praised by readers. Double rooms with breakfast £19. (8443444, (8442222.

Pension Öz Kalamaki (14), right in the centre. Beautiful building with pleasant staff. Very appealing terrace. 10 welcoming, bright rooms, almost all with balcony. Very clean. Double room with breakfast £27. (8443066, (8443433.

Pension Gül (4) has many user recommendations, especially on account of the friendly owner, the gorgeous view from the roof terrace, and the tasty food (great breakfasts, evening meal on request). Spotless rooms with balconies, air-conditioning, tiled floors and screens fitted to all windows. Double room £21, apartment for up to 4 people £50. (8443099, www.kalkangul pension.com.

Food and drink
(see plan opposite)

The grade of restaurant is usually relative to location: at the bus station there are the few remaining cheap *lokantas;* as you descend to the centre, the restaurants become more tasteful, culminating in the fairly pricey fish restaurants at the port. Nothing is really cheap in Kalkan anymore; note that most prices are shown in British pounds, not Turkish lira!

Paprika (8), cooking with an international accent — making good use of high-quality olive oil and fresh herbs. Turkish specialities (like *börek* with walnuts), but also Italian pastas. Main courses £7-14. Live jazz on some evenings. Yalıboyu Mah., (8441136.

Zeki's Restaurant & Coffee Shop (10), centrally located on Mustafa Kocakaya Cad. Elegant, modern décor straight out of London. John Le Carré ate here several times and was very pleased; his recommendations now hang on the wall. Small well-chosen menu (steaks with fine sauces and good desserts. Main courses £9-£15. (8443884..

Ali Baba (6), diagonally opposite the *dolmuş* station. This simple *lokanta's* priority is thoroughly honest casserole dishes without gimmicks. Frequented by a colourful mix of hungry bus travellers and curious tourists. Huge portions. Main courses £2.10-£3.50. You can also eat well at **Odak (6)**, just above Ali Baba on the first floor. *Meze, pide,* kebabs, *güveç*. Mains £2.40-9.

Of the many restaurants between the port and the beach, readers have recommended **Korsan (19)** with refined Turkish cooking and tasty fish dishes from £8-12. Lunchtime menus are less pricey. (8443622. Very fresh fish is also on offer at **Deniz Restaurant Palanın Yeri (19)** just next door; it's owned by the local fish-monger! Similar prices. (8443047. If you are looking for something really special, try **Aubergine (18)** — just a couple of tables where you can have superlative

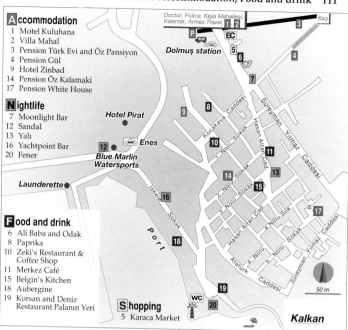

Accommodation
1 Motel Kuluhana
2 Villa Mahal
3 Pension Türk Evi and Öz Pansiyon
4 Pension Gül
9 Hotel Zinbad
14 Pension Öz Kalamaki
17 Pension White House

Nightlife
7 Moonlight Bar
12 Sandal
13 Yalı
16 Yachtpoint Bar
20 Fener

Food and drink
6 Ali Baba and Odak
8 Paprika
10 Zeki's Restaurant & Coffee Shop
11 Merkez Café
15 Belgin's Kitchen
18 Aubergine
19 Korsan and Deniz Restaurant Palanın Yeri

Shopping
5 Karaca Market

Kalkan

Turkish/international cuisine — from wild boar (!) with aubergines to swordfish with fresh herbs or poussin in brandy sauce. Main courses £9-11. (8443332.

Belgin's Kitchen (15) is another reader recommendation: top-quality Turkish home cooking, usually hard to find in Kalkan — like *mantı, güveç* and fresh *börek*. Lovely roof terrace with humourous decorations — like a giant stuffed donkey and a nomads' tent. Main courses £6-11. Yalıboyu Mah., (8443614.

Merkez Café (11), very popular café/restaurant. In addition to a licence to serve alcohol, the supply of sweets is guaranteed. From snacks to sticky pastries, breakfast and fresh-squeezed juices. Reasonable prices. Hasan Altan Cad.

Nightlife

There are some bars and discos, but no frenetic nightlife (the *jandarma* call time at 1.30am); relaxed boozing is preferred. Repeat customers like the **Yalı Music Café (14)**, with bar and terrace, on Hasan Altan Cad.; by your second visit you are greeted like a regular. In the upper part of town, on the corner of Kocakaya Cad. and Süleyman Yılmaz

---

Tip on trout!
At İslamlar, between Kalkan and Patara, signposted from Akbel off the old inland road (see touring map), there are several excellent trout restaurants, all raising their own fish. Readers particularly liked Değirmen (nice terrace) and the equally charming Çiftlik.

Cad. is the **Moonlight Bar (7)** with a cosy atmosphere and very long list of drinks. **Yachtpoint Bar (17)** by the Barakuda Diving Club at the port is where divers meet up in the evenings (next door there's a hookah café). **Sandal (12)** is a meeting place for yachtsmen and wealthy locals, with good (expensive) cocktails on the roof terrace. Quieter souls head for **Fener Café (21)** by the lighthouse, where you can lounge about on comfy divans.

Beaches and diving

In Kalkan itself there's only a small (but well maintained) beach next to the port, with crystal-clear water. In the new western district of Kalamar, the **Kalamar Beach Club** has a lido with cleverly designed natural stone platforms. But it's worth heading for the nearby beaches — especially **Patara** (see page 114) or the **Bay of Kaputaş** (see page 113).

Diving: The **Dolphin Scuba Team** at the Hotel Pirat has been in business 15 years. One day's diving with hired equipment costs £40, diving courses from £300. Open Apr.-Oct. (8442242, www.dolphinscubateam.com.

Watersports: **Blue Marlin Watersports** has an office in the Hotel Pirat ((8442783) and offers various 'Water Fun Specials', including waterskiing and jet skiing.

Practicalities A-Z

Barber: **Safter**, in a small wooden building beside the post office. For those who want to feel 'like a sultan' (according to his self-advertisement) you'll get a perfect haircut, including tea and

back massage for £4.75. Readers found it a 'relaxing holiday experience'.

Boat trips: The most popular boat trips take you to various local beaches and bays or to Kekova (some are combined with a bus trip to Kaş). *Be aware that it is best to book just a short time before departure:* the tour companies 'officially' limit the number of participants to a maximum of 20. But in reality they over-book, taking up to 40 people. If you already have a ticket, transferring into an empty boat is difficult, as they all leave at the same time. One-day boat trips cost from £12-17 per person including lunch.

You can also hire boats at the port to take you wherever you want to go. But unless you have a group to fill the boat, this is an expensive option.

Car and two-wheel hire: There are several options, for instance **Enes** near the Hotel Pirat. Cars start from £30 per day. (8443961, www.enesrentacar.net. There's a company hiring out **two-wheelers** at the entrance to the town near the *dolmuş* station.

Doctors and dentists, English-speaking: are available at the **Medical Centre Tuana** above the taxi rank on the road to Kalamar. (8442244.

Launderette: at the yacht club in the port. A 4kg wash and dry costs £5.

Newspapers: English newspapers and the like are widely available, for instance in the **Karaca Market** diagonally opposite the *dolmuş* station.

Organised tours: Of the various companies, one long-established firm is **Armes Travel** on the road to Kalamar about 200m above the *dolmuş* station (Cumhuriyet Cad. 10; (8443169, www.armestravel. com). They do day trips like a morning bus to Kaş, then on to Kekova by 'Glass Bottom Boat' (£30 with lunch) or to the Saklıkent Gorge and Tlos (£24 including lunch); their two-day tour to Pamukkale and Ephesus costs about £45 all in.

The **Dolmuş Cooperative** also offers tours: e.g. Saklıkent and Xanthos (£8), a Tuesday tour to the market in Fethiye and to Ölüdeniz (£9), and a bus/boat tour to Myra and Kekova (£11). The minimum number of participants is about 6 people.

Police: The *jandarma* is on the Kaş/Fethiye road; in an emergency call (156.

Post: The post office is close to the *dolmuş* station and is usually open on Sundays.

Shopping: Every Thursday there is a large market some 500m northwest of the roundabout by the mosque.

Sights around Kalkan
Bay of Kaputaş
This bay lies in the steep coast below the road from Kaş to Kalkan. Incredibly picturesque, it has a sand/shingle beach collaring a sea in all the blues and greens of an artist's palette — turquoise, emerald, aquamarine. But because it's so beautiful, tourists come *en masse* in high summer (by boat or *dolmuş*). *Getting there: regular* dolmuş *service from Kalkan and Kaş. If you drive, you can park beside the road.*

Gömbe
Several tour operators in Kaş, Kalkan and Patara offer Gömbe as a hilly inland destination. Many villagers here are still semi-nomadic, living on the coast in winter and in the mountains during the summer. The roads cross passes at 1000m and lead up to the heights of the Lycian Taurus. The landscape is wonderful. Naturally, as is usual with such trips, one can also buy carpets: Gömbe is famous for its kilims — woven, rather than knotted carpets.
Getting there: By car take the zigzagging 07-53 road from Kalkan to Gömbe (passing the start and end of Walk 5) — or the 07-52 from Kaş (via Kuruova Beli and Walk 4). Dolmuş *connections from Kaş every 2 hours, from Kalkan very sporadic. If you don't have your own wheels, it's best to take an organised tour.*

Yeşilgöl and Uçarsu
Lake Yeşilgöl and the Uçarsu Waterfall are the highlights of the landscape around Gömbe. The rugged Taurus mountains show their other face here — 'chocolate box' scenery. To get to these two sights, take an organised tour from Kaş or Kalkan. Or, if you have a car, from the central crossroads in Gömbe follow signs for 'Uçarsu/Yeşilgöl'. After about 3km the road loses its tarred surface, and after another bumpy 4km you come to a makeshift 'Otopark'. Leave the car here and set off on foot (signposted). After about 15 minutes, at an altitude of 1900m, you can see the deep green lake (*yeşil* means 'green'). After another 15 minutes you'll be looking at the 60m-high waterfall (*uçar su* means 'flying water').

4 PATARA

Accommodation/camping • Food and drink • Beaches •
Practicalities A-Z • Patara (ancient site)

Area code: (0242
Information: at the Kaş Tourist
Office (see page 63).
Connections: The signposted
turn-off for Patara is on the left,
14km west of Kalkan on the
coastal D400 highway; from there
it's a further 4km. All large cross-
country **buses** usually stop at the
turn-off. But several companies
have a branch in Patara and offer
a shuttle service; prices are about
the same as those to Kalkan.
Dolmuş: Regular connections to

Kalkan (£2.50) and Kaş (£3).
Timetables are posted at the
dolmuş stop in the centre of
Gelemiş. The *dolmuş* co-op also
runs tours to places like Gömbe,
Xanthos and Saklıkent (prices
depend on season/number of
participants; (8435117.
Taxis: The taxi rank is in the
centre of Gelemiş. Fares for
Xanthos or Letoon are about £30
return, Saklıkent £45. If you
bargain well, you should be able
to get a 20% discount.

P atara can be defined in three ways. First and foremost,
it is one of the most beautiful beaches in Turkey, very
long and totally unspoilt. Secondly, Patara is the ancient
city lying in ruins in the dunes behind this beautiful beach;
it was once one of Lycia's main ports. Finally, 'Patara' is
the common name for the settlement of guest houses and
small hotels scattered even further behind the beach, but
its official name is Gelemiş.

Patara Beach (often classed by tour operators as the best
in Turkey) is over 14km long and up to 400m wide; the
sand is almost white and in the summer burning hot. If
you are in search of absolute peace, you will find it here.
The surf rushes in a reassuring rhythm, the water is
crystal-clear, and bathing is just superlative. The beach is
a nesting place for loggerhead turtles, and the dune
landscape behind it a protected area for rare birds;
building here is prohibited. Signs alert you to the fact that
the loggerhead turtle is 95 million years old and should
be allowed to become even older. So Earth's younger
inhabitants, *Homo sapiens*, are only allowed here during
the day — and only on sand close to the water's edge.

Since the coastal strip is taboo, tourism is based 2km
behind the beach in Gelemiş, a fairly faceless accumu-
lation of small hotels, *pansiyonlar*, restaurants and bars —
of which the 'centre' is little Atatürk Park with its tea
garden and children's play area. There are, however,
plans afoot to pave some roads and create an open-air
theatre and a museum with finds from the Patara site.

Ancient Patara (see page 118), rather than the turtle, is

Patara Beach — 14 kilometres of pristine sand and never crowded

responsible for the lack of local infrastructure. Remains of the city are still found around Gelemiş — some visible, some still buried — so building has been officially banned for many years. Nevertheless investment continues, although the investors must always take into account that they may get a stop or demolition order at any time (that's why you will see some ruined buildings).

In 2004 a development plan for Gelemiş was finally submitted, which outlined where it may be developed in the future and what must be demolished. This plan also put an end to large hotel projects: each new building is limited to 150sqm, while the plot to be developed must be at least 600sqm. And the few local families who control Gelemiş keep an eye out to make sure that no bribes are taken, so that almost all existing pensions and hotels remain in their hands — they worry that large club hotels would put their customers off. As a result one probably has to accept that Gelemiş will never be 'perfect', but will remain a cosy refuge for those with simple tastes who want to leave the cares of the world behind in typical Turkish family-style accommodation.

Accommodation/camping

There are approximately 1800 guest beds. Almost all the guest houses and hotels can be recommended as good value for money, but many are only open from May until mid-October. **Patara View Point** is signposted

Loggerhead turtles

Weighing up to two hundred kilos and up to a metre long, the loggerhead *(Caretta caretta)*, like all sea turtles, spends its entire life in the water. The females only come ashore to lay their eggs. Like tourists, they are particular about their beaches, and they like fine sand — particularly from May to September. But while the tourists visit during the day, the turtles appear at night. If they are disturbed on their way to their nesting site by noise, light or any obstacles (like sunbeds), they sometimes return to the sea and lose their eggs.

The turtles dig a nest to lay their eggs. Afterwards they cover the table tennis ball-sized eggs with sand. After about 60 days' incubation under the summer sun, the hatchlings dig themselves free. This usually happens at night. To then find their way to the sea, the tiny turtles turn towards the brightest surface — usually the moonlit water. The females will remember this place for their entire lives: 20 to 30 years later, and from thousands of kilometres away, they return to exactly the same place to lay their eggs. This means that the few beaches that are still visited by loggerheads must remain in their natural state, so that the remaining population does not become extinct. Measures are taken to protect the species:

• Avoid the nesting beaches between sunset and sunrise.

• Don't use any artificial light sources behind the beach (campfire, headlights, etc.) — lest the fledgling animals crawl in the wrong direction and dry out painfully in the sun on the next day!

• When sunbathing, keep within five metres of the water. The turtles do not bury their eggs where the beach is wet. If you are too far back from the water, in dry sand, children could dig into a clutch of eggs or you could put up a parasol and extend the breeding period with artificial shade.

• Under no circumstances touch young, newly hatched animals.

left uphill at the beginning of Gelemiş. It's the best of the up-market selection; Turkish/English management, with a lot of British visitors. 27 rustic rooms, all with balconies and air-conditioning. Pool and appealing terrace with divans and open fireplace (some evening barbecues). Readers recommend highly. Doubles £30, singles £20. (8435184, www.pataraviewpoint.com.

Hotel Mehmet, family-run hotel high above Gelemiş (also a left uphill from the village entrance). Quiet setting. Restaurant, bar, pool, carpeted conversation area with fireplace. Clean rooms with shower/WC and balcony or terrace. Nimble Mehmet speaks good English. Open all year. All rooms with air-conditioning; prices include breakfast: doubles £24.50, singles £17.50. (8435032, www.kircatravel.com.

Hotel Sema (yet another left turn uphill from the village entrance). Readers recommend this hotel for its very friendly, helpful, family atmosphere. The hillside rooms have balconies with views over Gelemiş. The owner, Ali

Çörüt, is full of good tips for excursions in the area. 16 spotless double rooms with superb breakfasts £18 (singles £10), tasty evening meal from £4.50. ℂ 8435114, www.semahotel.com.

St. Nicholas Pension, near the centre — covered in bougain-villaea and with a vine-shaded terrace. Well-kept rooms with air-conditioning and balcony. Popular with the British. Good restaurant. Doubles £20. On the road to the beach (a bit noisy). ℂ 8435154, ℂ 8435024, www.stnicholaspensionpatara.com.

Zeybek 2 is a somewhat isolated 12-room guest house (sign-posted). There is no nearby building to block the view, so the outlook from the cosy roof terrace is delightful (unfortun-ately, no alcohol served). Nicely furnished rooms, all with balconies. Double rooms with climate control £14, without £9. ℂ 8435086, zeybek2pension@hotmail.com.

Flower Pension, long recom-mended by readers. On the right as you come into the village. The helpful owners Mustafa and Ayşe Kırca speak English and in the evenings run a very good family restaurant with Turkish home cooking. 9 cosy doubles with shower cubicles/WC, balcony or terrace, climate control and mosquito netting (£15 including a very good breakfast, singles £9). The family also rents out two colourful, rustic apartments (for 4-5 people) for £18-28 a night. Very pleasant courtyard with palm trees. Tea and coffee always on offer; washing machine available. ℂ 8435164, ℂ 8435279, www.flowerpension.com.

Rose Pension, another readers' favourite, in fairly large grounds (turn right at the village entrance). 12 simple but very friendly rooms with climate control, bath, WC. Nice shaded terrace. English spoken. Doubles £15, singles £9. ℂ 8435165, www.rosepensionpatara.com. On the way to Rose Pension you pass **Paradise Pension**, with just 8 rooms (same grade/prices, same friendly service, but less attractive terrace). Turkish home cooking on request. ℂ 8435190, www.paradisepension.com.

Camping: **Medusa Camping** in the centre opposite the *dolmuş* station offers long-distance walkers a roof over their heads. Otherwise it's pretty grim and spartan. At least there's a nice bar. £2 per person. ℂ 8435193.

Food and drink

The bulk of the restaurants and pension kitchens in Patara are recommended. You can find authentic Turkish food (but no beer, wine or *rakı!*) in the **Restaurant Tlos**. Readers also recommend **Sofra Restaurant** near the *dolmuş* station: the hostess is pleasant and there is an excellent mushroom salad starter. See also the 'Tip on trout' in the panel on page 111.

Beaches

The long beach is only accessible by a few approach roads. The southernmost access road is past Gelemiş and the Patara site; this leads to the most-visited (and most beautiful) part of the beach, where a charge is made. North of this is the section called Çay Ağzı and still further northwest Kumluova Plajı.

Patara Beach: There are patrols on the beach to ensure adherence to the daily opening times (summer from 08.00-19.30, winter 08.00-17.30). There is a fee of £2.40 for entrance to the beach (and the excavation site, which the beach road passes through). There's a snack bar on this part of the beach. Sun-shades and -loungers for rent, very cheap beer, and lifeguards.

Anyone coming from Gelemiş who wants to visit this beach and see the imposing dunes without paying, can do so by taking the following route (on foot or with wheels). From Gelemiş follow the signposts to the İlay Hotel. Pass this hotel (on your right) and 600m further on, where the road turns right, go left on a gravel track. This leads past a pine forest to the large dune area. From here to the sea it's still about 10 minutes on foot.

Çay Ağzı: This free public section of beach belongs to Ova district and is about halfway along Patara Beach. There is no public transport. To get there turn right 2km after turning off the D400 towards Patara (no signposts, but a lot of signs for pensions in front of a rock wall). Now it's another 6km of dirt road . Some summers a few primitive bars set up on this stretch of beach.

Kumluova Plajı: This marks the northern end of the 16km-long sandy beach. Usually this expansive dune landscape is virtually deserted — perhaps because the beach is narrower here. Follow signposting for Letoon (see page 128), then keep straight on past the site.

Those who prefer the alternative of a small cosy bay should make

for **Kaputaş** (see page 113) or go left along Patara's beach at the end of Short walk 11-2.

Practicalities A-Z

Car and two-wheel hire: available through **Kırca Travel Agencia Patara** (see 'Organised tours' below). Cars from £30 per day, jeeps £45, scooters £17.

Money: There are exchange bureaus, but at time of writing no cash machines. The nearest ATM is 5km from Gelemiş: it's at the first petrol station on the left on the D400 towards Fethiye, 1km past the Patara turn-off.

Organised tours: There are several local companies, including **Kırca Travel Agencia Patara** in the centre close to the *dolmuş* station. Possibilities include Saklıkent Gorge with Tlos and Xanthos (£20 per person including travel, guide and lunch). A canoe ride on the Xanthos River costs £20; a tour to the small mountain town of Elmalı (highly recommended) £25; Pamukkale tour £65; two-day tour to Ephesus £125. Various 'blue cruises' cost about £45 per person per day, including food. **Airport transfers to Dalaman** (£65 for up to 4 people) and **Antalya** (£95 for up to 4 people). (8435298, www.kircatravel.com.

Post: The post office is in the centre close to the *dolmuş* station.

Riding: Han Horse Riding, on the left at the entrance to the village, offers rides on Haflinger horses — along the beach or inland. They also accept beginners. £34 for 2h30min. (0536 5754593 (mobile). Also bookable through various travel agencies between Kaş and Patara (or Kirka above).

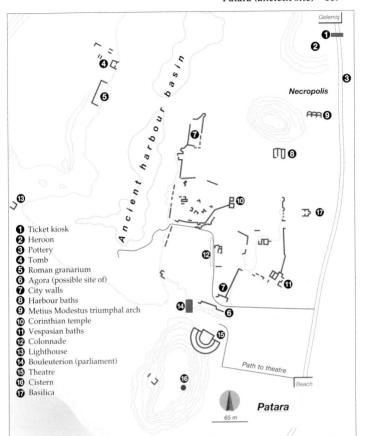

1 Ticket kiosk
2 Heroon
3 Pottery
4 Tomb
5 Roman granarium
6 Agora (possible site of)
7 City walls
8 Harbour baths
9 Metius Modestus triumphal arch
10 Corinthian temple
11 Vespasian baths
12 Colonnade
13 Lighthouse
14 Bouleuterion (parliament)
15 Theatre
16 Cistern
17 Basilica

Necropolis

Path to theatre

Beach

Patara

65 m

Patara (ancient site)

Patara, probably settled by the 7th century BC, was one of the prominent cities of the Lycian League. Like Tlos, Pınara and Xanthos, Patara had the right to three votes and also administered the federation's archives. At the same time Patara was one of the main ports in Lycia. Since all the dominant powers used this port for their fleets, Patara thrived throughout antiquity. During the era of the Roman Caesars, Patara became the seat of the governor of Lycia and Pamphylia and even surpassed Xanthos. This period was also associated with much building, and most of the ruins that are still visible today date from Roman times. The story of St. Paul the Apostle mentions Patara as a stopping point on his third missionary journey. St. Nicholas ('Father Christmas') was born here in around 290.

Over the ages the city continually fought against the sand, which constantly threatened to block the port entrance. Today that area is an arm of land deposited

Rustic bridge over the Eşen Çayı (Xanthos River), west of Patara

by the Xanthos River. When the port could no longer be saved, Patara's decline followed — the city was abandoned about 800 years ago.

Excavations have been undertaken again and again in recent decades. They intensified in 2004 under Professor Fahri Işık from Antalya's Akdeniz University. Thanks to the discovery of some stones covered with soot, he came across ancient Patara's 'genuine' lighthouse (at that time just thought to be another heap of stone). As a result, all plans of

Patara in travel guides must now be redrawn. By the way, some 5000 truckloads of sand had to be removed during the excavation of the lighthouse. Whether or not this lighthouse is the oldest in the world (as is being claimed), still needs to be proven. It seems to have toppled over as the result of a 'tsunami', rather than an earthquake as was previously thought. All the original stone are still there; work has already begun on rebuilding the 20m-high edifice.

Sights

Ancient writings report the existence of an oracle's site at **Apollo Patareus**, but so far no traces of this have been found in Patara. Perhaps they refer to the Apollo Sanctuary in the nearby temple city of Letoon. But even without the Apollonian Oracle, these ruins still offer much to be seen. **Short walk 11 describes a route taking in the whole site**, beginning the magnificent propylon shown on page 32. See the notes on page 123. When the walk finishes at the beach, head inland to see the sand dunes and the ruins on the far side of the harbour.

But it is not only the ruins which contribute to the attraction of this site. What is really fascinating is the singular combination of wild, expansive steppe country and indescribably beautiful beach backed by the turquoise sea. Paul Klee and August Macke would never have reached Tunis, if their journey had taken them via Patara…

Opening times and entrance fee: as for the beach (see page 117).

The Patara aqueduct south of Yeşilköy, showing the sealed pipeline

Walk 11: Yeşilköy • Delikkemer Aqueduct • Patara

Time: 4h15min
Grade: easy-moderate, mostly over good footpaths and tracks; overall ascents of 200m
Equipment: see pages 23-24; one drinking water spring early on in the walk, cafe/restaurant at the end, but carry plenty of fluid — much of the route is exposed to the sun, and temperatures can be high even in spring.
Travel: 🚐 *dolmuş* from Kaş to the Yeşilköy cement works* (half-hourly from May-October; journey time 50min). Out of season use the 🚐 Kaş/Fethiye service (hourly); alight at the Yeşilköy cement works. 🚗 by car, park at Patara and take a *dolmuş* to Yeşilköy to begin (15min).

Alternative walks
1 Yeşilköy — Delikkemer Aque-duct — Yeşilköy (2h45min; easy). Follow the main walk to the 2h15min-point, then turn right down the dirt road, back to the cement works at Yeşilköy.
2 Exploring Patara (1h45min; easy). Take the bus to Patara and start at the main gate. See 'Exploring Patara' (the last paragraph on page 123). After your walk, continue to the beach. Head inland to see the sand dunes and ruins on the far side of the harbour. Going left along the beach takes you over a headland to a more secluded beach.
3 Delikkemer Aqueduct to Patara (8h15min; moderate-strenuous, with overall ascents of 250m). Follow the main walk to the 1h20min-point, then continue along the dirt road and follow Lycian Way signposting, undulating round the coast through hamlets and on to Patara.

This walk follows the course of Patara's aqueduct, circumnavigating the hillside at the rim of the Xanthos Valley. The heavy stone masonry supporting the rock-cut pipeline feeding the ancient port with fresh water is an engineering feat, still standing 2000 years after it was built. The path passes through pine woods, meadows of wild flowers and groves of olive trees — with views over the Bay of Kalkan, the Anticragus coastal mountains and the fertile plain watered by the Eşen Çayı (Xanthos River). Patara was the birthplace of St. Nicholas, who went off to travel through Palestine before returning to become bishop of Myra. Excavation work is continuing to unearth major finds buried under sand for hundreds of years — like the lighthouse that once guided ships into the grandest of harbours.

Start the walk at **Yeşilköy**, opposite Albayrak Cimento (**cement works**), where the main D400 intersects with the Yeşilköy bypass.* Follow the highway to the left for 15 minutes, then turn right on a dirt road winding its way up to a saddle on the hillside. Nearing the saddle the road sweeps round to the right; if you look up left here, the aque-duct walls come into view. Take the footpath leading up through vegetation and pass through an opening in the heavy masonry wall of the **Delikkemer Aque-duct** (**50min**). Take in the view from the old olive (*Olea europaea*) grove out across the Bay of Kalkan.
Turn round to inspect this section of engineering mastery, shown opposite: the 12m-high wall is

*If the Yeşilköy bypass is open, you should be able to alight further east, opposite the road to the aqueduct.

made up of polygonal interlocking blocks supporting the sealed syphonic pipeline carrying water 12km from the main spring near Akbel to the great port of Patara. If you suffer from vertigo, go back down from this point and rejoin the path on the opposite bank. If you have a head for heights, you can inspect the aqueduct at closer range: walk up the right-hand bank to a break in the wall, clamber up on to the top of the aqueduct and walk across the span. The stone blocks were sealed together with iron staples and pointed with lime cement. Some of the blocks have inspection holes that would have been plugged, keeping the system airtight.

From the top, drop down left on the bank. From here the path recrosses the line of the aqueduct and descends left through olive trees to rejoin the **dirt road** (**1h20min**). Turn left, continuing up the hill. After five minutes take the **Lycian Way** footpath off the bend, going over the metal water pipe. The path veers right, following the line of the aqueduct and contouring the hillside — with fine views down the Xanthos Valley and over Yeşilköy village. The marshy section in the corner of the valley was a lake before modern irrigation channels were built to nourish this fertile land. Behind is fire-scarred Duman Dağı (Smoke Mountain). Continue round the hillside to a **spring** under an oriental plane tree. From the spring the path rises in a westerly direction, through lush rock roses, sweet laurel, kermes oak (*Quercus coccifera*) and the larger holm oak (*Quercus ilex*) cut back by the charcoal burners. The carob tree also thrives in the Mediterranean climate; called *keci boynuz* (goat horn) in Turkish, it is harvested at the end of August to make *pekmez*, a thick carob syrup. After about 15 minutes the path drops and switches back on itself, to cross a small olive grove and pass bee hives on the opposite bank. Here the path widens into a tractor track. Continue round the hillside through olive groves. The olives are picked from early November, when most are taken to the press/mill in Yeşilköy for oil and sold in the local markets. You pass what looks like a ruined tower, with a doorway at the back revealing an overgrown garden. Eventually the track descends through pine forest to a **dirt road** (**2h15min**).

Turn left; there is an old **cistern** on the left bank. Continue up the hill through to open farmland, passing a house on your right. When you meet a forestry track (**2h30min**), turn right, following the red/white flashes of the Lycian Way. Looking ahead, the sea comes into view over the treeline. The track enters young pine forest, contours round the hillside and comes to a **viewpoint** five minutes later. Looking up the centre of the valley, the sharp eye will spot the ruined walls of Xanthos. To the left (north-northwest), the Anticragus Mountains rise from the sea, Baba Dağı (1969m) being the highest — very popular with paragliders who land on the blue lagoon beach at Ölüdeniz. The continuing track becomes a tortoise motorway in springtime, after winter hibernation. At a sharp bend about 15 minutes past the viewpoint, take the higher track and continue through the forest. Later the track winds down the hillside, levels out in olive groves and *tarla*, and comes to a dirt road.

Do not follow the Lycian Way sign to Patara, but turn left towards Kalkan ('Yalı Burun'). Head towards the white house on the hillside, pass a street lamp and, approximately 300m after the signed junction (by an olive tree), turn right across a culti-vated field. Go round the edge of the wheat crop and drop over the terrace into the olive grove. The path cuts down the middle, over and round stone terracing and past a pine tree split by lightning. At the bottom of the valley, the path swings right to cross a concrete irrigation channel. Turn left along the adjacent track, contouring the hillside towards the sea.

Soon the view opens up over the ruins of Patara, with the theatre and harbour entrance visible in the distance. Look out for some red-tiled roofs and turn right down a dirt road past these buildings. These are the archaeo-logists' houses, with numerous headstones in the garden. (The black dog here is very friendly and might even escort you round the ruins for half a packet of biscuits!) Continue down the track to the triple-arched main gate to **Patara (4h15min)**, the propylon shown on page 32.

Exploring Patara (see plan on page 119): Facing the **Metius Modestus triumphal arch**, dedi-cated to the Roman governor of Lycia/Pamphylia, the wall run-ning up the hillside to your right was the line of the **aqueduct** as it entered the city. Down on your right is part of the **main colon-naded thoroughfare**, awaiting excavation; to your left is a Lycian-style **sarcophagus sur-mounting a house-type tomb**. From here, head to the recently excavated **harbour baths** next to a palm tree oasis. These are a

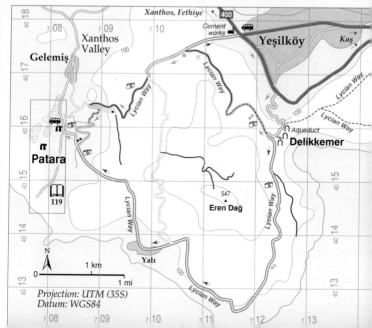

very elaborate affair, with the furnaces below on the side-street to heat the underfloor hypocaust system. Make your way back to the road and continue seawards. You pass a **basilica** on the right, with the windowed apse facing the road. Continue to the main track and turn right, past the **Emperor Vespasian baths**, with a triple-vaulted roof. Fork right over the hump to the **main street**. Excavation work is continuing in this area, exposing shops and offices — as well as columns in many varieties of marble, polished conglomerate (pudding stone) and pink granite, showing the prosperity of this major port. Head past the sunken end (popular with egrets and grey herons, as well as hundreds of frogs). Continue along the track to the **Corinthian temple**: the 8m-high doorway is decorated with egg and dart relief. From here the late harbour walls can be seen, a mix of different stonework, rebuilt through the ages.

Retrace your steps past the main street and continue by the probable site of the (still unexcavated) **agora** and **bouleuterion** to the main **theatre**. At the back of the stage you can see the excavation line, the grey stonework having been exposed to the elements, the white preserved by sand. As you enter the orchestra look up at the inscription on the side, naming one of the theatre's major benefactors. The high walls below the seats protected the audience; the recesses held caged wild animals, which were then set free to maul a gladiator (notice the carved relief of a gladiatorial costume on the lower walls). Climb the seats to the top of the second *cavea* and take in the magnificence of that era, its monuments still standing after 2000 years.

Just to the left of the centre of the top *cavea*, cross the open ditch and follow the footpath disappearing up into the bushes, up to the top of the hillock. Take the right fork to a first **viewpoint**, from where the plan of the ancient city is spread out before you. On the far bank of the **harbour** is the **granarium**, dedicated to the emperor Hadrian who travelled to the region in 131AD. Turning towards the sea, you can see the **lighthouse** protecting the harbour entrance. Further round is the ruin of a wealthy family's **mausoleum** watching out over the whole city. Retrace your steps to the viewpoint and take the path across the hillock. On your right is a huge **cistern** with a stone pillar in the middle to support the roof; it was built to keep a water supply in case the city was taken under siege. Continue along the path past the trig point to the next **viewpoint** over the 14km-long stretch of deserted golden sands. Not only do loggerhead turtles nest here (see page 116), but also green turtles and the endangered *Chelidonia myndas* species.

Take the path downhill and go over the trampled barbed wire into a **mimosa plantation**. Head down the sand bank into the hollow and turn left, working your way through the trees to find the footpath again, crossing more trampled barbed wire. (*Don't head towards the sea inside the plantation.*) The path descends past a house. Turn right by the prickly pear cactus and skirt the field, to the **car park** and **beach**.

5 BETWEEN PATARA AND ÖLÜDENIZ

Xanthos • Letoon • Sidyma • Pınara • Saklıkent Gorge • Tlos • Gebeler

Area code: (0252
Walk: 12

Connections and opening
times: see individual entries

Between Patara and Fethiye the main coastal D400 highway makes a deep inland sweep to the north, away from the coast. Close to the town of Kemer (not to be confused with Kemer in the Antalya region) it then turns west, back towards the coast. The first, northbound stretch of road runs across a cultivated plain and past isolated farming villages. To the west the plain is bordered by the Elmacık Dağı ridge, to the east by Akdağ and Yumru Dağı — their summits covered with snow well into April. But this route offers much more than beautiful landscapes. To the right and left of the road are several sites — Xanthos, Letoon, Sidyma, Pınara, Tlos. And between them, about halfway between Patara and Ölüdeniz, is the impressive Saklıkent Gorge.

Xanthos

This beautifully located World Cultural Heritage Site stretches along a rock outcrop high above the Eşen Çayı. The site is best known for its tombs. The theatre's orchestra is full of rubble, and many other, less-accessible buildings are decaying. Xanthos was one of the most powerful Lycian cities and controlled the Lycian League in late Hellenistic and Roman times. This federation consisted of some 20 cities and was governed by peoples' representatives and a kind of 'president', so that Lycians created the world's first 'republic'. The site includes ruins from Lycian, Hellenistic, Roman and Byzantine times. Considering that the city sustained heavy losses over thousands of years, it seems a miracle that so much still survives.

According to Herodotus, Xanthos was founded by colonists from Crete. The Xanthians were a courageous people and feared subjugation. Herodotus relates their heroic fight against the advancing Persians (545 BC), which led to the deaths of all the inhabitants except those who were absent from the city: 'Of the current Xanthians most are immigrants, except for about 80 families; these families were absent at that time and so remained alive.' Those men present had brought their families, ahead of the arrival of the fast-moving, far superior Persian army, into the acropolis and set the castle on fire; they themselves fought to the death.

The survivors and immigrants rebuilt Xanthos, but their work didn't last long: in the 5th century the city was completely destroyed by a large fire. The following generations were luckier: for some three centuries skillful diplomacy again and again secured autonomous periods for the Xanthians, and in addition peace and prosperity. That changed in 42 BC: Brutus,

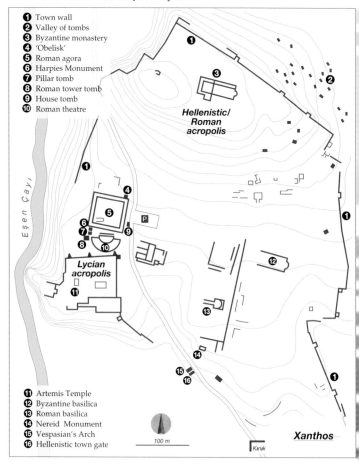

❶ Town wall
❷ Valley of tombs
❸ Byzantine monastery
❹ 'Obelisk'
❺ Roman agora
❻ Harpies Monument
❼ Pillar tomb
❽ Roman tower tomb
❾ House tomb
❿ Roman theatre

Hellenistic/Roman acropolis

Esen Çayı

Lycian acropolis

⓫ Artemis Temple
⓬ Byzantine basilica
⓭ Roman basilica
⓮ Nereid Monument
⓯ Vespasian's Arch
⓰ Hellenistic town gate

100 m

Xanthos

Kınık

Caesar's murderer, who was being hunted by Octavian, laid siege to the city. And with the seizure of Xanthos, history repeated itself. The men killed their wives and children and afterwards committed collective suicide. Brutus offered a reward for each Xanthian saved (!) and so protected 150 citizens from death. Under the Caesars, Xanthos became the provincial capital; in the Byzantine era it was a bishopric. Attacks by the Arabs in the 8th century brought the city's history to an end. It was only rediscovered (together with Tlos and Pınara) in the 1840s by Sir Charles Fellows. In 1988 UNESCO declared both Xanthos and Letoon World Cultural Heritage Sites.

Getting there/opening times/prices: Xanthos is signposted off the main D400 highway north of Patara. If you don't have your own wheels, it's best to take an organised tour. Open daily May-Oct. from 07.30-19.00,

Lycian rock tombs — landmarks of a puzzling people

The ancient sites between the Bay of Antalya and Lake Köyçeğiz are full of many strange and impressive graveyards — with pillar tombs, sarcophagi, and especially rock tombs, the like of which are not found anywhere outside Asia Minor. Many of the stone house tombs imitate timber constructions, with beams both cross- and lengthwise, a method also once used in the building of storehouses. The tombs were developed between the 6th and 4th centuries BC and are our inheritance from ancient Lycia.

For scholars the Lycian people are still a mystery. There is no reliable information on their ethnic identity nor any data regarding their origin. What *is* known, based on Attic tribute lists, is that the first inhabitants of the Xanthos Valley were called Lycians by the Greeks. The Lycians apparently took no notice of this, as they still called themselves Termilae in the 4th century BC on coins and tomb inscriptions.

It is also known that, due to their isolation behind the high Taurus

Interior of a Lycian tomb at Xanthos

Mountains, the Lycians had little exchange with other cultures in pre-Roman times. So this closed cultural landscape allowed Lycia to develop its own written and spoken language (the Lycian alphabet used 19 Greek letters and 10 of their own).

Today the question remains unanswered — what inspired them to build such strange graveyards and at such a height? Our knowledge of the Lycians is on firmer footing from the Hellenistic period, but this knowledge is little help — because the strange Lycian tomb architecture ended at the beginning of the Hellenistic era.

Nov.- Apr. 08.00-17.30; entry fee £1.50.

Sights

From the car park it's only a few steps to the **theatre**, which dates from the 2nd century BC. While the rows of seats are relatively well preserved, little remains of the former two-storey fly tower. But it must have been very lavish, since it was commissioned by Opramoas, one of the richest men in Lycia; he donated approx-imately 1200 aureen (equal to about 10kg of gold). The orchestra could only be entered from the eastern side; the western entrance was a fake. Behind the theatre is the **Harpy Monument** and a **pillar tomb** (see photograph on page 57). The four-sided flat-roofed monument to the Harpies consists of a 5.4m-high monolith, decorated at the top with reliefs of seated figures, between which are the fertility symbols (cock, egg, pomegranate). The demonic Harpy is depicted as half-woman, half-bird. These reliefs are considered characteristic of Lycian sculpture, despite the fact that they are copies (Sir Charles had the originals transported to the British Museum). Why the dead were buried at these airy heights remains an unresolved mystery. The pillar tomb beside it is a double tomb. The base of pillar dates from the Hellenistic era and is hollow in the centre — the most likely place to put a coffin. Centuries later a second stone sarcophagus with a pointed, arched roof was placed on top. Nearby there is also a Lycian house tomb.

The **agora** was once in front of the former stage housing of the theatre, and was surrounded by a colonnade. Now only the so-called **obelisk** shown on page 49 remains at the northeast corner. 'Obelisk' is misleading, however, since it contains a chamber. The exterior is covered with inscriptions. The 250-line text, the longest Lycian inscription found to date, lists the heroic acts of Kherei, son of the Persian Field General Harpagos: he defeated the Attic fleet in 429 BC. For those whose Lycian is not up to scratch, but who can understand some Greek, there is a 12-line Greek summary at the end. Those who have little grasp of either language have the same educational deficiencies as your authors.

Xanthos had one of its very finest finds spirited away by Sir Charles: the **Nereid Monument**, one of the most important tombs from southwestern Turkey. It also now resides in the British Museum; only the foundations were left behind. It must have been spectacular: a typically Lycian rectangular base with marble reliefs around the sides, surmounted by an Ionic temple. It is thought that it was the prototype for the tomb built for Prince Mausolos in Halicarnassos (today Bodrum), from which the term mausoleum is derived.

Letoon

Only 4km from Xanthos, Letoon was the main religious centre of the Lycian League, where people met every year for cult celebrations and athletic competitions. Today it is just a small field of ruins. First you see the **theatre**; despite the quite well-preserved rows of seats, it's nothing special. A few steps beyond the entry kiosk the bases of columns from a **portico** protrude from a pond; this would have been a magnificent gate, securing the com-

Leto and Lycia

Leto, Zeus's lover and pregnant by him, was pursued by his jealous wife Hera. No country in the world dared to take her in. Finally, on the island of Delos she bore the god's twins Artemis and Apollo. As she continued to move from place to place with her children, she came to the river Xanthos. She wanted to wash her babies, but herdsmen blocked her way. To their surprise, some wolves appeared and drove them off. In thanks, Leto called the place Lycia. Even though we know today that etymologically Lycia does not stem from lycos (wolf), the story is still a lovely one.

Letoon — north portico and some inquisitive tourists

pound's north side. Some beautifully carved stones lie in the shallow water.

Behind this are Letoon's three **main temples**, standing side by side. One assumes, due to an inscription on a sacrificial stone, that the main, western temple (30 x 15 m), nearest the road, was dedicated to the goddess Leto. It is currently being rebuilt. Little is left of the small Artemis Temple next to it (where the side walls extend forward, forming an entrance hall); only foundations remain. The same holds true for the most easterly temple, dedicated to Apollo.

South of the main temple lies the rubble of a ruined 7th-century **Byzantine church**, and to the west of it are the remains of a gigantic 'well' temple, part of the **nymphaeum**.

The most important find from Letoon now resides in Fethiye's museum — a stela discovered near the temple compound in 1973. Its inscriptions, in Aramaic,

Greek and Lycian, helped scholars decipher the Lycian language.

Getting there/opening times/prices: signposted from the main D400 highway north of Patara. IIf you don't have wheels, take an organised tour. Xanthos and Letoon are on the Lycian Way. Open daily May-Oct. from 07.30-19.00, Nov.-Apr. 08.00-17.30; entry fee £2.20.

Sidyma

Sidyma, a Lycian settlement dating from the 5th century BC, is not of major importance. Except for walkers following the Lycian Way, no tourists are likely to visit it. But a trip into this barren mountain world is an enjoyable experience nonethe-

❶ Theatre
❷ Temple
❸ Town wall
❹ Odeon
❺ Thermal baths
❻ King's Tomb
❼ Agora
❽ Rock tombs
❾ Former acropolis

Pınara

50 m

less. Scattered on top of and between the ruins (most of which date from the era of the Roman Caesars) are the dwellings and stables of the mountain peasants who live here today — a harsh life. The village boys will lead you to the tombs and other relics worth seeing. But what they really want to show you is their prowess with a catapult. Make sure they don't use them to knock sparrows out of the sky — these kids can really aim!

Getting there: There are no dolmuş connections. By private transport turn off the D400 at Eşen, north of Patara (signposted to Sidyma). From here it's another 17km, the last 2.5km on dirt track.

Pınara

Pınara, like Tlos, once ranked among the six most important Lycian cities, today it lies off the tourist route. Pity. Although the remains of this ancient city (with the exception of the necropolis and theatre) are quite modest, its breathtaking location, with views to the high Taurus Mountains, is spectacular.

Little is known of Pınara's history. According to ancient sources the city was founded in the 4th century by the offspring of people living in over-populated Xanthos. Other sources report that it was one of the few Lycian cities to capitulate to Alexander the Great without a fight. What occurred in Pınara's history during the Roman and Byzantine eras is little known, although it did become a bishopric. It is thought that the city was abandoned in the Middle Ages after an earthquake and that the inhabitants founded the nearby settlement of Minare Köy. Many houses were built there using ancient stone blocks. Pınara extended over several levels. The **theatre**, with its 27 rows of seats, stands on the lowest level, by the car park. Only the foundations of its orchestra remain. From the car park a path leads to the large **King's Tomb** (Kral Mezarı) — the car park attendant will point you in the right direction. The coffered façade is in a pitiful state. The doorway and entrance hall are covered with reliefs, those in the entrance hall depicting fortified cities. From here the path leads further uphill through an overgrown little valley with a stream and full of butterflies. You come to a rock terrace on which are the remains of the **agora** and **odeon**, which probably served at the same time as the **bouleuterion**. Both are almost completely destroyed. Behind the odeon is a sheer 450m-high cliff, honeycombed with more than 900 rock tombs. Rope ladders and cradles would have been lowered from above to build them. An **acropolis** once rose above the cliff, primarily serving as a place where the populace could take refuge. *Getting there/opening times/prices: No dolmuş connections. By private transport, Pınara is signposted off the D400 highway about 40km north of Kalkan and 48km south of Fethiye. The last 2km of road to the site is in* *bad condition. You can't see the ruins from the small car park, except for the rock tombs. The site (still unfenced) is open daily from 08.00-17.00. Entry fee £4.*

Saklıkent Gorge

This impressive canyon (see Walk 12) is halfway between Patara and Fethiye at the foot of the Taurus Mountains. Sheer perpendicular cliffs up to 300m high enclose a raging river. On one of the cliffs a secure wooden walkway leads into the ravine just above the river (depending on the water level); after just 200m this leads to a secluded restaurant awaiting hungry visitors. It's a great place to relax in the shade, listening to the sound of rushing water, enjoying a drink and a delicious grilled trout.

Most visitors make it to the 'restaurant corner'. Afterwards the gorge splits. Those who want to continue can take off their shoes and wade — the first kilo-metre of the 17km-long gorge is easily accessible and very im-pressive. It's also thought that the mud on the river bed has healing properties. If you plan to walk part of the gorge, either take suitable **footwear for wading** or rent waders at the ford by the restaurants. The gorge is also popular for **rafting** and **camping**: the **Gorge Club** at the exit not only has a good trout restaurant, but also runs a simple, cheap campsite (2 people with camper £5) and rents out simple but roomy tree house accommo-dation (per person with H/B £15). They also organise rafting trips (5km for £15). (6590074, www.saklikentgorge.net.

Getting there/opening times/prices: The gorge is on offer from virtually every tour operator between Kalkan and Fethiye. In summer there is also a regular dolmuş *to Saklıkent from the bus station in Fethiye (via Tlos; journey time 1h). From Patara or Kalkan, take a bus towards Fethiye and alight at the Kemer crossroads, then contine on the* dolmuş *from Fethiye. By car, the gorge is signposted off the D400 Kalkan–Fethiye highway. Open daily from 08.00-19.30; entry fee £1.50.*

Saklıkent Gorge: this couple hardly need waders, but usually the water is higher.

Time: 4h, plus time to explore the Saklıkent Gorge

Grade: easy-moderate; all downhill or on the flat; good paths and tracks; overall descent of 700m.

Equipment: see pages 23-24; wading shoes for the gorge.

Travel: 🚌 from Fethiye to Arsaköy (the first minibus service leaves Fethiye *dolmuş* station at 12.00; journey time 1h30min). This *does* give you enough time to do the walk and explore the Saklıkent Gorge, but if the timing is too rushed for your liking, it is possible to stay overnight in Arsaköy. There are currently no pensions, but it's possible to stay in a village house with Turan Akkaya's family (phone in advance on 0252-6584102 to make a booking and to let them know you are coming for dinner). They are used to tourists staying and also arrange guided walks up to the summit of Akdağ and another walk descending to the ruins of Tlos. Return from Saklıkent to Fethiye by *dolmuş* (half-hourly during the holiday season, infrequently in winter; journey time 45min).

🚗 travelling by car, from Fethiye take the Antalya road to just past the Kemer junction, then turn right following signs for Saklıkent. Cross the Eşen Çayı (Xanthos River) and, 13km from the junction, turn left on the signposted road up the mountainside to Arsaköy (under an hour's drive). If you don't wish to walk back to collect the car, drive to Saklıkent and take a taxi up to Arsaköy.

This walk explores the highland village of Arsaköy, picturesquely situated on the lower slopes of the mass of Akdağ above the split of the Saklıkent Gorge. *The snow melt waters the fertile farmland of the village and the Xanthos Valley below. The ancient ruins of Arsada are perched up on the cliffs with commanding views over western Lycia. Your path descends through terraced farmland, becoming an ancient mule trail skirting the cliff face. Once down in the valley, the walk continues along the base of the cliff, past old stone houses, to the dramatic entrance to the Saklıkent Gorge. The cold mountain springs rising in the canyon provide mains water for the farming communities, and for Kaş and Kalkan as well. The gorge runs 17 kilometres into the mountainside, one of the many defiles running off the slopes of Akdağ and feeding into the Eşen Çayı (Xanthos River) flowing to the sea at Patara Beach. The gorge is now a major tourist attraction, and it is possible to walk up it for a kilometre or so, to see the marble walls metamorphosed and sculpted over thousands of years by the immense water pressure.*

Start the walk from the main village square in **Arsaköy**: with the **mosque** on your left, head to the right-hand corner of the square by Yavuz Market. Descend past the market (the path is marked by **red flashes**) and cross the stream. The path follows the stream through lush vegetation, where narrow-leaved glaucous spurge (*Euphorbia rigida*) and arum lilies grow among the oak and poplar trees. Continue down past walled gardens with grapevines, through a dip, and alongside another walled garden. The path twists left to join a dirt road at the entrance to a house. Look back here to the mass of Akdağ, snow-

133

capped until early summer. Walk down the dirt road and, after a bend to the right, take the second left turn, down to a T-junction. Turn right and continue past houses, a water tap, and apple orchards to the next junction. Go straight over the road here, heading north-northwest on the track by the Valonia oak. The track cuts through cultivated land (*tarla*); anise is the popular crop cultivated in the surrounding fields. The track winds down the hillside by a terraced *tarla* and olive grove; up on your left, atop the rocky hillside, is the ancient site of Arsada.

The track bends sharply left: after 10m take the path dropping into the pine trees on your right. Follow the **red arrows** as the path zigzags down to the farmland below. Cross the *tarla* to reach a track and turn right. (But first, if you wish to explore the ruins of **Arsada**, turn left on the track up to the saddle, then take the path up the hillside to explore the ruins; return the same way.) Continue down the track through terraced farmland until the track ends. Then follow the path running diagonally right across the field and continue around the edge of the field. The sound of rushing water comes up from the ravine below on your right. You are now on the **ancient mule path** leading down to the Xanthos Valley, and views open out across the plain, with the Eşen Çayı flowing through its centre to the sea.

The path zigzags down, eventually **crossing the ravine** via a gate on a bridge dating from Ottoman times. The path then rises slightly, passes through a gap near a huge 'sculpted' boulder, then quickly descends towards the valley. Views around here take in the farming village of Kayadibi; scrubby oak, spurge, Jerusalem sage and oregano edge the path. At the bottom, the path continues by the edge of a stony field planted with young olive, peach and pomegranate trees. When you meet a track, fork left and descend to a junction, then follow the **concrete irrigation channel** through to a **dirt road (1h45min)**.

Turn left and continue along the dirt road, descend past the village **cemetery**, and turn left by an old stone house. After 20m drop to a path cutting right, heading back towards the cliff face. The path passes tall pine trees and wheat terraces. When you meet a track, turn right and descend across a **bridge**. The water below runs down from Arsaköy and the ravine you crossed earlier. The track now contours round the hillside following the irrigation channel. In early February colourful anemones dot the route (whereas higher up, on the mule trail, ice 'stalactites' may well be hanging down from the hollows in the cliff face!). Across the valley are the Anticragus coastal mountains, where snow-clad Baba Dağı peaks at 1969m. The track skirts the edge of **Kayadibi** village. Above you, on the lower slopes, olive groves bank up to the cliff, and a patchwork of rich farmland blankets the plain. January is lambing season so, if you're walking here in February or early March, the farmyards will be full of lambs, young goat

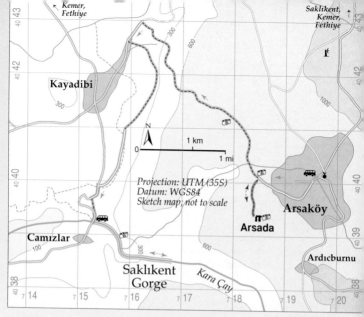

kids, and cows and donkeys tethered to their grazing spots. Turn left when you come to a wide dirt road and follow the **larger concrete irrigation channel** round the hillside. The dirt road eventually drops down to an **asphalt road (3h35min)**. Turn left along the road, then cut left into the pine trees to some beehives and a bee-keeper's hut. Then pick up the track that winds down through the forest to come out on the asphalt road once more. Turn left downhill to the bridge at the entrance to **Saklıkent (Hidden Place) Gorge (4h)**. From the **ticket office** just below the bridge follow the walkway to the restaurant inside the canyon. Once in the gorge, there are many springs rising from the cliff face, so to venture further in, you have to cross the icy current. Having crossed, continue up the gorge with its precipitous cliffs towering more than 200m above you on either side, and the stream, aptly named 'Kara Çay'

(Black Stream), disappearing into the narrow defile. The stream rises on the slopes of Akdağ and enters the gorge near the village of Çamlıköy at a height of 800m. It then drops 17km over dozens of waterfalls to the gorge entrance.

As you walk further into the gorge the rock formations become more fascinating, formed by the immense water pressure pulverising the rock and fallen boulders wedged into the crevices. It's possible to ascend some of the small waterfalls, but impossible to walk the whole of the canyon. For the very fit and adventurous, canyoning tours are available, taking two days to complete the whole canyon. These take place during August and September when the water level is at its lowest. Another popular activity is tubing — following the main course of the stream over mini-rapids — half-sitting, half-lying on an inflated inner tube, with a paddle to steer.

Tlos

This ruined city lies some 65km north of Kalkan and 42km southeast of Fethiye near the hamlet of Döğer. Archaeological finds such as a bronze hatchet lead scholars to assume that its origins date back to the 2nd century BC. According to 14th-century BC Hittite sources, there was a settlement here called **Dalawa** at that time. Coins indicate that in Lycian times it was known as **Tlawa**. Tlawa was one of the most powerful cities on the Lycian coast, having three votes in the Lycian League. From their hill — still crowned today by the surrounding walls of a Byzantine castle — the inhabitants had strategic control of the best location in the entire Xanthos Valley.

During the time of the Roman emperors (starting from the 2nd century) Tlos was known as the jewel in the Lycian crown. In the Byzantine era the city was still a bishopric, but after that it rapidly declined and many inhabitants emigrated, with only the castle remaining occupied. Tlos had a sad renaissance in the 19th century, when an Ottoman feudal lord (the descendant of a notorious robber) built a winter home in the acropolis: Kanlı Ali Ağa ('Bloody Ali') spread suffering throughout the entire Xanthos Valley with his raids and acts of violence. He also drastically changed the face of the castle, part of which he had rebuilt as stables and barracks.

Sights

The ruins date from Lycian, Roman and Byzantine times. They are partially overgrown by poplars, rampant shrubs and grass, so can only be made out with difficulty. Still, you can't miss the acropolis, where the ruins of the **Byzantine fortress** rise above the foundations of a Lycian castle. The remains of the walls on the eastern side, which are still quite high, were part of 'Bloody Ali's living quarters. In the sheer cliff below, a Lycian **rock necropolis** catches the eye. This graveyard is the high point of the site — as you can see from first glance. It is at its most beau-

Tlos — the castle hill and necropolis

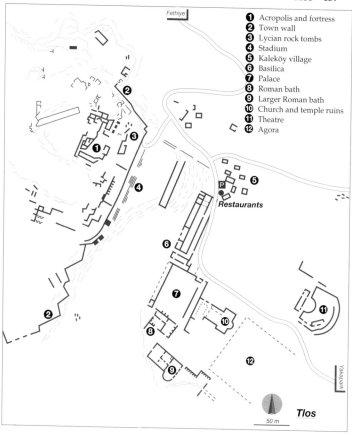

1. Acropolis and fortress
2. Town wall
3. Lycian rock tombs
4. Stadium
5. Kaleköy village
6. Basilica
7. Palace
8. Roman bath
9. Larger Roman bath
10. Church and temple ruins
11. Theatre
12. Agora

Fethiye

Restaurants

Yakapark

Tlos

50 m

tiful in the morning light, but be careful clambering around after rain, it's very slippery! Behind the façades of the tombs you'll often find entrance halls adorned with reliefs depicting battles; some with inscriptions. Best known is the **Tomb of Bellero-phon**, with a temple-like facade and two unfinished columns. The reliefs here naturally include motifs from the life of Bellero-phon (see panel overleaf).
The relics from the Romans, who settled in the flat valley to the east of the hill, are mostly in dreadful condition. Just below

the acropolis is the **stadium**, of which only a few stone seats remain. Parallel to this is a 160m-long **basilica** with three naves; once it would have been two storeys high. South of the basilica are two **Roman baths**; only a few ivy-covered arches remain from their barrel vaulting. Opramoas, one of the wealthiest men in Lycia, probably financed them (see also page 127). The splendid **larger baths** consisted of three huge adjacent rooms with enor-mous windows through which the bathers enjoyed a wonderful view of the Xanthos Valley. Some

The Bellerophon legend

Bellerophon was the legendary Greek hero who tamed the winged horse Pegasus. He was set three impossible tasks by the Lycian King Iobates. (Why? That's a long story, detailed in the 'Antalya to Demre' guide — and in the Euripidean tragedy.)
He completed all three and married the king's daughter. From their offspring came the later rulers of Lycia.
But Bellerophon became the victim of his own hubris. He believed that he could ride Pegasus to Mount Olympos, realm of the gods. His presumption so infuriated Zeus that he caused the horse to throw its rider, and Bellerophon fell to earth.

100m further east (by the roadside) is the overgrown **theatre**. With its semicircular cavea and 34 well-preserved rows of seats, it is a textbook example of a Roman theatre. Amazingly it was built in the centre of the plateau and not into the side of the slope. Inscriptions reveal that it took 150 years to build.
Getting there/opening times/prices: In summer there is a regular dolmuş to Tlos (en route to Saklıkent) from the bus station in Fethiye (journey time 1h). It's also offered by most tour operators between Kalkan and Fethiye. By private transport, it is signposted off the D400 highway north of Patara; coming from Fethiye, first drive east on the D400, then turn left on the D350 towards Korkuteli and Antalya; soon a brown sign points the way. The site (although unfenced) is officially open daily from 08.00-17.00; entry fee £2.20.

Accommodation

Mountain Lodge, on the road to Tlos from Patara or Fethiye, is a quiet spot. Comfortable carpeted rooms with rustic furniture spread around several buildings in a pleasant garden. Pool. Mostly British guests. Per person with breakfast £28. (6382515, www.themountainlodge.co.uk.
Berghof, a small idyllic spot in the middle of nowhere, signposted off the Tlos road. Lovely pool area (expect some naturists). 7 well-furnished rooms, two with kitchens. Sauna. Restaurant with German and Turkish dishes. Per person £19 with breakfast. (6382444, brigittekochs@ hotmail.com.

Food and drink

'Yakapark' is an area about 2km above Tlos with several trout restaurants (signposted). You sit under old maple trees, enjoying the rush of mountain streams.

Gebeler

The hamlet of Gebeler lies on the way from Tlos to Fethiye. Its main attraction is an underground thermal bath with gushing warm (38°C) water — good for the stomach and intestinal problems, hair loss, haemorrhoids, fertility, rheumatism, gout, spots, sweaty odours and whatever else ails you. But the bath, always neglected-looking, was up for sale at time of writing. Not far from it are two caves, the larger allegedly 7km long (but only 400m is accessible).
Getting there/opening times/prices: Access as for Tlos above; you pass Gebeler en route. Opening times and prices for the bath under potential new ownership not known; to visit the caves £0.40.

6 ÖLÜDENIZ

Accommodation/camping • Food and drink, nightlife •
Practicalities A-Z • South of Ölüdeniz • Kayaköyü • Gemiler Bay

Area code: (0252
Information: The **Ölüdeniz Tourism Cooperative** close to the *dolmuş* terminus in Belcekız is primarily geared to finding accommodation at its member establishments.
Connections: A *dolmuş* runs (in summer) between Fethiye and Ölüdeniz every 5-7 minutes from 07.00 till 01.00 (the terminus is at Belcekız Beach): fare £1.20. You

can also board at Ovacık or Hisarönü Köy — if it's not the 'rush hour' in that direction. The **taxi** fare from Belcekız to Fethiye is about £15, to Hisarönü Köy £6.50, to Kayaköyü £9.
Parking: motorists who want to bathe in the lagoon can use the car park just in front (£4.50 per car for the day). Entry to the **beach** is £1.20.
Walks: 13-15

When visualising the dream-like lagoon of Ölüdeniz, one thinks of the turquoise waters of the South Seas and a deserted, almost snow-white sandy beach below a fissured cliff, with a magnificent yacht anchored off the shore. But Turkey's best-known beach (shown on the cover), only delivers what the brochures promise in winter.

Ölü Deniz ('Dead Sea') — no way! It teems with people from April until the end of October; in high summer thousands throng to the bay every day. Nor is the lagoon dead in the biological sense — it's just that there are no waves. The photogenic beach formed by the lagoon is appropriately called 'Kumburnu' ('Sand Nose') in Turkish, and you have to pay a small charge to use it. Flying over the lagoon is just spectacular; Ölüdeniz is the Mecca for paragliders, and a tamdem flight is almost a 'must'.

Over the last couple of decades, Belcekız, a well-kept holiday resort laid out like a chessboard, has been developed behind the southern half of the roughly 3km-long beach. Before there were only a few campsites in this area. Belcekız isn't beautiful, but neither is it ugly (there are no 10-story hotels) — it's just a bit sterile. Since space on the lagoon and in Belcekız is limited by nature, the touristic infrastructure stretches several kilometres inland: on the Fethiye road, some 15km away, the two small resort towns of Hisarönü Köy and Ovacık offer plenty of accommodation, but little character or flair.

Accommodation/camping

Behind the beach at Belcekız are mostly mid-range hotels and more up-market club resorts. Campsites have priority right by the lagoon but, increasingly, the

site owners are limiting the space allocated to camp facilities in favour of more lucrative bunga-low rental. The bulk of British package tourists stay in the faceless resort towns of Hisarönü

Köy and Ovacık. The season for most hotels and pensions only lasts from April to mid-October.

Beside the lagoon: The sandy beach is very narrow and 'concreted over' with sunbeds. Along the side-road signposted to 'Hotel Meri', there are plenty of places to stay, interspersed with beach clubs.

Sugar Beach Club, previously called Ölüdeniz Camping. In the summer it's the meeting point of young international travellers. Has a good beach bar (loud noise until about midnight), shop, good restaurant, children's play area. Small and large bungalows with bath and climate control; also simple cabins without bath. Camping in an adjacent shaded area; good sanitary facilities. Bungalow for 2 people £40-52, cabin £25, 2 people with camper van £15. Ölüdeniz Cad. 20, (6170048, (6170752, www. thesugarebeachclub.com.

Suara Lagoon Beach, a clean campsite where there's always a free space. Large area with a couple of olive trees and little shade. Good piece of beach and good restaurant. Simple sanitary facilities. 2 people with tent £7, with camper van £18. Ölüdeniz. (6170123.

Front Lagoon Beach Motel, 12 large rooms, all separated from the sea by an attractive garden. Doubles with climate control £35, without £30. Ölüdeniz. (6170383, genc-frontlagoon@hotmail.com. Just past here is **Green Park,** which belongs to the Hotel Meri (6170001, www.hotelmeri.com), and **St. Nicholas Genç Beach** (6170088, www.stnicholashotel. com). Both rent mobile homes; at St. Nicholas they are less tightly

packed — and are also a bit cheaper: £40 for 2 people. There's a good beach restaurant too. The string of campsites comes to an end at **Osman Çavuş Camp** (6170028), a mini-estate crammed with spartan huts (no baths, 2 people £24).

In Belcekız: Except for the White Dolphin, all the following hotels are reached the same way: coming from Fethiye, turn left past the Ata Lagoon Hotel on 226 Sok. and then take the first right (224 Sok.).

Beyaz Yunus (White Dolphin), a new (2007) little luxury hotel on a hill between Belcekız and Kıdrak Bay. Only 7 large rooms, all tastefully decorated and comfortably furnished. Pool with fabulous view! A dream hotel. Doubles from £135. Kıdrak Yolu Üzeri 1. (6170244, www.beyaz yunus.com.

Oyster Residences Ölüdeniz, almost on the beach; 16 rooms divided between two buildings (a lot of natural stonework). Comfortable and individually furnished in some style; wooden floors. Lovely pool area. Double rooms £115. (6170765, (6170762, www.oyster residences.com.

Jade Residence is just next door; opened in 2005. It's another good tip, also peaceful. Up to you to decide which has the lovelier pool area! But for sure Jade has the prettier breakfast terrace, with sea view. Same prices. (6170690, (6170692, www. residence.com.

Hotel Karbel Beach, about 100m from the beach as the crow flies. 30 rooms with tiled floors, divided between two buildings around a pool. Pleasant service, a lot of young Turkish guests. Double with climate control £60, single £45. (6170013, (6170096, www.karbelhotel. com.

Hotel Bronze, friendly place with 23 airy rooms. Small pool and garden full of greenery. All rooms with balconies. Always praised by readers. Double room £42. (6170107, (6170182.

Oba Motel, a little bungalow village one street back from the sea. Although the little cabins and bungalows are quite tightly packed, there is a lot of greenery. The accommodation ranges from spartan (but with private sanitary facilities) to extremely comfortable (with seating nook, separate sleeping area below the roof, fine bath, climate control, fridge and verandah). Good adjacent restaurant. Bungalow for 2 people £30-90, depending on fittings. (6170470, (6170522, www.oba hostel.com.

At Ovacık: **Ocakköy**, signposted on the left (the sign is small!) at the entrance to Ovacık (when coming from Fethiye); from there it's about another 1km. This is an idyllic place, under Turkish/German management. Five hectares of land with 25 stone-built cottages (beautiful studios for 4 people maximum), with cooking areas and sometimes open fireplaces. The whole complex has been built over the ruins of a Greek village. Lots of flowers, a shop and several pools. For 2 people from £38 without breakfast. (6166157, (6166158, www.ocakkoey.de.

Food and drink, nightlife

In Belcekız there are steak houses, pizzarias and Chinese restaurants. At night you can relax in bars with open fires and soft piano music or visit noisy disco pubs. The selection is enormous. In Hisarönü Köy there are primarily pub-style restaurants offering full English breakfasts in the morning. The motto seems to be 'all you can eat' buffets along with Sky Sport. The only cheap thing here is the beer.

Eating in Belcekız and at the lagoon: **Oyster Residences**, beach restaurant at the hotel mentioned above, the most up-market place in the area. Tastefully designed terrace restaurant, where even monied Turks eat out. Unusual, constantly changing, but limited menu. Swordfish kebab is one of the specialities. Main courses £9-17. (6170764.

Buffalo's Steak House, a Dutch-run establishment belonging to the Flying Dutchman Hotel. Large open-air steak house (huge portions of meat and burgers) in American style. Small menu in 'cowboy hat' format; often live music (folk or Latino). Mains £8-15, including a good *meze* and salad buffet. Çarşı Cad. 6, (6170441.

Oba Restaurant, at the hotel recommended above. Garden restaurant. Together with Kumsal (see below), one of the few places still serving Turkish food. The *köfte* and *güveç* variations are especially tasty. Middle price range.

Kumsal Restaurant, one of the oldest places in Belcekız. Once it was just a beach restaurant, but since the recent renovations, it has a pseudo-chic atmosphere. But the quality of the food and the fair prices remain the same: fish, steaks, *pide* from wood-burning ovens and kebabs. At the southern end of Belcekız Beach. ℂ 6170058.

Another good place with fair prices is the restaurant at the **Sugar Beach Club** (see above), where you sit beside the lagoon, with 'easy-listening' music.

Nightlife in Belcekız: From the **Buzz Beach Bar**, nice terrace bar (good view). Good cooking served in the restaurant down-stairs. Full of good-humoured customers, lounge music. Very popular. On the beach promenade.

Help Beach Lounge, right next to Buzz Beach Bar and another very popular haunt. Brightly decorated terrace bar with a lot of wood. All kinds of beers and coffees, international dishes, including burgers and Mexican. Happy hour from 18.00-20.00.

Cloud Nine, on the promenade at the beginning of pedestrian-ised Çarşı Cad. Pseudo-chic bar and popular meeting point for the paragliding fraternity. The cocktails are a bit disappointing.

Crusoes, also on the promenade is well liked for outdoor dancing.

Tequila Cocktail Bar, on Çarşı Cad. in the middle of town. Cosy bar with all kinds of tequila and other cocktails, also beers. If it's really hot, you can jump into the bar's very own pool.

Nightlife in Hisarönü Köy: There are plenty of bars and pubs; people even come over from Fethiye. **Time Out** and **Grand Boozey** were the most popular places at time of writing — at least with the karaoke fans.

Practicalities A-Z

Boat trips: There are day trips to **Gemiler Island** (see page 147)

and a few sea caves and beaches in the area; these cost about £9 including a meal. Another popular tour runs to **Butterfly Valley** (see opposite) and costs about £7.50. Boats leave from near the *Jandarma*.

Car hire: Various tour companies also rent cars, starting from about £35 per day.

Doctors and dentists, English-speaking: There is a **medical centre** on the shore road to the lagoon in Belcekız (between the police station and the post office). **Esnaf Hastanesi,** a private medical facility based in Fethiye, has branches in Belcekız on Çarşı Cad. and in Hisarönü near the turn-off to Ölüdeniz. Both can be reached at ℂ 6166513.

Money: There are cash dispensers in Belcekız near the *dolmuş* station and on the main street in Hisarönü Köy.

Organised tours: Almost all trips from Fethiye (see 'Organised tours', page 165) can be joined at Belcekız or Hisarönü Köy. Most tour companies offer a pick-up service from the hotels.

Police: The *jandarma* in Belcekız is on the shore road to the lagoon; emergency number ℂ 156.

Post: The post office is also on the shore road to the lagoon.

Shopping: Every Monday there is a market at the Ölüdeniz/ Hisarönü Köy road junction. Hisarönü Köy also has some 'pound shops' where, as the name implies, you can only pay in pounds sterling.

Sports

Diving: The **European Diving Center**, based in Fethiye (see 'Diving', page 161), has branches in Hisarönü Köy (on the main promenade) and Belcekız (at 226

Sok., visible from pedestrianised Çarşı Cad.).

Paragliding: At the beginning of the 1990s paragliding enthusiasts discovered **Baba Dağı** (1969m) high over the Ölüdeniz lagoon. It wasn't long before tandem flights with professional pilots were added to the programme of local tour companies. Since then Baba Dağı has become a mecca for paragliders. The '**Air Games**' take place every year in the second half of October — a sort of five-day 'flying circus'. Flying conditions at Baba Dağı are definitely *not* for beginners. Year after year the winds are under-estimated, resulting in accidents and even deaths. There are many companies offering tandem flights between April and November; one of the best known is **Sky Sports**; the cost is about £90. Their office is in pedestrianised Çarşı Cad. in Belcekız, (6170511, www. skysports-turkey.com. While the flying time is usually at least half an hour, experts can make it last up to two hours and with favourable thermals get as high at 2500m. The landing strip is the grassy area behind the beach at Belcekız. From here you can also suss out the pilots — some glide down from Heaven beautifully, others end up in hedges. So watch these landings and choose your pilot accordingly!

Even if you're not flying, a trip to Baba Dağı with its fire-watch station is a great experience; the views are just awesome. If you *are* flying, it's worth asking the operator if you can go to the top in a vehicle an hour before the flight begins, otherwise your time up there will be very short.

By the sea, at the foot of Butterfly Valley

South of Ölüdeniz

A 14km-long road winds through the magnificent coastal landscape south of Belcekız (see map on page 152). It's tarred as far as Faralya, then gravel. To join it, follow signposting for the 'Lykia World' club in Belcekız. After about 2km you pass **Kıdrak Bay** with its wonderful beach (entrance fee). Some 6km further on you come to the group of houses called **Faralya**, a spread-out farming community with cultivated terraces overlooking the sea and **Butterfly Valley** *(Kelebek Vadisi)*. The view down over this small valley, with its beautiful beach framed by steep mountain slopes, is very impressive. The valley, full of fluttering butterflies, is a protected nature reserve. It is *possible* to descend the 500m down to the beach, but the path, which begins at the George House Pension, is difficult and potentially dangerous. You must be absolutely sure-footed with a head for heights, and don't try it with a heavy pack or after rain — there have been fatal accidents. The path is waymarked with some red dots and there are some fixed ropes. A much safer way to explore this area is to do Walk 14 and take a boat trip to the beach one day. The bar at the beach rents a few tree houses with shared sanitary facilities (H/B £19 per person; mobile ☏ 0555 6320237, www.butterflyvalley. blogspot.com.). Faralya has opened its arms to tourism, and there are several places to stay, from basic family-run pensions with camping and bungalows in the gardens to up-market accommodation. There is also a small market.

The road ends about 6km further on at a tiny 'car park', where you can turn round. Home-made wooden signs point the way from here down to a simple tree house campsite in the **Bay of Kabak**. It takes 20 minutes to get down to the idyllic little sand and shingle beach, and 30 minutes to get back up. This will appeal to those with Robinson Crusoe fantasies; there are no creature comforts — apart from cold beer.

Although the Bay of Kabak is also a nature reserve, it has been built on illegally, so how long this idyll will last is open to question.

Getting there/prices: In summer a dolmuş runs 5 times a day from Fethiye via Ölüdeniz and Faralya to Kabak (at time of writing at 07.00, 09.00, 11.00, 16.00 and 18.00, returning 1h30min. later). In winter it runs twice a day. A taxi from Ölüdeniz to Kabak costs about £24. There are also boat trips from Ölüdeniz to Butterfly Valley; boats leave at 11.00, 14.00 and 18.00 from opposite the Jandarma (price about £6.50 per person return).

Accommodation in Faralya

Wassermühle (Watermill), under German/Turkish manage-ment. Coming from Ölüdeniz, turn left uphill just before Gül Pension. This is one of the most beautiful places to stay in the area, a babbling-brook paradise with 7 tastefully decorated suites and 2 double rooms, some of which have great balconies and delightful views. Large garden area with (chlorine-free) pool. Restaurant, five-star service. You have to book early; the minimum stay is one week. Closed in winter. The only disadvantage is that while the sea is in view, it's a long and tiring walk away. Double room with H/B from £42 per person. ☏ 0252/6421245, www.natur-reisen.de (site is also in English).

Accommodation in Kabak Bay

All the accommodation here uses shared showers/WC. It's best to reserve in advance, since it takes so long to get there and back. **Kabak Natural Life**, the 'most comfortable' of the spartan facilities, next to the beach. Wonky huts romantically sited on terraces, blending into the natural surroundings (per person with healthy H/B £25). Comfy nooks to sit in, natural pool. If you ask ahead, they will send a donkey up to the road to carry your baggage down. ☏ 6421181, www.kabaknaturallife. com.

Nearby is a simpler camp, **Oli's Garden**, with tiny wooden huts; no pool.

Turan Camping has a pool, but it's not as 'perfect' as Natural Life. 17 simple bungalows with mosquito netting; lovely restau-rant, open-air library. Bungalow with balcony £19 per person, without balcony £11. ☏ 6421227, www.turancamping.com.

Sultan Camp doesn't have the charm of those above; 11 simple bungalows beside vegetable plots. H/B £17 per person. (6421238, www.sultancamp.com. **Reflections Camp** is the most spartan site of all, but has a very pleasant atmosphere. 7 simple open-sided bungalows, under which you can pitch your tent. Dotted with banana trees; sanitary facilties with a view to die for! With H/B £17 per person. (6421020, www.reflections camp.com.

Kayaköyü

This village lies in a valley off the main road between Ölüdeniz and Fethiye — it was an old Greek settlement called **Livissi**. The Greeks who lived here were re-settled in the Peloponnese during the population exchange after the Turkish War of Independence in 1922. The place was abandoned, became a ghost-town, and was then devastated by an earthquake in 1957. Today the shells of the houses in this once-stately town rise in grey rows up the slopes. Salamanders and lizards rustle through the weeds between them, and scorpions doze in the shade of the stones. What hasn't crumbled over the last 80 years is still crumbling ... but once it was found to be a tourist attraction, it was declared a 'museum area', and so now an entrance fee is charged. It's not only day trippers who have shaken the ghosts from the place, however: people are also settling here again — both foreigners and Turks, who are building bars and cafés, small pensions and boutique hotels in or between the ruins. All the nearby holiday

Kayaköyü's church

resorts have tour companies offering trips to Kayaköyü, but to visit it on your own, why not follow Walk 13?

Getting there/opening times/prices: In summer from 07.00-22.00 dolmuşes every 30 min. from Fethiye to Gemiler Bay via Kayaköyü; in winter hourly till 19.00. By car, access is via Fethiye: take the one-way road (Çarşı Cad.) sign-posted to Kayaköyü (see plan on

Greeks and Turks — neighbours, learning to love each other again

At the beginning of the 20th century the Greeks were the largest non-Muslim minority in the Ottoman Empire. In Istanbul they formed approximately a quarter of the inhabitants, and many places on the Mediterranean and Black Sea coasts, as well as in central Anatolia, were in Greek hands. Over centuries they had lived together peacefully with the Turks; tensions were the exception, not the norm.

But with the end of the Ottoman Empire after the First World War and the attempt by Greece to seize Asia Minor (see 'History' on page 60), the situation changed. The Turkish War of Independence followed, at the end of which came the so-called 'population exchange' — a driving out and/or ethnical cleansing: some 1.4 million Greeks had to leave Turkey, while about 350,000 Turks moved in the opposite direction from Greece.

The only Greeks allowed to remain were those in Istanbul (without them, the city's economy would have broken down almost at once) and the inhabitants of the Aegean islands of Tenedos (today Bozcaada) and Imbros (today Gökçeada). But even they turned their backs on Turkey over the following decades: the new Republic levied non-Muslims with discriminatory taxes, and those who either couldn't pay or refused to pay ended up in labour camps.

In the 1950s the Cyprus conflict intensified the ill feeling between Greeks and Turks to such a degree that peaceful cooperation was no longer possible. The Menderes regime particularly stirred up mob hatred by blowing up the house in Thessaloniki where Atatürk was born, blaming the Greeks. This resulted in the 'Istanbul Pogrom': on the night of 6/7 September 1955 thousands of Greek shops and homes were plundered and burnt, as well as 70 churches and 20 schools. This resulted in yet more emigration.

The improvement in relations between the two nations has only come about in recent times with, for instance, each offering the other help with severe earthquakes and wildfires. Greece is now a proponent of Turkish entry into the European Union.

---

pages 158-159). Kayaköyü is open round the clock; during the day (in season) the entry fee is £2.20.

Accommodation

Ekizoğlu's Place, a reader recommendation received too late for us to check out. 4 large cabins with fridge, gas cooker, shower/WC and verandah, set round a small but immaculate pool. £29 for up to 3. (☎ 6180134).

Food and drink

The restaurants near the ruined area live from the day-trippers. For an evening meal you may prefer to seek out **Kaya Wine House**, an old stone building signposted off the Fethiye road. There's a wine cellar on the ground floor and two comfy intimate dining rooms above, each with private terrace. Only open in the evening and only by reservation (☎ 6180454). It's tiny, private and magical, but the romance doesn't come cheap.

Gemiler Bay (above) and (right): St. Nicholas church on Gemiler Island

Organised tours

Seven Capes Sea Kayak Centre, Dean Livesley's company (see page 9 for details), is based at Kayaköyü. Contact him on ☏ 0252 6180390 or ☏ 0537 4033779 — or see the web site: www.seven capes.com.

Gemiler Bay

Gemiler Bay is some 7km south-west of Kayaköyü, with an island of the same name lying just off the shore. There are always a few yachts anchored between the bay and island, with regular boat trips arriving. But this once-idyllic spot is now on the route of jeep and quad safaris, and the restaurants (which also rent sunshades and beach chairs) feature burgers and fish 'n chips. You can camp in the olive grove behind the beach, if you first ask permission from the restaurant owners.

On **Gemiler Island (Gemiler Adası)**, also known **St. Nicholas Island**, there are two ruined

churches which were once connected by an underground passageway. Today, several sections of the once 500m long tunnel have collapsed. In one of the churches, you can still see parts of frescoes.

Getting there/prices: See under Kayaköyü for dolmuş connections. Plenty of boat trips from Fethiye or Ölüdeniz. By private transport take the road out of Kayaköyü signposted 'Gemiler Adası'; the final 4km is unsurfaced, but easily driven. Entry fee for the beach £1.10, for the island an additional £2.50 — and for a boat to get you to the island £5 return.

Walk 13: From Kayaköyü to Ölüdeniz

Time: 2h50min
Grade: easy-moderate; good, well-waymarked footpath underfoot (a few slippery sections).
Equipment: see pages 23-24.
Travel: 🚌 from Fethiye to Hisarönü (fairly frequent; alight at the junction at the top of the hill), then (less frequent) 🚌 to Kayaköyü. Return from Ölüdeniz on shuttle *dolmuş* to Fethiye.
Alternative walks
1 Ölüdeniz to Kayaköyü (3h 20min; moderate; some slippery sections underfoot). Use the map to ascend, rather than descend.

2 Fethiye — Kayaköyü — Ölüdeniz (8h15min; moderate, with some slippery sections underfoot). Start the walk in Fethiye at the tombs of Telmessus sculpted into the cliff face. Follow the old cobbled road up the hillside. The path cuts across many bends in the road, taking a more direct route through the forest. As you pass through a saddle, Kayaköyü can be seen on the opposite hillside. Skirt the valley, to the ticket office and café at the base of Kayaköyü and follow the main walk from there.

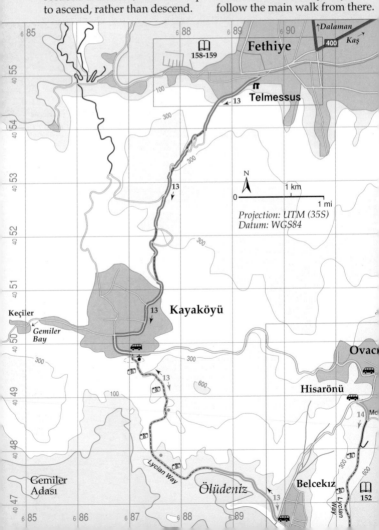

During the population exchange (see panel on page 146), thousands of people were uprooted from their homes. For a deeper insight into Turkey's modern history, read Louis de Bernières' novel 'Birds without Wings'; he uses Kayaköyü as his fictional village Eski Bachce for the main location of the book. This walk climbs through ruined and deserted Kayaköyü, then follows an old mule trail round the dramatic coastline, with fine views over Gemiler Island. You then descend through pine and wild olive with occasional glimpses to the lagoon and Baba Dağı. Ölüdeniz is crowded in summer, but out of season herons and egrets feed in the lagoon, and in spring wild flowers abound, with several orchid species colouring the way.

Start the walk by the ticket booth at the **main entrance to Kaya-köyü** (with café and toilets). Walk up the paved and cobbled, walled street, past ruined houses, to the large 17th-century **church** with its pebble mosaic courtyard and vaulted roof with interlocking patterns on the stuccoed walls. Continue up past the ruined buildings; the path, waymarked with the red/yellow flashes of the **Lycian Way**, is lined with fig trees; oregano, daphne and spurge grow amid the uninhabited houses.

As the route winds up the hillside, look back for fine views over this ghost town and the farmed fields of the valley below. Rising through young pine trees, you cross a **crest** (**35min**) and, looking south, have your first views of the sea and the dramatic shoreline of Yedi Burun (Seven Capes). Continue along the rocky path, gently descending into pine woods. Beyond the jagged coastline is Gemiler Adası, popular with boat trips from Fethiye and Ölüdeniz.

The path contours along the wooded slopes, passing a domed **cistern** on the left, then zigzags downhill — now a well-worn mule trail. The trail sweeps left towards a saddle on the headland, goes into a dip and through sage, pine and sweet laurel. You then ascend to a **clearing** (**1h15min**) by stone walls. From here the path turns left, past large carob trees, and crosses a **saddle**, to emerge beside a large **water deposit**. Here the path forks left and gradually descends through pine and wild olive (*Olea europea*), before continuing left round the hillside through shady pines.

After passing over a small **rise** (**1h45min**) the idyllic lagoon of Ölüdeniz comes into view through the trees. Continue twisting down the wooded hillside as more of the beach opens up, with mighty Baba Dağı (1969m) towering in the background. As you reach another vantage point, the turquoise waters become even more inviting. The path now descends steeply, zigzagging through the trees. (*Take care: there is slippery loose scree underfoot in places.*) Continue down to an enclosure full of mature olives. Turn left before the locked gate, go through a dip and round the fenced area, to a **park area** by the water's edge (**2h30min**). Turn left and follow the road round the lagoon, to the main beach at **Ölüdeniz** (**2h50min**). *Dolmuşes* for Ovacık, Hisarönü and Fethiye wait at the sharp bend in the road.

Time: 9h30min
Grade moderate, on good
footpaths; overall ascent of 400m.
Equipment: see pages 23-24.
Travel: 🚐 Ölüdeniz shuttle
dolmuş from the *dolmuş* station in
Fethiye (every 10min); alight at
the 'Montana Resort' sign just
past the start of the descent to
Ölüdeniz. Return on *dolmuş* from
Kabak (end of the line, where the
dolmuş turns round and returns
to Fethiye via Faralya village;
service five times a day in
summer, twice a day off season;
see page 114). By 🚗 park at
Ovacik and return to your car by
the same *dolmuş* service.
Alternative walks: Faralya and
Kabak can both be reached by 🚐
dolmuş (as above under 'Return').
1 Ovacik to Faralya (6h45min;
grade as main walk). Follow the
main walk to Faralya.
2 Faralya to Kabak (2h30min;
moderate; overall ascent 200m).
Follow main walk from Faralya
to Kabak.
**3 Faralya — Kabak Beach —
Faralya** (7h15min; moderate;
overall ascent 400m). Follow the
main walk from Faralya to
Kabak. Then pick up Walk 15 on
page 153. When you get back to
Kabak, vary the return by taking
the dirt road back to Faralya.

*This walk follows the start of the
Lycian Way through the stunning
scenery of the western Lycian coastline, high on the shoulders of Baba
Dağı. You follow an ancient mule
trail through the hamlets of Kozağaç
and Kirme, before descending to
Faralya, above the precipitous cliffs
of Butterfly Valley. The route
continues through lush vegetation,
pine forest and terraced farmland to
the idyllic setting of Kabak.*

Start the walk at the **'Montana
Resort' sign**: turn left towards
the Montana Pine Resort, passing
the sign for the start of the Lycian
Way. After five minutes the road
bends sharply left uphill towards
Sun City Villas; here take the
track that runs straight ahead
(right) off the bend. At the next
bend, past a water cistern, again
fork right and continue along a
footpath. This path is part of an
ancient route and runs through
lush vegetation and pine forest,
contouring round the lower
slopes of Baba Dağı. The route
becomes a terrace-supported
mule trail, with splendid views
down over the lagoon beach and
resort of Ölüdeniz and away to
Gemiler Island. The trail steadily
ascends round the mountainside,
with a ravine disappearing down
to the sea. Spectacular views over
the dramatic coastline abound as
you ascend southwards, high
above the coast.
The trail is mainly exposed to the
sun, but you can take a break at a
group of **shady oaks by a water
cistern** (615m; **2h05min**), perhaps
in the company of wild ponies. If
you look south-southeast from
here, you will see a lone tree at a
pass — where you are heading.
As the trail continues onto the
mountain, take the waymarked
fork to the right. Nearing the
pass, climb the stile over the wall,
then zigzag up to the **pass** (740m;
2h35min) you saw from the
cistern.
You now leave the view of
Ölüdeniz behind and look up to
the snow-streaked (in spring)
summit of Baba Dağı (1969m).
The path levels out and runs past
some new developments near the
hamlet of Kozağaç. The path

opens into a dirt road and passes a fenced garden and newly built mansion. Keep uphill on the track; then, by a shady tree, descend right, heading south-southeast — first across old terraces, then through a young olive grove and across a bulldozed area. Look for the red and white flash waymarks to rejoin the path and head back into the vegetation. Some **shady pines (3h30min)** make an excellent picnic spot, with the dramatic cliffs of Baba Dağı above and a deep ravine on your right.

As the path continues past old terraces, fork right on a lower path through scrubby oak, back to the dirt road (used by para-gliders to drive to their take-off point). Turn right and descend the road towards the hamlet of **Kozağaç**. Turn right again, dropping off the road towards pine trees, then turn sharp left into a dip, towards the houses. Turn right alongside a stone wall; this path leads to a track. Turn right at the junction and follow the track downhill. At the next bend, turn left on a footpath. Turn right at the next waymark, heading over rocks. At a rise, go left, towards the mountain. The path now descends through pine trees and round a poplar plantation in a hollow. Cut right through oleander and cross scree, then rejoin the dirt road by some **plane trees (4h15min)**.

Follow the road to the right, to a drinking water **spring**. Baba Dağı's smooth-faced cliffs are up on your left, and there are many scattered boulders that have fallen as recently as 1957, when the area suffered a huge earth-quake that flattened Fethiye. Continue along the road, steadily ascending, then take the right-hand track (under the electricity wires). Take the path to the left, running parallel with the road but below it, ascending through the pine forest. The path drops right, then rises to rejoin the dirt road at a **pass (4h50min)** from where views open out to terraced farmland and the village of Kirme, with Faralya below. Continue along the dirt road as it descends towards the main village. Ignore the first right turn past the old **schoolhouse** and continue to the next junction, with a shady seating area (kösk) and a huge mulberry tree set above the main **Kirme village springs (5h15min)**.

Descend past the springs, forking right down a walled lane through the village. After five minutes, take the walled footpath descending to the left, past a Lycian rock **tomb** on your right and a young olive grove. At the next junction go right downhill, towards pine trees and through a dip where there is another potable **spring**. The path becomes a track; at the next junction, turn right, following the Lycian Way waymarks. Further on, veer right off the track on a path alongside a dry stream bed, heading towards an old water mill. The path zigzags down through lush greenery past the **mill** (now a hotel; see page 144), where you join the main village road in **Faralya (6h45min)**. You are now above famous Butterfly Valley (see notes on page 143, 'South of Ölüdeniz').

Turn left along the road, past the **mosque** and several drinking-

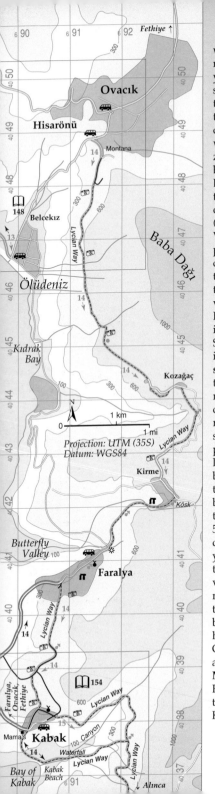

water **springs**. After about 20 minutes, past some **tombs** up on your left, look for the Lycian Way sign (on a bend) and ascend the track on the left. Just 10m up this track, turn left uphill on a path dotted with oregano and lined with grafted olive trees. The path zigzags up between limestone boulders, with views over to Baba Dağı. The path rises through a junction and past an old terraced clearing, to a **saddle** (**7h45min**).

Veer right over the saddle; you pass some old terracing and come to an old olive tree. Then the path drops to a track: follow this round the hillside, with good views over the southern end of Faralya village — as well as the island of Rhodes on a clear day. Swinging left, the track descends into a hollow, then rises past a **spring** and farmed terraces on the right. Continue up the track, now with views over the Turkish coastline, where line upon line of ridges, each a different shade, stretch out to the horizon. Once past a huge oak tree, the track levels out and sweeps right: look behind you here, for a fine view to Ölüdeniz. Continue round the bend and descend through pines; the track bends right again: after 50m take the **footpath** (**9h**) descending into the woods on your left. Wind down through the woods, with views of Kabak's valley below and pine-cloaked mountains above. Emerging from the woods, the path runs between stone walls and ruined houses (some with grass roofs). Coming onto track, go downhill at a junction, to the dirt road by **Mama's Pension** (**9h30min**). Enjoy refreshments on the lovely terrace, with stunning views over Kabak Beach and the valley.

Time: 8h45min
Grade: moderate, with about 850m ascent/descent, mostly on good footpaths
Equipment: see pages 23-24; the springs en route are likely to be dry in summer, so take plenty of fluid. Refreshments available at Alınca or down near Kabak Beach at one of the camp/bunga-low sites. You can even stay overnight in Alınca, but you must book in advance: contact Bayram Ali at his house in Alınca: 0252 6791169.
Travel: 🚐 *dolmuş* from Fethiye *dolmuş* station to Kabak and back (five times a day in summer, twice a day off season; see page 114). 🚗 Travelling by car, park near Mama's Pension in Kabak.

Alternative walks
1 Kabak canyon loop (5h20min; moderate, with 450m ascent). Follow the main walk as far as the 2h-point. Turn right here and follow the walk from the 5h50min-point to the end.
2 Kabak — Kabak Beach— Kabak (2h15min; moderate). Use the map and, guided by Lycian Way waymarking, walk down to the beach (the main walk in reverse) and back up. Perhaps also explore up the canyon.

This stunning walk follows an ancient mule trail from the pictur-esque village of Kabak, traversing and climbing into the mountainside cliffs through lush pine forest. You rise to the village of Alınca, perched high on cliff-top terraces, for specta-cular views overlooking Yedi Burun (Seven Capes) and the dramatic shoreline of western Lycia. From here you descend through a canyon, for a refreshing swim on a sandy beach. The trail leads back up to the start at Mama's Pension, where you can enjoy refreshments while awaiting the dolmuş.

Start the walk from **Mama's Pension** in **Kabak**. Turn left, then right, ascending the track from the Lycian Way signpost. Turn right at the T-junction and continue past terraced gardens and ruined houses to the old village **mosque** with a *kösk* (seat-ing platform) built under the shade of an oak tree. From here take the path past prickly pear cactus and terraced olive groves, soon forking left on a track rising towards the mountain. Watch for your ongoing path up the terraces.* It takes you up to an old stone house with millstones in the garden. Turn right through a tunnel of vines, to the next house, rising over terraces, then forks right (by a **spring**) on the **ancient mule trail**. The trail rounds the cliff face, into the jaws of a canyon, and runs through pine and sage to the next **spring**. Contouring round the mountainside, you cross a stream bed, then ascend to the right on the **opposite side of the canyon** (320m; **1h45min**). The path undulates through strawberry trees, past a shepherd's grave and another **spring**.

At a **junction with a Lycian Way signpost** (**2h**), take the left fork (*but go right for Alternative walk 1*). The path twists up round the cliff face, past a square-cut cavern and streaked rock buttresses. Zigzag up between the boulders, rising

---

*A new dirt road in this section (not on our map), may cause problems. Just below the first spring is a new white water tank. The old mule trail starts just above this building. The route should have red/white Lycian Way marking by 2009.

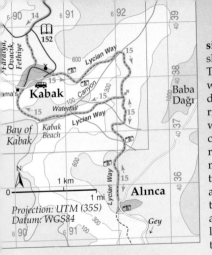

back through pine trees, to a *zeytinlik* (small olive grove) below the towering cliffs. Go through the wooden gate and up the forested slopes to a circular terrace (530m). This is an ideal campsite with a **spring** just below and fantastic views over the valley and beach with the mountain towering behind. Continue up through the pine forest towards a pass. Just below the saddle, the path forks left, then twists uphill before skirting the edge of the forest to the next pass (look back here, for good views over Gemiler Island). The path swings left, then right, out of the forest. Then it opens out into track, running alongside a brushwood fence and open farmland into the village of **Alınca** (725m; **4h05min**). The second house on the right, your refreshment stop, has a shady *kösk*, from where you can relax and enjoy the magnificent views, looking south over the rugged coastline of the Yedi Burun. The village of Gey — the next stopping point along the Lycian Way — is also visible perched high above the sea cliffs. From Alınca retrace your steps back down to the **Lycian Way**

signpost (**5h50min**) near the shepherd's grave and spring. Turn left and follow the woodland path winding its way down into the canyon. The path rises through a small clearing, where you fork right and continue contouring along the rim. Patterned *siklamen* (cyclamen) leaves cloak the ground as the route zigzags down a path to a splendid (seasonal) **waterfall** in the gorge. It then continues alongside the stream bed, past a log bridge. After another stretch through lush vegetation, the path crosses the stream, then runs past a terraced olive grove. You cross the stream bed again and continue through young pines into open land at the bottom of the valley. Follow the left side of the stream bed past an old threshing circle and on to a small graveyard at **Kabak Beach** (**7h30min**). If you've brought your swimming kit, this is an ideal opportunity to bathe in the turquoise sea!

Turn right along the beach and take the steps between walls. Veer left behind the house, then turn left uphill on the track winding up the slope. Take the right fork, following the red and white waymarks above the terraced olive grove. Then take the path forking hard back to the right, zigzagging up the hillside. Soon a right fork takes you along to an unfinished building. The path winds up the terraced slope, then cuts left through a small farmyard. Turn right on the track running past the buildings, then take the path round the cultivated land. Emerging on another track, by a wooden cabin, turn left and continue uphill, back to the main dirt road in **Kabak** by **Mama's Pension** (**8h45min**).

7 FETHIYE

History • Accommodation • Food and drink • Nightlife • Beaches and diving • Sights • Practicalities A-Z • Kadyanda • Oineanda

Area code: (0252

Information: The Tourist Office is next to the Hotel Dedeoğlu (before the marina). In winter daily from 08.30-12.00 and 13.00-17.30, in summer Sat./Sun. only from 10.00-12.00 and 13.00-16.00; İskele Karşısı, (6141527, (6121975.

Connections: the **bus** station is a few kilometres east of the centre, at the junction of the roads to Ölüdeniz and Muğla/Antalya. From there you can get to the centre (Fevzi Çakmak Cad.) by *dolmuş* (look for the sign 'Taşyaka/Karagözler'). There are also good connections round the clock to Antalya (4 hours, inland route; £7.50), Pamukkale (5h, via Denizli; £9), Selçuk (4h30min, usually via Aydın; £8), Kaş (2h 30min; £5) and Marmaris (3h; £7).

Airport bus: Havaş is the company running to Dalaman airport (see page 171), 50km northwest of Fethiye. 2-4 buses a day leave from opposite the police station; fare £9. (7925077, www.havas.com.tr.

Dolmuş: The *dolmuş* station is about 2km east of the centre. You can also pick up any *dolmuş* for Çalış, Ölüdeniz, Üzümlü, Kayaköyü, Saklıkent, Göcek or Kabak at the *dolmuş* stop by the mosque on the corner of Atatürk Cad. and Gaffar Okan Cad.

Water *dolmuş:* In the summer every 30 minutes to Çalış, as well as regular sailings to nearby Şövalye Island.

Travel agents: Lama Shipping Travel Agency, in the old town at Hamam Sok. 3/A, (6149985, www.lamatourism.com.

Parking: It's best to use the paid car parks between the promenade and Atatürk Cad.

Taxis: There are stands on Atatürk Cad. The fare to Dalaman Airport is about £43, to Ölüdeniz £18.

Walks nearby: 13-16

Fethiye is one of the magical names on the Turkish coast. But it's the nearby beach at Ölüdeniz which is the great attraction, rather than the city of 52,000 inhabitants. Another of Fethiye's attractions is its marina: together with Göcek, this is one of the major yachting centres between Antalya and Marmaris.

Today's Fethiye extends over what was ancient Telmessus, from which up to 20 rock tombs set in a steep wall are the most important remains. A visit to these tombs is a must, not least because of the wonderful views over the city and the Bay of Fethiye. The remaining ruins were to a large extent destroyed by the two big earthquakes of 1856 and 1957. These earthquakes were also responsible for the fairly sterile layout of much of the city, where only a few palms brighten up the roadsides.

The centre of Fethiye is completely geared up for tourism. Every evening crowds of sun-bronzed holiday-

Evening at Fethiye harbour

makers from the surrounding beach resorts crowd into town. Most are British, followed by Germans. First you stroll past the tour boats at the dock. From there you continue through the lanes of the quite well restored old town — past endless carpet, jewellery, leather and souvenir shops. Afterwards you visit a restaurant or a bar. *Everyone* follows this sequence — as if there were punishments for contravening the norm.

The most famous beach in the area is at Ölüdeniz (see page 139). But the time when one could be alone there with nature belongs far in the past. The beach at Çalış, approximately 4km north of the city centre, is less attractive. Behind it there's a large area full of package-tour hotels and everything that goes with them.

History

Telmessus is mentioned as a member of the Attic-Delos Federation for the first time in the 5th century BC. In the 4th century BC the city was under Lycian rule and afterwards was conquered by Fleet Commander Nearchos on behalf of Alexander the Great. After Alexander's death it came under the influence of Ptolemy. Telmessus was famous at that time for its school of visionaries; the reputation of the so-called 'snake-men' reached far beyond Asia Minor. Many rulers searched for advice here, among others King Croesus.

After Manisa's defeat of the Syrian King Antiochos (190 BC) Telmessus became part of the Kingdom of Pergamon; 57 years later the city fell to Rome. But the

Romans regarded Telmessus as little more than one of many pirate haunts along the fissured Lycian coast and took no notice of their new acquisition.

In the 6th and 7th centuries Arab raids devastated the city, and in Ottoman times it led a shadowy existence. During the Middle Ages the city was called **Makri**. The Knights of St. John from Rhodes established the castle as a base in the 15th century; later, it was also used by the Genoese. In 1922 the predominantly Greek population had to emigrate in the population exchange (see panel on page 146), and soon after the small town was renamed Fethiye ('Conquest').

After the Second World War Fethiye experienced an industrial upswing by shipping chromium mined in the hinterland. But in 1957 an earthquake almost completely destroyed the city. Very few inhabitants died, however: shortly before the disaster, the mayor — acting either on incredible intuition and/or his internal seismograph — used loudspeakers to call on the inhabitants to leave their homes and so prevented many deaths. The city was rebuilt in a fairly plain style; it's not beautiful, but it 'works'. Today Fethiye is booming and, like any typical hot coastal town, thrives on tourism. This creates prosperity and work. The number of inhabitants rises three-fold in the summer. It's estimated that around 5000 foreigners also live in and around Fethiye.

Accommodation

(see plan on pages 158-159)
There are over 650 registered

The Telmessian horse

Nearchos, Alexander the Great's Fleet Commander, knew the history of the Trojan horse and used a similar trick in the conquest of Telmessus. He asked Antipatrides, the ruler of Telmessus, for permission to enter the port with one of his ships, saying that he wanted to allow captured slaves and musicians to return to their city. Antipatrides consented after a brief inspection of the crew. Thus Alexander's soldiers, disguised as Sarotti Moors, rowed undisturbed into the heart of the city. Once on the acropolis, they pulled their knives from flute cases and shields out of drums and baskets … and forced the surrender of the surprised Telmessians.

places to stay around Fethiye. What's on offer in the city itself is not usually appealing, but there are some good hotels and guest houses of varying categories at the marina, on the slope above it, and a bit further west, above the *Jandarma*. Less expensive places are along Ordu Cad.: go west on Fevzi Çakmak Cad. and turn left at the *Jandarma*, then take the next right. There are good *dolmuş* connections to the centre; look for the 'Taşyaka' sign. If you are looking for a place on the beach, then book somewhere around Ölüdeniz (see page 139). There are also innumerable mid-range hotels behind Çalış Beach; this is only 'second-best' when compared with Ölüdeniz. There are *no* campsites in Fethiye; again, look to Ölüdeniz, which has a wide choice.

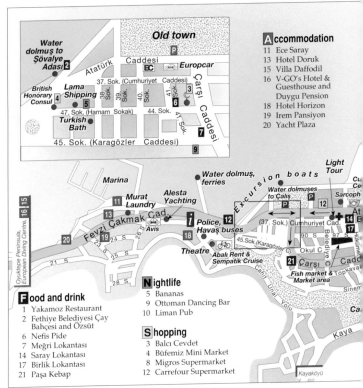

Accommodation
11 Ece Saray
13 Hotel Doruk
15 Villa Daffodil
16 V-GO's Hotel &
   Guesthouse and
   Duygu Pension
18 Hotel Horizon
19 Irem Pansiyon
20 Yacht Plaza

Food and drink
1 Yakamoz Restaurant
2 Fethiye Belediyesi Çay
  Bahçesi and Özsüt
6 Nefis Pide
7 Meğri Lokantası
14 Saray Lokantası
17 Birlik Lokantası
21 Paşa Kebap

Nightlife
5 Bananas
9 Ottoman Dancing Bar
10 Liman Pub

Shopping
3 Balcı Cevdet
4 Büfemiz Mini Market
8 Migros Supermarket
12 Carrefour Supermarket

Ece Saray (11), a posh resort hotel located at the eponymous marina. This is the top place in the city, built to resemble a sultan's palace on the Bosphorus. High-quality restaurant, 'wellness' centre. Double room from £180, singles from £150. 1. Karagözler Mevkii, (6125005, www.ecesaray.net.

Hotel Doruk (13), above the marina. 30 standard rooms with carpeted floors and air-conditioning, some with lovely sea view. Nothing special. Pool. In high season almost always fully booked, usually by British package tourists. Double room £48, single £32. (6149860, www.hoteldoruk. com.

Villa Daffodil (15), friendly house with 28 small but pretty rooms somewhat away from the centre at Fevzi Çakmak Cad. 115. *Dolmuş* connection to the centre. Pool, nice terrace, a lot of wood. Double £47, single £23. (6149595, www.villadaffodil.com.

Yacht Plaza (20), above the marina. 30 rooms with air-conditioning and large balconies, roomy and with big wooden furniture. Pool. Ask for a room with sea view: a lovely outlook and quiet. Double £40, single £28. Karagözler Mah., (6125067, www.yachtplazahotel.com.

Hotel Horizon (18), family-run hotel well above the centre of the city. Rooms with stone floors, all

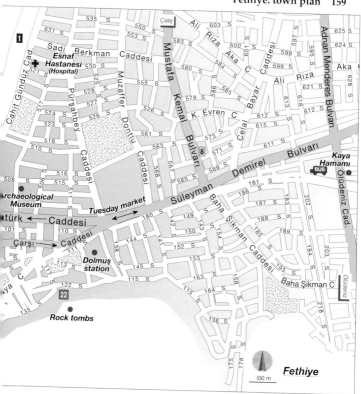

Fethiye

100 m

with balconies and most with delightful view over the marina. A bit tired; the walls could do with a coat of paint. Pool. Double room £30. Abdi İpekçi Cad., (6123153, (6126508.

V-GO's Hotel & Guesthouse (16), in the Karagözler quarter above the *Jandarma*. Amply large, comfortable rooms, all newly done. Well-kept pool surrounded by bougainvillaea. Friendly staff and very popular (best to book early). Double room £30. Ordu Cad. 66, (6144004, (6122109, www.v-gohotel.com.

Duygu Pension (16), also very popular with guests from many countries. Nicely decorated but very simple rooms (no cup-

boards, no hand towels). But immaculately clean and with a well-kept pool. Double with climate control £24, without £20. Ordu Cad. 54, (6143563, www.duygupension.com.

Irem Pansiyon (19), family-run, with 22 clean, well-kept rooms, 13 of which have balconies and 4 with sea views. Nice (but fairly noisy) breakfast terrace. Double room £20 with breakfast, single £14. Fevzi Çakmak Cad. 45, (6143985, (6145875, www. irempansiyon.com.

Food and drink

(see plan above)

Most of the more sophisticated restaurants are in the old town and on the waterfront promenade. Just as good, but less expensive (as long as you're not ripped off) are the simple *lokantas* in Çarşı Cad., Dispanser Cad., and at the bus station. Note that in Fethiye it's common for many restaurants to serve hors-d'oeuvres without being asked. If you don't want to find these on the bill, send them back again.

Kızılada Restaurant, a fish restaurant on the eponymous island just off the coast. Delightful terrace — wonderful at sunset. Great cooking (there is also meat) in the higher price bracket: reckon on £45-65 per person for a top-class meal with drink and speedboat transfer. (0532 2312665 (mobile).

Yakamoz Restaurant (1), is known for its good fish dishes, but it's fairly pricey. Inside a long bar with wicker chairs. Outside, you can choose between cosy seating nooks or tables right on the water. Somewhat outside the centre, on the shore promenade near the Esnaf Hastanesi Hospital — an enjoyable short walk to get there. (6124226.

Meğri Lokantası (7), on Çarşı Cad. *Not to be confused with the restaurant with the same name in the old town!* Popular with both Turks and tourists. Huge choice of freshly prepared casseroles, many of which are suitable for vegetarians. Also kebabs and fish. Efficient service. Main courses £4-9.

Only a few steps away is **Paşa Kebap (21)**, offering huge portions of meat, *pide* and *lahmacun*. Simple and well-loved.

Birlik Lokantası (17), somewhat away from the main action on Hükümet Cad. Varied dishes —

apart from the usual and steaks, there are also casseroles, different kebabs, and *pide* from a wood-fired oven. Another big plus here is the service, just like the friendly, attentive waiters in the Anatolian hinterland. Simple and economical.

Saray Lokantası (14), near the Birlik on the corner of Atatürk Cad. and Hükümet Cad., but somewhat more up-market. Choice of dishes about the same, and equally inexpensive.

Nefis Pide (6), a simple local with outdoor chairs near the mosque in the old town. *Pide, lahmacun* and kebabs in earthenware pots, good quality at realistic prices. The 'worm in the apple': no beer, no wine, no spirits…

Tip: Fishmarket
You can buy your own fish at the market north of Çarşı Cad. — a kilo of sea bream (çipura) costs about £4.50, of giant prawns £20 — and then take the fish to one of the nearby restaurants to be cooked for you. That only costs £2.50, including bread, salad and garlic butter (entrées and drinks obviously cost extra). This is a popular treat with tourists, but none the less fun for that — there are musicians around and the atmosphere is very relaxed.

Fethiye Belediyesi Çay Bahçesi (2), is the cheapest and simplest restaurant on the promenade. Run by the city council; only sells snacks.

Özsüt (2), nearby, is part of a country-wide chain well known for its good sweets and baked goods. Nice inside and out.

Nightlife

Most bars are located in the old town, with the odd one on the slope above. If you're looking for more choice and conversation, make for Hisarönü Köy or Belcekız.

Bananas (5) is the city's disco — opposite the *hamam* in the old town. A lot of house and all the usual. A good place during the day, too, when you can sit outside and enjoy a water pipe.

Just behind the *hamam*, along **45. Sok**, there are several bars. Another little street with bars is near the **cultural centre** (Fethiye Kültür Merkezi). There's something for everyone on this street — bars, cafés and restaurants, all with good prices.

Liman Pub (10), a Turkish-style rustic beer hall. There is also food, but people come for the cheap beer (0.7 litre for £2!). It's also near the cultural centre.

The **Ottoman Dancing Bar (9)**, near Meğri Lokantası, has an oriental atmosphere. If you don't want to dance, you can sit out on the terrace with a hookah. Not cheap.

Beaches and diving

The only place to swim on the doorstep is the **harbour basin**. The next closest place of any merit is on the **Oyuktepe Peninsula** (see 'Sights' on page 164). As an alternative you can take a **boat trip**. The best-known is the '12 Islands Tour' (see 'Boat trips' on page 164), during which they lay anchor several times, for instance in front of the small group of islets called **Yassıca Adalar**, where you can swim from islet to islet. On the largest of these there's a beach shaped like a raindrop stretching out into the sea and in the centre of the beach a natural 'pool' — this is a wonderful paddling place for children. Other anchoring spots are **Deliktaş Adası** (good for snorkelling), **Tersane Adası** (with Greek ruins) and **Haman Koyu** (a bay with monastery ruins in the water).

Other boat trips head **towards Ölüdeniz** and anchor at various bays and islands. Bear in mind that sometimes this trip can be a bit uncomfortable because of the sea-swell. One of the places visited on this route is **Gemiler Island** (see page 147).

Other wonderful swimming spots you can reach by *dolmuş* or hired car include the popular beach of **Ölüdeniz** in the south (see page 139), and the bays of **Katrancı** and **Günlüklü** in the north (both described on page 169).

Long, grey-pebbled **Çalış Beach** (4km north of the centre) is mostly used by tourists from the package hotels behind it. There are a lot of bars and a wide choice of water sports. There is also an **aquapark** in Çalış (entry fee £11), which can be reached by water *dolmuş* from Fethiye.

Diving: There are various caves and reefs off the Fethiye coast. The largest firm offering diving is the British **European Diving Center**, on the way to the Oyuktepe Peninsula. Karagözler Mah. 133. ℂ 6149771, www. europeandiving.com.tr, with branches in various places in the area. One problem is that there are usually very large groups. There are various teaching levels, from beginner to international diploma. Some prices: day trip with three dives, hotel transfer and lunch £70, taster course with rented equipment £70, three-day diploma course £380.

Water sports: At Çalış Beach there's parasailing, banana-boating, water skiing, and surfboarding.

Sights

Lycian rock tombs: Fethiye's major attractions are the graves in the crag to the east above the city; the **Tomb of Amyntas** in particular catches the eye. It is thought that this temple tomb in Ionic style was carved from the rock in the 4th century BC for the son of a local prince. Behind the two columns, which hold a decorated architrave, is a richly ornamented fake-stone door, which hides the burial chamber. Several smaller rock tombs are arranged around this one, some of them originating from the 6th century BC. The purpose of a necropolis is particularly obvious in Fethiye: those who could afford to do so had a whole city built while they were still alive, so they could live on after death in familiar surroundings high above Telmessus.

Getting there/opening times/prices: Take the one-way street, Çarşı Cad., leading out of town — it's sign-posted 'Kaya mezarlan (Rock Tombs)'. The Tomb of Amyntas is open daily from 08.30-17.00; entry fee £3.80. Those who are economizing can go in the evening or at night — the tomb is illuminated, and can be seen just as well from the distance.

Lycian stone sarcophagi: Just keep your eyes open when you walk around Fethiye, and you will see several relief-decorated stone sarcophagi standing on bases. These were built to hold the remains of Lycians from the upper classes. Because of their pointed roofs, which look like upside-down boats, they are also called **ship-keel sarcophagi**. The most beautiful of these compact little house tombs is next to the district administrative office (Fethiye Kaymakamlığı), just by the post office. Until the middle of the 20th century this sarcophagus was standing in water, since the coast here had dropped over the course of thousands of years (see Kekova on page 96). By the end of the 1950s deposits of earth had shifted the local coastline seawards, so it's now back on dry land.

Theatre: Built during the late Hellenistic period and later extended by the Romans, the theatre lies in the southwest of the city, near the Tourist Office. It once had 28 rows of seats and seated 6000. There are still some richly ornamented architectural fragments to be seen. Today occasional performances still take place in the theatre during the summer.

Castle of the Knights of St. John: Only a few pieces of rubble remain from this 15th-century castle built on a hill above the city; a visit is only worthwhile for those with scholarly interests.

Museum: Fethiye's museum consists of a relatively large archaeological collection and a small ethnographic section. The latter has on display a beautifully carved wooden swing-door from Kayaköyü (see page 145), as well as a loom, traditional costumes and embroideries. In the more interesting archaeological department, the collections include statues and busts of rulers and divinities, ceramics, glass and metal objects, large and small stelae, amphorae and coins, and a tomb with beautifully worked reliefs. Another pleasant touch is the collection of oil lamps dating from Hellenistic to

Tomb of Amyntas

Byzantine times. The terracotta coffin, complete with some bones, is a fairly macabre inclusion.

Getting there/opening times/prices: The museum is on a side-street off Atatürk Cad., on the way out of town (signposted). Open daily (except Mon.) from 08.30-17.30; entry fee £1.40.

Şövalye Island and the Oyuktepe Peninsula: These are two places near Fethiye which are very appealing for walking, swimming and snorkelling.

Şövalye Island, in the Gulf of Fethiye, is a tranquil spot with the summer homes of wealthy Turks; it's easily reached by water *dolmuş* from the port. After two hours you will have seen the whole island. There's also a small hotel and restaurant, the ruins of an old church and cisterns. The beaches are quite small.

You can round the whole **Oyuktepe Peninsula** to the west of Fethiye in about three and a half hours on foot: follow Fevzi Çakmak Cad. past the marina, to the end of the bay (with a wharf), and then signposting to the 'Letoonia Club and Hotel'. (A *dolmuş*, signed 'Taşyaka', leaves from diagonally opposite the tourist office and goes as far as the wharf.) Then just continue along the coast. You pass several idyllic shingle beaches framed by pines (some charge, like **Küçük Samanlık Koyu** and **Büyük Samanlık Koyu**). There are beautiful views of Fethiye and offshore islands. When you come to the access road for the Hillside Beach Club, high above the sea, turn left, back to Fethiye. The whole stretch is tarred, so can be done by car or scooter.

Practicalities A-Z

Boat trips: Strolling about in the evening, you can compare all the offers at the quayside: dozens of brightly illuminated tour boats with route maps will be touting for business. One of the most popular excursions is the all-day **12 Islands Tour** (see 'Beaches' on page 161), which explores the islands off Göcek's rocky coast (with lunch about £12). Unfortunately in high season about 10 boats take off at the same time and hit the same islands at the same time, so the beaches are more like public swimming pools full of screaming teeny-boppers. Another tip: take along your own drinks — on the boats and the islands, where there is a monopoly, the prices are outrageous. For something a bit different, you can go by **ship to Rhodes**. The easiest way is to book tickets at the **Lama Shipping Travel Agency** in the old part of town, Hamam Sok. 3/A, (6149985, www.lamatourism.com. There are daily sailings from May to Sep. at 09.00, returning at 16.30. The sailing takes 1h35min. Day return tickets £60; longer stays £88.

Car hire: There are various local firms (cars from £30) opposite the marina at the start of Fevzi Çakmak Cad. **Avis** is there, too (at No. 9; (6123719, www.avis.com.tr). **Europcar** (contact via Real Tour) is at Atatürk Cad. 40, (6144995, www.realtour.com.tr). Car hire from the international firms starts at about £55 a day.

Doctors and dentists, English-speaking: at Lykia Medical Assistance Service at Atatürk Cad. 104 (near the Light Tour Travel Agency); also the private hospital, **Esnaf Hastanesi**, on the coast road in Çalış, opposite the Yakamoz Restaurant, (6126400.

Launderette: **Murat Laundry**, at the marina between the Yacht Hotel and Hotel Doruk (on the sea side); £7.50 per load.

Newspapers: English-language daily and weekly papers, also magazines, etc. are on sale at the **Büfemiz Mini Market (4)** on Atatürk Cad. among other places.

Organised tours: Of the various tour operators, one of the longest established is **Light Tour**, Atatürk Cad. 104, (6144757. Two-day tours to Ephesus and Pamukkale with them cost about £80, one-day tours to Dalyan and Caunos £17, to Tlos and the Saklıkent Gorge £17, jeep safaris £26. Most of the Fethiye companies running the longer tours also have branches in Çalış and Ölüdeniz, or even in Patara. Price differences between the various firms are insignificant.

Paragliding: See under Ölüdeniz, on page 143. Most organisers in Fethiye just take a commission and pass you on someone in Ölüdeniz.

Post: The post office is on Atatürk Cad.

Police: next to the Tourist Office; (6141040.

Riding: You can book horse-riding with various organisers or direct with **Perna Ranch** on the road between Hisarönü Köy and Kayaköyü. British management. They also accept beginners. For two hours allow £22. (6180182, www.pernaranch.co.uk.

Shopping and souvenirs: The search for souvenirs is one of the highlights of an evening stroll. Go to the **old town** — one large bazaar. The shop fronts are decorated with carpets, and jewellery glitters everywhere, cheek-by-jowl with 'United Colors of Benetton' T-shirts and shops selling cheap imitation watches.

Balcı Cevdet (3) is one of several good honey shops, selling for instance pine honey and *pekmez* (thickened grape juice). Large portions. 42. Sok.

Otherwise the **main market area**, north of Çarşı Cad., is worth a visit (open daily except Sun.). Everything's on sale, from legs of mutton to underpants. Some fish restaurants line the sides of the market (see 'Food and drink' on page 160).

A large **market** is held each Tuesday in the market quarter near the *dolmuş* station, and that's a lot of fun!

A large **Migros Supermarket (8)** is located outside the centre on Mustafa Kemal Bul., and there's a **Carrefour (12)** in the centre on Atatürk Cad.

Travel agency: **Lama Shipping Travel Agency** (see under 'Boat trips' opposite).

Turkish bath (hamam): Fethiye's famous **historical** *hamam*, 400 years old, is located in the old town. Separate sections for men and women. Daily from 07.00-24.00; entry fee £12; rose oil massage £9 extra. Newer **Kaya Hamamı** by the bus station has similar opening times and prices.

Two-wheel hire: **Abalı Rent** has an office near the amphitheatre in front of the port. Scooters start at £12, 600cc cross-country bikes at £38. (6128812, www.abalirenta car.com.

Walking: Besides Walks 13-15, see notes on page 164 about

Şövalye Island and the Oyuktepe Peninsula. Walk 16 to the site of Oineanda is also within reach.
Yacht charter: Alesta Yachting at the marina is one of the best (℄ 6141861, www.alestayachting. com). Yachts for 6 passengers with crew start from £550 per day (without food).

Kadyanda

A day trip to the atmospheric ruins at Kadyanda, 27km north-east of Fethiye and at a height of 1000m, is worth the trip just for the wonderful view over the Bay of Fethiye. The Taurus forests have recaptured this forgotten city; trees grow in and around the ruins, pine needles coat the collapsed columns, and roots entangle fragments of reliefs. Little is known about Kadyanda, which is not mentioned in any chronicles. From some inscriptions it is known that a Carian ruler once levied taxes on Lycian cities, including Kadyanda. Kadyanda was not small — as you will see if you make the trip to this long-forgotten world, which is rarely visited (other than by people who come to plunder the ruins).

A circular route leads through the site, and it's a good idea to keep to this (especially if you are on your own), since there are several open cisterns. If you climb uphill from the right-hand side of the car park, you come to an impressive **polygonal wall**, which was both the city wall and the retaining wall for the theatre above. The **theatre**, embedded in a shady slope, dates from Roman times and is in quite good condition (apart from the orchestra). The seats for the city's dignitaries had backrests. About 200m further on you find yourself walking on a very long, narrow and relatively even surface and may imagine that there was once a road here, but it was in fact the **stadium**. Above this, to the right, is an area with large underground cisterns: this may have been the **market place**. Further up, also on the right, are the remains of a **Hellenistic temple** and, opposite, the site's best-preserved ruins — **baths** dating from the 1st century. The **agora** once lay further downhill; now it's just a field of rubble. The way back to the car park offers panoramic coastal views and leads past various **tombs**. In places you'll see some interesting architectural fragments under the canopy of pines.

Getting there: Kadyanda (signposted 'Cadianda') is reached via the sleepy small mountain village of Üzümlü, 20km northeast of Fethiye. Üzümlü is on the main road to Denizli, signposted off the D400 coastal highway. From Üzümlü it is 7km further to the site; the last 3km of road is unsurfaced. At this point there is a quarry and an unsign-posted fork; keep left. Note that after heavy rainfall this little road can be catastrophically eroded! There is a dolmuş connection as far as Üzümlü, but then you have the 7km walk up to the site, with a height gain of 400m (remember to fork left at the quarry).

Oineanda

While this site is further away from Fethiye, it makes an excellent focal point for Walk 16, which is easily accessible by bus and a fairly undemanding walk. See notes about the site opposite.

Time: 5h
Grade: moderate, but parts of the descent (on a pathless section) are rough and stony; ascent/descent of about 250m.
Equipment: see pages 23-24; walking boots essential. In winter, make sure you have warm clothing — the temperature can be 10°C cooler than on the coast.
Travel: 🚌 from Fethiye (any bus heading to Altinyayla, Denizli or Gölhisar); alight at the Seki junction (journey time about 1h10min). Return on any bus heading back to the coast and Fethiye.

Shorter walk for motorists (3h20min; grade as main walk). 🚗 Drive from the Seki junction to İncealiler and park near the tea house by the bridge. Ascend to the ruins but, on the descent, fork left on a main path and that will bring you back to the village by a different route. You could also visit the less-frequented sites of Balbura and Bubon, both scattered amongst cedar and juniper trees in refreshing mountain settings —ideal picnic spots. And note that there is an old Roman bridge under 2km northeast of the junction which was the site of Termessos Minor.

Oineanda commands a strategic position overlooking the Seki plain and the pass on the route down to the ancient port of Telmessus (modern-day Fethiye). The city formed a tetrapolis with Kibrya, Bubon and Balbura — the north-western frontier of ancient Lycia, controlling one of the access routes down into the Xanthos Valley. Things were not always so favourable for the Oineandans' Lycian

neighbours, as they sided with the Roman general Brutus when he laid siege to Xanthos and destroyed the city in 48 BC. Lycia was then taken into the Roman Empire. In this region, steeped in history, you have spectacular views of varied Lycian landscapes, while enjoying the fresh mountain air.

Start the walk at the **Seki junction**, where you alight from the bus. Walk 1km down the road, then turn right towards Ceylan. After walking another 1km, take the right fork past a marble **quarry**. Another 2km of road-walking brings you to the village of İncealiler (4km; **1h05min**).

Pass the **mosque** and turn right over the **bridge**; the village shop and tea house are situated here. Continue along the dirt track through the village; take a left fork, then keep right, uphill. When you come to a pile of rocks, turn right on a footpath and follow it alongside a stream, leaving the village. The path heads northwest up to the ridge; there is a confusion of paths here, but they all lead up to the saddle and walled ridge. Views open up as you climb, towards the many snow peaks of Akdağ and down over the Seki plain. (A new ski centre has now opened up on Eren Tepe above the village of Ceylan, but snow had fallen when I visited and, without chains, it was too treacherous to investigate.)

When you reach the **saddle** (1450m; **2h10min**), the massive fortified walls of the site come into view. Make your way to the wall which defended and supported the **aqueduct** into the

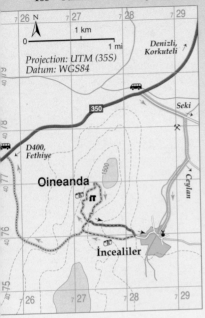

Projection: UTM (35S)
Datum: WGS84

1 km
0
1 mi

Denizli,
Korkuteli

350

Seki

D400,
Fethiye

Oineanda

1500

Ceylan

İncealiler

theatre to a large flat area slightly to your left: this was probably the **agora** or market place, surrounded by a stoa with fallen columns.

Cut right across the agora and find a path that contours round the hillside, back to the citadel walls. You can climb through one of the slits and make your way back to the **aqueduct wall** (**3h15min**).

Go through the aqueduct wall and descend west-southwest. Fork right by a rocky outcrop, then fork left by the next rock outcrop. Follow the stream bed down through the trees. There is no path on this section, but continue down, picking your way around the trees. When you come to a small clearing, fork right on a goats' path and follow it to the right, rounding the hillside and crossing the stream. Go down through a dip, then rise round to some open land with a scattering of ancient faced stonework. From here the path turns sharp left, descending back to the course of the stream. Cross to the left side of the stream and continue onto the plain. Keep right by a fenced area, and continue to the **main D350 road** (**5h**), where you can *flag down* a bus bound for the coast.

main city of **Oineanda**. Turn right along the wall, through junipers.

Keep left along the ridge by the main **fortification walls** worked by a Hellenistic chisel some 250 years before Christ. The fortifications were built with defence in mind, since the city overlooked and controlled the pass and ancient road down to the port of Telmessus.

Moving along the ridge, you now descend through cedar and juniper towards the city centre. As the ground levels out, you are walking on the stone-slabbed **main street**. Continue in a northerly direction past the **public buildings**, still half standing, with their huge block-work still intact.

Climb again, up to the **theatre** (**2h40min**), which looks over the city and the mass of Akdağ beyond. Drop down from the

8 GÖCEK AND THE AREA BETWEEN FETHIYE AND DALYAN

Bay of Katrancı • Göcek • Dalaman Airport • Osmaniye • Ortaca

Area code: (0252
Connections: hourly **dolmuş** between Göcek and Fethiye; **bus** information at several agencies in the centre. **Taxis** are available in Göcek at the square with the mosque; to Dalaman Airport costs £17, to Fethiye £19.

J ust 65km separates Fethiye from Lake Köyceğiz and its outlet to the sea, a delightful delta where you'll find the town of Dalyan. The main road between Fethiye and Dalyan runs parallel with the coast as far as Göcek, leading past several wonderful places to swim.

Beyond Göcek the road leaves the coast and heads inland via the new Göcek Tunnel (although you can also go via the Göcek Pass at 345m). You pass the turn-off to Dalaman Airport and Sarıgerme, a small, fairly character-less resort-in-progress. Beyond Ortaca and some citrus plantations, you come to Dalyan; its beach, İztuzu, attracts both turtles and tourists in equal measure.

The bays of Katrancı and Günlüklü

Some 17km north of Fethiye (13km south of Göcek) a signpost indicates the turn-off to the picture-book **Bay of Katrancı**, with a beautiful picnic area and campsite under pines (£5 per tent or camper; tents for hire; mobile (0535 4092069). Simple sanitary facilities, changing rooms, and a small restaurant facing the clean, clear water — even a water-slide. A further 3km north is the **Bay of Günlüklü**, with a couple of palms on the beach. It's as lovely as Katrancı, with a shady picnic area and campsite (a bit more expensive than Katrancı's). There are bungalows, too (see below), mostly booked by party-loving Russians who like techno beats. Entrance fees are charged at both beaches. Outside the Turkish holiday season the bays are quite quiet; in season they are very full. Between the Bay of Günlüklü and Göcek you will pass several more beautiful bays, but they are hard to reach by land.

Accommodation: The Bay, at the northwestern end of Günlüklü Bay. Modern (2007), comfortable bungalows, some with jacuzzis and open fireplaces. Nice greenery. 2 restaurants. Doubles from £75. (6336200. (6336272, www.thebaybeachclub.com.

Göcek

Accommodation, food and drink, nightlife • Practicalities A-Z

The first hotel in Göcek, 30km northwest of Fethiye, opened about 15 years ago. Since then not many more have been added, since there are no good beaches. But by boat you can head for some of the fantastic bays in the area. As a result, the welcoming town of 3100 inhabitants has concentrated almost entirely on yachting tourism.

There are four marinas! Various agencies and service centres look after their interests. On the wide

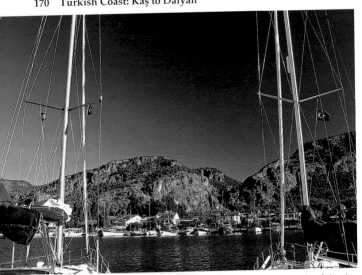

One of the marinas at Göcek (top) and fishermen off the coast early in the morning

palm-lined esplanade, you can stroll past yachts from all over the Mediterranean, then have a drink in one of the cafés or bars nearby. Everything here is a little tidier and more sophisticated, since they cater for the yachting fraternity rather than the package tourist.

Many of the beaches in the Bay of Göcek are included in the popular '12 Islands Tour' from Fethiye (these islands lie practically on the doorstep). There are also a few good

bathing bays to the southwest of Göcek, which can be reached either by a long hike or by jeep.

Accommodation/camping, food and drink, nightlife

The cost of accommodation, food and drink is about 30% higher in Göcek than in Fethiye or Dalyan. Almost every second house on the esplanade offers a few simple rooms for rent.

Accommodation/camping: Hotel A & B Home Hotel, also on the road parallel with the shore promenade. Family-run, well kept, comfortable hotel with 10 rooms, yellow inside and out. A lot of wrought-iron furniture, but unfortunately the fleecy carpets don't contribute any Mediterranean flair. Small pool area with a Harley Davidson between the sunbeds (the owner is a big Harley fan). Double room £75.

(6451820, www.abhomehotel. com.

Villa Danlin, opened in 2004 on the road parallel with the shore promenade. Friendly place with nice rooms in two small buildings separated by a pool. Double room £60, single £50. (6451521, www.villadanlin.com.

Başak Pansiyon, on the promenade (but its sign is at the back, on the street parallel with the promenade). Very clean, simple rooms on the first floor; shared terrace with lovely view. Friendly management. Double £35. Marina Yanı, (6451024.

Star Pension, a little place on the promenade in the western part of town. Simple, almost spartan rooms with tiled floors. But try to get one of the two rooms with balcony and port view, they are super! 2 restaurants — a simple one at the back and a posher one at the front. Double £30. Cumhuriyet Mah. 59. (6452024.

Camping: There are spartan camping possibilities behind the promenade at the western end of town.

Food and drink: Almost all the restaurants in Göcek can be recommended.

Can Restaurant, cosy restaurant with shady terrace on the promenade. One of the best places in town for fresh fish and good Turkish cooking. Huge choice. Fair prices: meze £1.20, main courses £3.50-8. (6451507.

Antep Sofrası, Göcek's best kebab house, with 20 kinds of kebabs (£4-£7.50), prepared while you watch. If you don't want a mountain of meat, order *pide* or *lahmacun*. On the road parallel with the promenade. (6451873.

You can also eat cheaply and well at **Mercan** opposite, a simple little *lokanta*. Pizza, *mantı*, grills and daily tasty lunch menu at only £2 (popular with locals).

Café -Restaurant Rocca, a reader's tip, is on the same street, opposite the Tansaş Supermarket. Delightful breakfast and good coffee.

Practicalities A-Z

Boat trips: almost identical to Fethiye (see page 164); top of the list is the **12 Islands Tour**.

Car hire: There are local firms on the road behind the shore promenade. But they don't own their own vehicles; they get them from Fethiye and charge a fat commission, so it's better to rent in Fethiye itself (see page 164).

Shopping: Sunday is **market** day.

Police: The *jandarma* is on the road parallel with the promenade, near the Can Restaurant. In an emergency call (156.

Post: near the main square.

Launderette: There are several, like **Dolphin Laundry** on the road parallel with the shore promenade; one wash £5.75.

Yacht charter: One firm is **E.G.G. Yachting**, on the esplanade next to the Can Restaurant, (6451786, www.eggyachting.com. The cheapest yacht, for 4 people, costs £1700 per week in high season (without skipper). You can see their boats under www.yacht booker.com.

Dalaman Airport

Open round the clock in summer, the airport lies in the middle of nowhere, about 7km south of Dalaman, an unappealing little city of 20,000 inhabitants. Saturdays and Mondays in particular are peak periods, when the planes spit out bleached-white, stressed-out passengers from all over Europe every 20 minutes. If you land here, before passport control you can buy **duty frees** (cheaper than duty-free at home). The **Tourist Office** in Arrivals is staffed round the clock in summer, in winter only when planes land. There also also **exchange bureaus** and **car hire** firms like Avis, Europcar and Hertz. The international terminal is 500m from the national terminal.

Connections: There is no public transport from Dalaman; if you aren't met by your tour operator or one of the **Havaş buses** (see 'Airport bus', page 155), a **taxi** will set you back £22 to Göcek or £32 to Fethiye. It's cheapest to take a taxi to Dalaman's centrally located bus station (about £9.50), for onward travel by bus or *dolmuş*. *Dolmuşes* only operate till 20.00, but the cross- country buses between İzmir and Antalya run all night.

Railway station without trains
Dalaman is probably the only city in the world with a railway station but no trains. At the beginning of the 20th century, the Egyptian ruler Abbas Hilmi II commissioned a hunting lodge for his Turkish estate and a station for his private railway in Egypt. His Parisian architects mixed up the two plans. Thus the hunting lodge ended up as a railway station in Egypt, while the station became a hunting lodge in Dalaman. Abbas Hilmi, an equally enthusiastic hunter and railway buff, eventually gave in and got used to the error.

Accommodation: There's nothing at the airport itself, but several on the airport access road. Readers recommend the **Hotel Burç** about 2.5km from the airport. 26 large, clean rooms with tiled floors and simple baths. Pool. Restaurant with canteen atmosphere. A bit noisy, but okay for one night. Double room £35. (6922935, (6922020.

Sarıgerme

This village, about 12km southwest of Dalaman, lies close to several ponds (breeding grounds for mosquitoes). It has been transformed from a sleepy farming village into the busy centre of a small resort (though hens still stroll with the tourists). The tourists are attracted by the wonderful, wide sandy beach 1km past the town. There's a small island off the shore and several all-inclusive resorts inland… with more every year. Luckily the beach is so large that you can usually find spot away from the crowds. There's also a small, well-maintained park with children's playground, picnic benches and a bar set in a grove. *Getting there:* dolmuş *connection via Ortaca (see below). If driving, it's signposted off the airport road.*

Ortaca

There is little of touristic interest in this district town of some 12,000 inhabitants. Multi-storey apartment blocks border broad, dreary avenues. But at the end of May/early June Ortaca comes to life with the colourful **Domates Festivalı** (Tomato Festival): processions, folklore, athletic contests, handicraft exhibitions, and a large market.

9 DALYAN AND SURROUNDINGS

Accommodation/camping • Food and drink • Nightlife • Beaches and diving • Practicalities A-Z • Sights around Dalyan• Köyceğiz • Bay of Ekincik

Area code: ℭ 0252

Information: The Tourist Office is in the city hall beside Gerda's Café. Very friendly and competent staff. They can also tell you all about the turtles. Open daily in summer from 08.00-19.00 (except for the odd weekend), in winter Mon.-Fri. from 08.30-17.00. ℭ/℡ 2844235, www.dalyan.com.

Connections: *Dolmuşes* start a few metres from the dock with the boat trips. At least one *dolmuş* runs every day to Fethiye (1h30min; £9 return) and Marmaris (2h; £9 return). More frequent connections exist to Köyceğiz (£4.25 return) and Ortaca (£0.90 single); from Ortaca's bus station you can travel virtually anywhere on the southwest coast. *Dolmuşes* run to İztuzu Beach at least hourly (£1.90 return).

Water *dolmuş*: to İztuzu Beach (via Caunos) £4.85 return. These take twelve people and set off when full; the same is true for the return.

From the small landing place 200m by the Caria Hotel you pay £1 (return) to cross the river in a rowing boat. From the far side of the river you can walk to Caunos in about 20 minutes. (A bridge will be built here eventually; the question is, *When?*)

Taxis: Dalyan's taxi drivers have fixed prices: İztuzu Beach £12, Dalaman £25, Köyceğiz £32, Marmaris £58 and Fethiye £52.

The small town of Dalyan (4100 inhabitants) lies on the eastern bank of the river-like inlet which connects Lake Köyceğiz with the Dalyan Delta. Lycian rock tombs lining the sheer cliff face are clearly visible on the opposite bank, and the remains of the ancient site of Caunos are bit further away.

Despite not being on the coast, Dalyan has a lot of flair. And although the small town is 10km inland, don't expect an oasis unaffected by tourism. During the day activities focus around the comings and goings of the boat trips at the quay; in the evenings visitors (mostly German and Dutch) stroll from bar to bar.

Not very long ago, Dalyan had a population of under 1000, who lived from fishing and agriculture — sesame, cotton and fruit. But the town hit the headlines at the end of the 1980s, when plans were revealed for a 2000-bed resort on İztuzu Beach which shields the Dalyan Delta from the sea. This beautiful beach is a nesting site for the loggerhead turtle (see panel on page 116), so the project caused uproar among conservationists around the world. The plans were fought, and the project was abandoned. But by this time the gorgeous beach was on everyone's

Boat trip on the Dalyan Delta

lips, guaranteeing Dalyan's rapid rise as *the* inland resort.

Development began on a large scale; new buildings, extensions, more storeys. Miraculously, given the number of architectural sins committed, Dalyan has remained modest. Within a few years over 100 places to stay were built in the countryside, as well as restaurants, souvenir shops and bars. The author of this rapid upswing has not been forgotten: in a small square by the quay there's a bronze monument depicting a happy family of turtles.

In the meantime the town's fishermen have all learnt the boat tour business. In season they carry thousands of guests every day through the Dalyan Delta to the famous beach, a remarkable natural paradise with approximately 150 bird species, including eagles, kingfishers, cormorants and pelicans. But this daily armada is endangering the ecological balance of the delta.

Accommodation/camping

(see plan on page 176)
There's a large selection of rooms for every budget, despite the fact that there are only 7500 guest beds. The loveliest places are in the south on the river, but you may be plagued by mosquitoes at night. On the other hand, nights in the centre can be very lively.

Happy Caretta (21), a lovely place south of town in a garden full of palms and cypress trees; right on the water, with a little boat/leisure dock. Turkish cooking in the evening if you like. The doubles (£50) are small, but well kept. Friendly service. Ada Sok. (2842109, www.happy-caretta.com.

Dalyan Garden Pension (18), about 20 min. on foot from the centre, in an idyllic spot. Readers' tip. Run by a friendly Turkish/English couple. 8 large, well-kept rooms. Lovely garden with palm and banana trees, 2 pools and bar. Bicycle rental. Doubles £45-£55. On the way to İztuzu Beach, signposted. (2843196, www.dalyangardenpension.co.uk.

Mandal-inn (10), about 300m from the river at 11. Sok 1. Small hotel with 22 rooms (the newest rooms on the upper floor). 3 rooms have jacuzzis — on of the has a jacuzzi on the balcony! All rooms are very large, clean, bright and pleasantly cool. Marble floors. Pool with small bar. Open all year. Double rooms £39-52 (good value for money). (2842286, (2842049, www.mandalinnhotel.com.

Pension Dervişhan (1), about 20 min. north of the centre (signposted from the start of the village). Right on the river, with loungers on the bank, flower-filled garden with hammocks, gorgeous terrace — paradisial. 9 rooms. They will cook in the evenings if you wish. Doubles with climate control £42, without £38. Gülpınar Mah. 101/A, (2842479, (2843539, www.dervishan.com

Hotel Caria (14), friendly place near the river. Large roof terrace with view to the rock tombs, 20 rooms with air-conditioning and large balconies, some over-looking the river. Doubles £24, singles £18. Yalı Sok., (2842075, (2843046, www.cariahotel.cjb.net.

Pension Midas (16), with a nice terrace right on the river, garden with hammocks. 10 simple but pleasant, air-conditioned rooms. Double £22. Maraş Mah. Kaunos Sok. 30, (282195, (2843154, www.midasdalyan.com.

Gül Pension (13), at 10. Sok. Very well kept, discreet atmos-phere. Very good breakfast with honey from their own hives. View to the rock tombs from their roof terrace. Pleasant rooms with bath and small balcony; 3-bed rooms for families. Double rooms with air-conditioning £25. (2842467, (2844803.

Camping: **Dalyan Camping (22)**, in the south of Dalyan near the Sweet Discobar (you can hear the beats!). Lovely location right on the water. A small, simple place with a couple of trees and okay plumbing. They also rent bunga-lows (large with bath £22, small without £12). Camping for 2 people with van pretty pricey at £18. Maraş Cad. (2842872, aksu@aksumakina.com.

Outside Dalyan: Villa Gökbel **(17)**, near the village of Gökbel, signposted off the road to İztuzu Beach. An architecturally interesting country house. From the lounge with its large fireplace there is a fantastic view to the delta. 8 huge, very comfortable rooms, but the thick carpets, heavy furniture and garish prints may not be to everyone's taste. Pool in the garden. Very friendly owner. Per person £28; tasty supper cooked for you if you like. Only suitable for those with private transport. (2890046, www. villagokbel.com.

Food and drink
(see plan above)
There are dozens of restaurants at the quayside, on the long parallel road behind it and

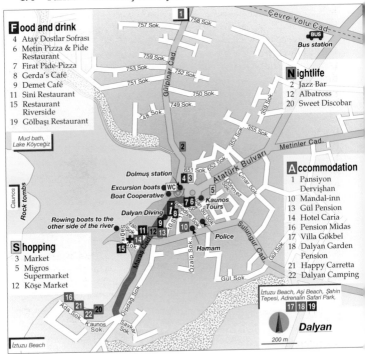

Food and drink
4 Atay Dostlar Sofrası
6 Metin Pizza & Pide Restaurant
7 Fırat Pide-Pizza
8 Gerda's Café
9 Demet Café
11 Sini Restaurant
15 Restaurant Riverside
19 Gölbaşı Restaurant

Nightlife
2 Jazz Bar
12 Albatross
20 Sweet Discobar

Accommodation
1 Pansiyon Dervişhan
10 Mandal-inn
13 Gül Pension
14 Hotel Caria
16 Pension Midas
17 Villa Gökbel
18 Dalyan Garden Pension
21 Happy Carretta
22 Dalyan Camping

Shopping
3 Market
5 Migros Supermarket
12 Köşe Market

Dalyan
200 m

around the *dolmuş* station offering Turkish and international food in all prices ranges. The specialty is fish from Lake Köyceğiz. The most idyllic places are the cosy restaurants by the river.
Restaurant Riverside (15), on the river. Lovely ambience in the large garden, view to the rock tombs. Large choice of starters; lamb, fish and seafood. Good service. Readers love it. Mains £4.50-12. (2843166.
Sini Restaurant (11), another place always praised by readers. Anatolian specialities like *çöp şiş* (a dish with tiny bits of lamb), *testi kebap* (kebab from a clay pot) or *Hünkar Beğendi* ('The Ruler Liked It' — meat with purée of aubergine). Mains £6.50-9. Geçit Sok. (Yalı Sok.) 12, (2845033.

Metin Pizza & Pide Restaurant (6), very plain inside, but lovely terrace on the far side of the street. Good steaks, *meze*, kebabs und *pide* — at fair prices. Excellent service, without being pushy. Another readers' favourite. Mains £3.75-9. San Su Sok., (2842877.
Fırat Pide-Pizza (7), hidden on a side-street off Maraş Cad. Same choice and prices as Metin; the *güveç* is especially tasty.
(2844585.
Atay Dostlar Sofrası (4), diagonally opposite the *dolmuş* station. Grills, tasty meze, casserole dishes, *mantı* and cheap daily menus. Many dishes are suitable for vegetarians. Inexpensive. (2842156.
Gerda's Café (8), near the town

hall. Nice garden café under German management (so there's always some home-made cake!).
Demet Café (9), in pedestrianised Maraş Cad. Another tip for those with a sweet tooth. Very good coffee and excellent baklava. Recommended by readers.
Outside Dalyan: Gölbaşı Restaurant **(19)**, about 3km outside Dalyan on the road to İztuzu Beach. Super-idyllic terrace restaurant with wooden jetties over the river. Steaks, fish, *meze* and *gözleme* in the middle price range; good breakfast. Turtles, ducks and peacocks in the grounds. Pedal boats for exploring the delta… but don't forget the mosquito repellent! Another readers' favourite. Free collection from your hotel.
☏ 2844410.

Nightlife

There's much more going on in town at night than you would guess from a daytime visit. Popular spots include:
Albatros (6) with 'hippy sound', and street-side counters.
Jazz Bar (2) on Gülpınar Cad. north of the *dolmuş* station; small rustic bar with open fireplace and vine-covered terrace. Live music Mon./Wed./Fri./Sat.
Dalyan's disco is **Sweet Discobar (20)**, in the southern part of town (on the river).

Beaches and diving

The 4km-long **İztuzu Plajı** (also called **Turtle Beach**) separates the delta from the sea. This is a fine sand beach facing out to very calm, child-friendly waters, and it's long enough to find a spot where you can't smell your neighbour's sun-tan oil. Sunshades and sunbeds for rent. Life guards. The western end of the beach is reached by road (10km, *dolmuş* connections; parking fee if you come by car). You can reach the eastern end of the beach by boat (see 'Boat trips' opposite) starting from Dalyan; the sailing takes about 45 minutes. The turtles have their bathing rights, too: the beach is *closed* from 20.00-08.00.

Aşi Koyu (Aşi Beach): This idyllic beach can only be reached with private transport. The gorgeous bay, framed by rock, has a beach of tiny grey pebbles. A little ramp leads into the water, and there is a taverna as well, with top-quality home-cooked Turkish dishes (unfortunately, quite pricey). The charge for the beach is £4 per car, £0.80 per person. You can also camp. To get there, follow the road to İztuzu Beach, but turn left after 7km (signposted). After another 5km, not far past the Mergenli village sign, turn right. Go right again at the T-junction 1.7km further on. Soon the road is unsurfaced and it's another 6.5km on a gravel track.

Kargıcak Koyu (Bacardi Beach): A sand/pebble beach, about 150m long, surrounded by cliffs. Completely untouched! To get there (about 16km from Dalyan), follow the road to İztuzu Beach, then signposting to Café Şahin Tepesi. Pass this café on the left (a nice place for a drink at sunset) and just keep ahead downhill on the gravel track. About 2.5km past the café turn right on another gravel track and park after another 500m, before this track descends in zigzags (and deteriorates badly). From here it's about 20 minutes on foot. A nice variation (again, if you have your own transport) is a trip to the beach at **Ekincik Bay** (see page 182).

Diving: Dalyan Dive, on Maraş Cad., offers two diving programmes with equipment and lunch for £54; 3-day beginners' course for £260. (2882332, www.dalyandive.com.

Practicalities A-Z

Boat trips: There is so much on offer that it can be very confusing, but everything will be very patiently explained at the **Boat Cooperative's** information stand on the quay ((2842094). There are boats to the mud bath (return £7.50), Caunos (£7.50), the Monday market in Köyceğiz (£7.50), and even boat trips that visit all three (£12). Of course there are bird- and turtle-watching trips (£7.50). There is a fun evening trip with barbecue (£12 per person); if you get stung by a mosquito, you only pay half price! Apart from the Boat Cooperative, private skippers also tout for business, but with the exception of those who learned how to sail at the Marrakesh bazaar, they are a lot more expensive.

Car hire: is offered by various travel agencies. Kaunos Tours (see 'Two-wheel hire' below) for instance offers **Europcar**; the cheapest vehicle starts from about £35 per day.

Doctors and dentists, English-speaking: The local **medical centre** is by the river near the Riverside Restaurant. (2842033.

Newspapers: English-language newspapers are available at the

Köşe Market near the Albatros bar on Maraş Cad.

Organised tours: Coach trips to all nearby and far-off sights are on offer; prices everywhere are similar, for example: Saklıkent Gorge (£20), Fethiye/market and Ölüdeniz (£20), jeep safari (£26), Dalyan tour with İztuzu Beach and mud bath (£13), two-day trip to Pamukkale and Ephesus (£75).

Police: The *jandarma* is on Belediye Sok. (2842031.

Post: in the centre.

Shopping: It's easiest to look for souvenirs and the like in the evening, when Maraş Cad. is transformed into a pedestrianised 'shopping mile'. Food can be got at the **Migros Supermarket (5)** on Atatürk Bul. near the Shell station. There is also a Saturday **market (3)** opposite the *dolmuş* station.

Turkish bath (hamam): The **Kiparis Park Hotel** runs a modern, tourist-orientated bath on Belediye Sok. What's on offer is completely different from a classical *hamam*: 30 min. with massage £12; 45 min. with aromatherapy massage £19; 45 min. with chocolate massage (!) also £19. They can collect you from your hotel. (2842424.

Two-wheel hire: At **Kaunos Tours** opposite the post office they rent mountain bikes for £10-13 per day. (2842816, www. kaunostours.com. A lot of places rent scooters, but the addresses change frequently.

Water sports: Kaunos Tours (see 'Two-wheel hire' above) offers **sea-kayaking** for £30 and **rafting** on the safe Dalaman River, including transfer and lunch for £40 (except in summer, when there may not be enough water!).

Sights around Dalyan

Rock tombs: On the far side of the river, in the steep cliffs facing Dalyan, Carian kings' tombs have been carved into the rock face. Ionic in style, they resemble Greek temples. Some once had colossal doors that opened. When building these tombs the stone-masons usually carved down-wards from above, as can be seen in the photograph on page 6: the most imposing tomb (at the right) was never finished; only the beginnings of columns show below the capital. Although not originally intended, several people were eventually entombed here over the course of centuries.

Caunos: Not very long ago, the ancient site of Caunos was just another unheralded ruined city with a few scattered remnants of antiquity. The ruins are still modest, but now the whole world suddenly wants to see them. The reason is simple: in the absence of any other cultural attractions in the Dalyan region, this rubble field was intensively promoted to the public by some Turkish tourist boards (Marmaris in particular), so that for the last decade Caunos has become a 'must-see'. The boat trip through the Dalyan Delta to the site is still by far the most interesting part of the trip.

The **acropolis** lies above the ruins on the hilltop. Those who take the trouble to climb up are rewarded with beautiful pano-ramic views. The **Roman theatre** and the rather plain **nymphaeum** are however still in relatively good condition. The **agora** is now nothing more than an attractive old circle in the burned grass.

The late-Roman **baths** were once one of the largest public baths in Asia Minor. Nearby are the remains of an early Christian **basilica** with the bases of columns, ornamented capitals and architectural fragments with Greek inscriptions inside. Historically Caunos, a modest small country town on the border between Caria and Lycia, never played an important role. The people lived from shipbuilding and from exporting salt, slaves and the resin of the liquidambar tree (*Liquidambar orientalis*). Over the centuries two chief problems plagued the inhabitants and eventually brought about the town's demise: the mosquitoes which carried malaria and the progressive silting-up of the port. *Getting there/opening times/prices: Caunos lies diagonally opposite Dalyan on the far side of the river. You can get there by taking a rowing boat (200m downriver from the port) and then walking for 20-25 minutes to the site, or join a boat trip on the delta (see 'Boat trips' on page 178). Caunos is open daily from 08.00-18.00; entry fee £3.80.*

Mud bath: This attraction, on the left of the river on the way to Lake Köyceğiz, was developed commercially to tie in with the boat trips. It's fun to go back to childhood and wallow in mud, but it won't take any years off your life. The mud is actually brought in from elsewhere because there are so many visitors (1000 a day in high season). *Note:* It's not recom-mended for those with a heart condition!

Opening times/prices: daily from 08.00-19.00; entry fee £2. In the morning the bath is still in shade.

Köyceğiz

Area code: (0252
Information: The Tourist Office is in the main square. Open Mon.-Fri. from 08.00-17.00; Atatürk Kordonu, (2624703.
Connections: The bus station is far outside the centre, near the coast road (a taxi to the centre costs £2.50). **Buses** run several times a day to Marmaris and Antalya, hourly to Fethiye and half-hourly to Muğla.

At first sight the small dozy town of Köyceğiz makes a welcoming impression: a palm-lined avenue leads into the centre. But once they see the empty seats on the esplanade and the bleached postcards in the kiosks, some tourists feel a bit melancholic and move on to Dalyan.

Köyceğiz, with about 7000 inhabitants, is one of the few places that refuses to participate in the profitable tourist trade. Only a few Turkish families stay at the hotels in summer, which makes this small lakeside town attractive for those keen to avoid the busy resorts; it is still unspoilt. Some inhabitants hope that Köyceğiz never changes — they see what happened to Dalyan. But others look down on the lake shore with envy.

Accommodation/camping

Flora Hotel, in the western part of town on the lake-side road. Bright, green, tidy rooms. Friendly service; bar. Double room £35. Kordon Boyu 98, (2624976, www. florahotel.info.
Hotel Alila, on the promenade. 20 rooms with air-conditioning; only two without lake views. Looking a bit tired lately. Restaurant. Small pool. Open all year. Double room £25, single 18. Emeksiz Cad. (/(2621150.
Oba Pension, somewhat off the beaten track at Gümülü Cad. 10, signposted off the main avenue into town. Simple family-run guest house with 10 rooms, all with balcony. Open all year. Double room £15 with breakfast. (2624181, (2624972.
Tango Pension, on the road parallel with the shore road. Clean doubles with bath (£22); dormitory (per bed £7). Nice garden bar in front. Alihsan Kalmaz Cad. (2622501.
Camping: Delta Camping, a peaceful oasis 1.5km west of town on the shore road opposite Delta Plajı. A lot of shade from high trees, moderate sanitary facilities, tennis, mini-zoo. Cheap: 2 people with tent or camper van £4. (2625502.

Food and drink, nightlife

There a several simple, good *lokantas* in the centre. Fresh fish from the lake (kept in an aquarium until you choose it) can be had in the **Thera Restaurant**. Large terrace, separated from the lake by just a narrow strip of grass. Fish from £6, *meze* from £1.20. (2623514.
Mona Lisa, right on the lake, serves good snacks (recommended by readers).
Yuvarlakçay Restaurant, in the woods, is the best tip. They've

built a terrace out over a stream which babbles away while you dine. Fresh trout from the stream or their famous *tandır kebap*, a roast mutton speciality. After a hot day it's beautifully cool. To get there follow the D400 towards Fethiye for 10km, then turn left (signposted); the restaurant comes up after 5km, on your right, in the woods. (There are other restaurants a bit further along this road.)

Nightlife: Apart from the cicadas, there's not much noise at night. The only disco, **Han 48**, near the Hotel Özay, is nothing special. So you get a good night's sleep in Köyceğiz and the next morning can enjoy your breakfast in the tea garden at the lake.

Practicalities A-Z

Beaches: The only place to swim in Köyceğiz is small **Delta Plajı** opposite Delta Camping. It's slightly salty fresh water, usually flat as a pancake and quite a change — instead of swimming out towards endless sea, you look across the lake to the mountains.

Boat trips: These leave from the small port by the promenade at Paşa Parkı. The standard day trip takes in İztuzu Beach, Caunos, the Sultaniye thermal baths and the mud bath (per person £7).

Car and two-wheel hire: **Özay Turizm Travel**, opposite the mosque in the main square, has cars starting from £35 per day, scooters at £12 and bicycles at £6. (2621822, www.ozaytours.com.

Doctors and dentists: The town's **hospital** is on the road to Marmaris. (2624718.

Events: The **Altın Arslan ('Golden Lion') Film Festival** (a local

Lake Köyceğiz

Lake Köyceğiz, 65 square kilo-metres and connected by a narrow river to the sea, is an inland bay. The lake is not fed by a river but warm springs. Most of its banks are edged with reeds, making it difficult to find a way in for a swim.

In addition to its almost totally unspoilt nature and unique fauna, the lake provides a culinary specialty: when the sea rises, sea water flows into the lake and brings with it flathead grey mullet (kefal) and perch (levrek) that spawn in the calm water. Since few find their way back into the open sea, they are caught in the narrow river and tastily prepared.

Botanic rarities in the swampy areas around the lake include meadows with liquidambar trees (Liquidambar orientalis), a member of the witch-hazel family with plane tree-like leaves. While these trees usually reach up to 45m in height, here they rarely achieve half that size. These rare trees yield a resin ('liquid amber') which is used in perfumery, as an expectorant, inhalant and in the treatment of skin diseases.

festival for Turkish films) takes place in the middle of August over five days.

Police: on the main avenue into town, (2623766.

Post: The post office is west of the main avenue; coming into town, take the penultimate turn to the right.

Shopping: The best shopping is at the **Monday market**, one of the largest and most beautiful in the region — even those based in Dalyan don't miss this!

Sights around Köyceğiz

Sultaniye Baths: Lake Köyceğiz is fed by a sulphureous and mildly radioactive spring (39°C) some 10km from Köyceğiz, on the southwestern shore of the lake. The baths were originally Roman, but were substantially changed by the Ottomans who also used them for cures. In recent times outdoor baths, a mud bath and cafeteria have been added for tourists. It is claimed that the water helps depression, bilious complaints, intestinal illnesses and the like. *Getting there/prices: Only accessible by private transport (signposted off the road to Ekincik Bay) or boat trip. No dolmuş. Entry fee £1.40.*

Bay of Ekincik

This calm bay, framed by high mountains, lies about 40km southwest of Köyceğiz. The trip is worthwhile not only for the crescent-shaped, reddish-brown pebble beach, but for the drive alongside Lake Köyceğiz. The bay is traditionally a stopping-off point for yachts and boat tours from Marmaris: passengers on their way to the Dalyan Delta transfer here into smaller boats. Behind the beach and on the approach road there are a few nice guest houses and hotels, a makeshift campsite, and the somewhat forlorn ruins of an unfinished resort. Otherwise the tourist infrastructure is still in its infancy — so it's very pleasant for those seeking a good beach where they can read a good book in peace and quiet. Ekincik village itself lies a few kilometres behind the coast.

Getting there: From Köyceğiz head west on the shore road (past Delta Plajı). Beyond some orchards you come to the little village of Hamitköy. Turn left at the end of the village (watch for signs to various guest houses). 1km further along you're on a good road to Ekincik. At time of writing there was only one dolmuş a day (summer only) between Köyceğiz and Ekincik, leaving Köyceğiz at 09.30, returning at 17.30.

Accommodation: Ekincik Hotel, on the beach. 27 air-conditioned rooms — okay, but nothing special; it's the location that makes it. Per person with H/B £40. ✆/✆ 0252-2660203, www.hotelekincik.com

Hotel Falcon Crest, endlessly recommended by readers. High above Ekincik. In 12,000sqm of protected land; pure peace. 38 large comfortable rooms with terrace. Lovely pool area. Shuttle bus to the beach. Between Apr.-Oct. you must reserve ahead. Excellent value for money: doubles with H/B £40. ✆ 0252-2660221, ✆ 0252-2660003, www.hotelfc.com

Pension Ekincik, 5min from the beach. 17 very clean, plain rooms; 1 apartment, most with balcony or terrace. Friendly owners, delicious food. Double room with H/B £40. ✆ 0252-2660179, www.ekincikpansiyon.com.

Hotel Akdeniz, 5min from the beach. Big, bright, well-kept rooms with balconies and air-conditioning. Super roof terrace. Very clean and friendly. Per person with H/B £36. Excellent cooking, open all year. ✆ 0252-2660255, www.akdenizhotel.com

● Index

Only geographical names are included here; for all other entries, see Contents, page 3. **Bold type** indicates a photograph; *italic type* indicates a map or plan; both may be in addition to a text reference on the same page. *RAM* refers to the walking map on the *reverse of the area map*.